WRITING THE WRONGS OF HUMAN RIGHTS

In LETTERS, WORDS, SENTENCES

Edward Horgan

Copyright © 2023 Edward Horgan. All Rights Reserved

No part of this publication may be reproduced, distributed, or transmitted in any form, or by any means, including photocopying, recording, or other electronic or mechanical, methods without the prior written permission of the author, except in the case of brief quotations embodied in reviews and certain other non-commercial uses permitted by copyright law.

I wish to dedicate this book to the millions of children who have died due to wars since the end of the Cold War, when peace should have been created for all of humanity. It's a crime to kill an old person but an old person killed is denied just a small part of their life. If a child is killed most of their life is destroyed, and they are denied the right to bring children into the world.

Edward Horgan

Acknowledgements

My first and sincere words of thanks must go to the editors of all newspapers who have published over 300 of my letters and articles. The practice of writing letters to the papers has existed at least since the 18th century. Such letters have become more important in recent times as they offer a sort of bridge between mainstream media and alternative media. They help to give a voice to ordinary people.

My thanks is also due to Eamonn Farrell of RollingNews.ie and Photocall Ireland for permission to use the photo on the cover of this book. The pen can sometimes be mightier than the sword.

And a special thanks to Laurence O'Bryan, BooksGoSocial, for the Trojan work by him and his team in helping to get this book through the onerous tasks of editing, formatting, and ready for printing.

Contents

Introduction 19

No. 1. BLITZKRIEG by Capt. E.J. Horgan 27

No. 2. Today's Tank Squadron and Tomorrow's 33

No. 3. Armour Developments in an Irish Context.......................................35

No. 4. Committing Our Troops to EU Force Clear Breach of Neutrality...........42

No. 5. Irish Army Officer Returns Medals in Iraq Protest 46

No. 6. Time to Face the Nightmare Scenario 49

No. 7. Aftermath of Iraq Invasion 52

No. 8. State Not Neutral by Any Credible Definition 54

No. 9. Heads Have to Roll at US Leadership Level 57

No. 10. Battlegroup Bait Just Another Threat to Peace 61

No. 11. 'un gilipollas integral'..65

No. 12. Annan's UN 'Reforms' Fall Short of Needs 65

No. 13. People Are Being Softened Up to Send Their Children to Fight for the West Against the Rest..68

No. 14. CIA Is Still Using Shannon for Torture Flights...............................72

No. 15. US Military Aircraft Opening a Second Front at Knock May Prove to Be No Apparition 73

No. 16. Should We Let US Troops Land at Shannon En Route to Iraq? 75

No. 17. World War Commemorations...77

No. 18. 'Clinical' Killings Are Heinous Crimes 79

No. 19. Why Irish Troops Are in The Wrong Part of Africa?.....................80

No. 20. FF Double Standard on Gay Marriage..81

No. 21. Army Tied into Questionable Peace Missions................................82

No. 22. No Mention of Neutrality in Constitution.......................................85

No. 23. High Price of Corruption, Greed, And Incompetence 86

No. 24. We Have All Become Passive Victims of Crimes 88
No. 25. Paras' Leader Should Be Stripped of His OBE 89
No. 26. Irish Defence Forces – We Must Defend Them 90
No. 27. Dáil's Tail End 94
No. 28. Guess How Long It Takes to Pick Up €50bn? 95
No. 29. National Strike 96
No. 30. Complicit in Torture 96
No. 31. Incontrovertible 97
No. 32. Pubs Going to The Wall Is a Positive Thing for Our Society 97
No. 33. Irish Army Personnel Should Quit Afghanistan 98
No. 34. Is There Anyone Accountable for Sorry Mess? 99
No. 35. Shannon Transit Breach of International Law 99
No. 36. Committing Treason Against Our Grandchildren 100
No. 37. To Prepare New York For Next Sandy, Move to Higher Ground 101
No. 38. Neutrality and the Triple Lock 102
No. 39. Politicians Just Support the Elite 103
No. 40. Abolition of Seanad Could Pose Increased Dangers for Peace and Neutrality Issues Say Campaigners 104
No. 41. Irish Sea Coast at Risk of Nuclear Disaster 106
No. 42. A New Party's Policies 106
No. 43. Release Whistleblowers Like Margaretta D'Arcy 107
No. 44. Gardaí Should Admit Mistakes and Resolve Them 107
No. 45. Moral and Physical Hazard in Unfair Imposition Of Levy 108
No. 46. Gilmore Not Entitled to be EU Commissioner 109
No. 47. Ireland Should Be Humane and Offer a Home to Guantanamo Prisoners 109
No. 48. Ireland Should Take More Guantanamo Prisoners 110
No. 49. US Bomb Attacks in Iraq Contravene UN Charter 112

No. 50. Junior Academic Staff Are Exploited at Universities 113

No. 51. Centenary of Armenian Genocide 114

No. 52. Questions Remain About Shannon Stopovers 115

No. 53. The Garda Síochána needs to downsize. 116

No. 54. Irish Neutrality Is a Good Example for Europe 116

No. 55. A Powerful Easter Message from Edward Horgan of Shannonwatch . 117

No. 56. Mary Lou McDonald is Acting in the Public Interest 118

No. 57. EU Should Face Court Over Its Cruel Policy on Mediterranean Refugees 118

No. 58. It Is Shameful the Government Failed to Commemorate Genocide 119

No. 59. Irish Have Long Sought Refuge Overseas and So Must Offer Refuge 120

No. 60. Afghan and Iraqi Wars Exacerbate Conflicts in Middle East and Africa 121

No. 61. Unjustified Wars Cause Hatred, Further Violence, and Terrorism 121

No. 62. Austria Shows Us the Way with Show of Neutrality 123

No. 63. Don't Damage Peace to Score Points on Sinn Féin 123

No. 64. Our Role in US Wars Helped Provoke Crisis 124

No. 65. Conflict Resolution is Key to Solving Migrant Crisis 124

No. 66. Ireland Should Recognise the Armenian Genocide 126

No. 67. Ireland Can't Distance Itself from the US Bombings Which Kill Children 126

No. 68. President and Taoiseach Absent from Funerals. Why? 127

No. 69. Having Fire Extinguishers in Cars is Dangerous 128

No. 70. Low Rank Arrest in Relation to Bloody Sunday Killings 128

No. 71. Syria and Terror Attacks on Paris 129

No. 72. Ireland Must Make Peace and Not War 130

No. 73. Prepared For a Terrorist Attack? 131

No. 74. It's Shameful That We Can't Find Room at the Inn 132

No. 75. Bankers Were Guilty of False Imprisonment 132

No. 76. Ireland Must Do More to Help Rid the World of the Nuclear Risk 133

No. 77. UN Forces Should Not Still Be in Golan Heights 134

No. 78. Israeli Illegal Annexation of the Syrian Golan Heights. 135

No. 79. We Need to Re-Address The Regional Imbalance 136

No. 80. Permanent Members of the UN Security Council Are Above the Law
.... 136

No. 81. Petitions Committee Publish Final Report on Irish Neutrality 137

No. 82. We Need to Ensure a Referendum on Neutrality Is an Election Issue 138

No. 83. Irish Politics Ignores Global Issues to Its Peril 139

No. 84. The Refugee Crisis Has Shown Just How Much the EU Has Lost Its
Way 140

No. 85. Ireland Complicit in Irradiation of Iraq 141

No. 86. Irish Neutrality is Breached by NATO and US Military Aircraft at
Shannon 141

No. 87. We Must Recognise Armenian Genocide 142

No. 88. New States of Independence 143

No. 89. Charity Thieves Are Worse Than Robbers 143

No. 90. New Threat of Militarisation 144

No. 91. We Need Irish Version of Chilcot 144

No. 92. Sentencing for Child Rape 145

No. 93. Americans are Insulting International Law on Irish Land 146

No. 94. Direct Provision Exacerbating Refugee Suffering 148

No. 95. Good Work at Shannon Airport? 148

No. 96. Israeli Shoot to Kill Policy Designed to Terrorise 150

No. 97. 700km Wall Will Be a Barrier to Peace 150

No. 98. John Kerry and Tipperary Peace Prize 152

No. 99. Peace an Unattainable Goal in the Middle East 152

No. 100. Complicity to Refuel any Warship 153

No. 101. Ireland Needs to Help Reform UN 154

No. 102. American Revolution – Coming to Terms with Donald Trump, the President-Elect of the United States 155

No. 103. Most Irish Would Agree with Higgins About Castro 155

No. 104. Visit of Naval Vessel Was Not Welcome 156

No. 105. Only Democracy is the Answer 157

No. 106. Why is Navy Taking Break from Med? 158

No. 107. Migrant Deal with Libya a Non-Runner 158

No. 108. Killing Other Human Beings Is Never Heroic and Irish Citizens Must Resist Joining Foreign Forces 159

No. 109. Apologies For Growing Old – Turns Out I'm Ruining the Country . 160

No. 110. Smuggling Armies as Well as People 161

No. 111. Torture Simply Does Not Work and Can Never Be Justified 162

No. 112. Our 'Turning a Blind Eye' Policy 163

No. 113. RAF Has No Right to Irish Air Space 163

No. 114. Supporting the Air Corps in its Mission 164

No. 115. The UN, Saudi Arabia, and Women's Rights 165

No. 116. Peacekeepers and the Drones 166

No. 117. Neutrality, 'Sacred Cows', and Brexit 167

No. 118. Britain Has Lost Its Way 168

No. 119. Manchester Terrorist Attack 168

No. 120. The World, and Ireland, Must Wake Up to Genocide in Yemen 169

No. 121. Neutrality Must Mean Making Peace, Not War 170

No. 122. Varadkar Must Do Better for Our Unfortunate Asylum Seekers 171

No. 123. UN Day In Support of Victims of Torture 171

No. 124. Leo's Shannon 172

No. 125. An Erosion of Neutrality? 173

No. 126. War of Words Between North Korea and US 174

No. 127. EU Army an Alternative to the NATO-Led Army? 175

No. 128. O'Loan Has Shown She's Up to the Task 179

No. 129. Square-Bashing Brainwashes Gardai 180

No. 130. Legacy of Cosgraves is Multi-Faceted 180

No. 131. Irish Naval Service Purchase of Ships 181

No. 132. Exposing the Truth with Regard to Wrongdoing Often Imposes Costs on the Whistleblower 182

No. 133. Commemorating Wars 183

No. 134. All Citizens of the World Should Be Equal Before the Law, Including War Criminals 184

No. 135. No Security for Us Without Neutrality 185

No. 136. The Plight of The Homeless Is A National Concern 185

No. 137. The Slaughter of So Many Innocents 186

No. 138. Police Adding Jam to the Cake 187

No. 139. UN Peacekeeping Missions 187

No. 140. Neutral Stance a Positive Move 188

No. 141. Human Rights Abuses Began Before the Holocaust 189

No. 142. It Is Not Good Enough for Witnesses to Be Silent 189

No. 143. Our Troops Are Being Put at Risk 190

No. 144. Neutrality and Unlawful Orders 190

No. 145. Ireland Over-Hasty in Joining the Rush to Expel Russian Diplomats 191

No. 146. Where Are Our Rugby Heroes Gone? 192

No. 147. False Flag War Crimes in Syria? 192

No. 148. Army Ranger Wing Served with NATO in Afghanistan 193

No. 149. Irish Health Service Mismanagement 194

No. 150. Militarisation of a 'Peaceful' Europe 195

No. 151. Incorrect Registration of Births 195

No. 152. 'Clinton Blackens TCD Name' 196

No. 153. Helping the Vulnerable in Syria 197

No. 154. UN Security Council Bid: Campaign Intensifies 198

No. 155. Belgian Apologies to the Congo? 199

No. 156. Never Too Old to Make a Difference 200

No. 157. Security, Defence, and Neutrality 201

No. 158. Mainstream Media Not to Be Trusted. 202

No. 159. The Agony of Yemen Getting Worse. 203

No. 160. Ireland's Record on Torture Prevention 204

No. 161. Immunity for US Soldiers in Ireland? 204

No. 162. 'IRA Song' Inappropriate for Hurlers' Celebration 205

No. 163. Facilitating the Killing of Children in the Middle East. 206

No. 164. Peaceful Ways to End War Crimes 207

No. 165. Nuclear Watchdogs are Failing to Bark 208

No. 166. Genuine Reform of Garda Force Needed 209

No. 167. Up to 1,000 Die on Day of Peace 209

No. 168. Accountability for Economic Crash 210

No. 169. Zappone Commands the Moral High Ground, Unlike So Many 211

No. 170. La Francophonie and Cultural Colonialism 212

No. 171. Media Ignoring Majority Interests 213

No. 172. The Role of Individuals in Promoting International Peace and Justice
.... 214

No. 173. Ireland Does Little to Help with the Famine in Yemen 225

No. 174. Why Do Laws Stop People Voting? Votes for Irish Citizens Living
Abroad 226

No. 175. Should Scouting Ireland be Disbanded? 227

No. 176. Crises Facing Our World Are the Fault of Humankind, Not God or Religion 228

No. 177. Revoking Irish Citizenship 229

No. 178. Irish Army Ranger Wing is Likely to be Sent to Mali 230

No. 179. Intervention by US Has Left Nations in Chaos 231

No. 180. It is Time to Suspend Work on Children's Hospital 232

No. 181. Punish Corruption in the Here and Now 232

No. 182. Ireland Complicit in Deaths of Yemeni Kids 233

No. 183. Irish Troops Need to Stay Out of the Golan Heights 234

No. 184. Neutrality Has Never Been More Important 235

No. 185. Julian Assange Facing Conspiracy Charges 236

No. 186. We Are All Complicit in US Aggression 237

No. 187. Irish Troops and a War in Mali 238

No. 188. Our Defence Forces Need to be Treated with More Respect 239

No. 189. When Will State Take Some of the Blame for America's Wars? 240

No. 190. Solving the Beef Farming Crisis 241

No. 191. The Celtic Interconnector with France Connects to Nuclear Energy 242

No. 192. President is Right to Speak Truth to Power 242

No. 193. Tough Laws Needed 243

No. 194. Rescuing Refugees in the Mediterranean 244

No. 195. Europe's Vision Includes War 245

No. 196. Concerned at Fracking Extremists 246

No. 197. By Our Silence And Inaction, We Are Complicit 247

No. 198. Parties of Law and Order? 248

No. 199. Coronavirus Threat at Shannon Airport 249

No. 200. International Women's Day? 249

No. 201. Us Military Should Not Be Using Shannon Airport 250

No. 202. Need to Question Draconian Decisions 251

No. 203. For the Future of Democracy, It Is Vital That Sinn Féin Are Part of the Next Government 252

No. 204. Criticism in a Crisis Can Help Save Lives 253

No. 205. SF Deserves to Be Invited to Join National Government 254

No. 206. Too Many Compromises 254

No. 207. Varadkar's €10M Military Transport Plane.......................................255

No. 208. Civilian Control of Defence is Democratic 256

No. 209. Ireland's Place on the UN Security Council......................................257

No. 210. Ireland Has Blood on Its Hands for Letting US Military Use Shannon 258

No. 211. 'Rule of Law' in EU 259

No. 212. 175 Years On, We Still Have a Lot to Learn from the Famine 259

No. 213. Abuses Of Human Rights Off the Scale 261

No. 214. Apologies Are No Substitute for Justice..262

No. 215. What of Culpability of the Fathers?...263

No. 216. An Effort to Right the Wrongs or a Bid to Limit the Damage?.........263

No. 217. Time to Ground Shannon Stopover 264

No. 218. Shannon and US Military's COVID Risk..265

No. 219. COVID-19 Exemptions for US Military at Shannon Airport? 265

No. 220. US Abused the Law 266

No. 221. Ireland Needs to Help in Myanmar..267

No. 222. Why We Must Speak Up to Prevent More Genocides 268

No. 223. Ireland's Neutrality Should Not Be Undermined 269

No. 224. Weapons Transport at Shannon Airport 270

No. 225. Death of Donald Rumsfeld 271

No. 226. Very Little Justice for Victims of Abuse 272

No. 227. Diplomacy Trumps Force 273

No. 228. Links Between Climate Change and Our Security 274
No. 229. Human Cost of US, EU, UN Sanctions 275
No. 230. Further Steps Needed Towards Taking Violence Out of Irish Politics 276
No. 231. Inappropriate Assertion... 277
No. 232. Why Are Irish Soldiers in Mali? 278
No. 233. Accountability for Torture 279
No. 234. What About All the Western Military Operations Near Us? 280
No. 235. International Neutrality Project... 281
No. 236. Simon Coveney Chops and Changes the Rules 289
No. 237. We Must Not Become a Stopover on Way to War 289
No. 238. US Sanctions on Syria and Cuba Are Described as Aggression by Irish Peace Activist 290
No. 239. We Should Facilitate Peace, Not US Troop Movements 291
No. 240. Ireland Must Use Active Neutrality to Promote Peace in Ukraine ... 291
No. 241. President's Statement Not Reported in Media 296
No. 242. Putin Knows He Won't Face Justice for His War Crimes 297
No. 243. Push for Peace 298
No. 244. The European Peace Project?.. 299
No. 245. Neutrality Gone AWOL? 300
No. 246. French Ambassador is Not Helping Matters 301
No. 247. Choosing Which Refugees Not to Welcome Is Racist...................... 301
No. 248. International Law Has Been Flouted by the Irish State For Years ... 302
No. 249. Human Rights Abuse in Sahara 303
No. 250. Western Nations Failing to Uphold Marine Obligations 304
No. 251. Aggressive EU Pushback Policies 305
No. 252. Unreasonable Criticism... 306
No. 253. Sinn Féin Not Only Ones Who Seek to Justify Political Violence ... 307

No. 254. If EU Sends Troops to Ukraine, Then Ireland Should Refuse 308
No. 255. Don't Rush to Judgement 309
No. 256. Silence of the Sheep 310
No. 257. Gas Pipeline Retaliation 310
No. 258. Apologising for Past Violence and Renouncing It into the Future Will Unite Us – Not IRA Chants 311
No. 259. Irish Neutrality Suffering Death by a Thousand Cuts 312
No. 260. NATO and EU Military Alliances Compromise Neutrality 313
No. 261. Justice Comes, Albeit 53 Years Too Late for Dónal de Róiste 313
No. 262. Death of an Irish Peacekeeper 314
No. 263. In 2023, Ireland Must Do What Is Right for Humanity 315
No. 264. Rescue Response in Syria Will Be Lesser Due to World Politics 316
No. 265. We Should Learn from the Swiss on Neutrality 317
No. 266. All Human Lives Are Equally Important. 317
No. 267. Too Many Women Are Being Forced Out of Irish Politics. 318
No. 268. Irish Government Active in Supporting War 319
No. 269. The International Criminal Court 320
No. 270. Remaining Neutral in All Aspects of War 321
No. 271. Ireland, Neutral, Non-Aligned, or NATO Belligerent? 321
No. 272. EU Bombs for Peace 333
No. 273. We Must Advocate for Peace Worldwide, Not Just at Home 334
No. 274. Are Mistakes of Rwanda Being Repeated in Sudan? 335
No. 275. Where is 'Register of Damage' For Victims of US Conflicts? 336
No. 276. Second-Hand Ships Not Up to the Task for Naval Service 337
No. 277. Environmental Crisis Needs to Be Tackled Not Neglected 337
No. 278. At a Crossroads on a United Ireland 338
No. 279. Med Mission Leaves Gap Off Our Coasts 339

No. 280. Ireland and Its Neutrality 340

No. 281. The New RTÉ Will Have to Be Independent 341

No. 282. Never Too Late to Do What Is Right.. 342

No. 283. Sinéad Was a Woman of Peace, So Warplane Tribute Was Deeply Inappropriate.. 343

No. 284. Two Wrongs Do Not Make a Right... 343

No. 285. Affairs of the Nation, Pillars of Society, Edward Horgan 344

No. 286. Thesis Edward J. Horgan, University of Limerick, 2008 The United Nations – Beyond Reform? The Collective Insecurity of the International System and the Prospects for Sustainable Global Peace and Justice............... 352

Introduction

Polonius: 'What do you read my Lord?'
Hamlet: 'Words, Words, Words.'

I decided to put this book of letters together, not just to record my past writings on matters that I considered to be of public interest, but also to help draw attention to the many wrongs that I have become aware of throughout my life. I was privileged to grow up on a small farm in Co Kerry, the seventh of eight siblings, with two grandparents, and two altruistic and very industrious parents in the immediate aftermath of World War II. I was just a few weeks old when the United States unjustifiably dropped atomic bombs on Hiroshima and Nagasaki. In the early 1960s, issues of international peace were highlighted by struggles for independence from abusive European colonial powers, as well as by the Irish Defence Forces' involvement in the United Nations peacekeeping, or peace enforcing mission in the Congo, and by the Cuban missile crisis. Tolstoy's *War and Peace* was one of the books I read as a teenager, so helping to contribute towards international peace seemed like an interesting career choice. I applied to join the military academy of the Irish Defence Forces and was fortunate to be accepted. In 1966, I served as a young lieutenant on a peacekeeping mission in Cyprus.

Most of my travels around the world have been to conflict regions and my research in recent years has focused on the colossal suffering these conflicts inflicted on so many innocent people, especially children, who are the most innocent of the innocent. I have survived so far without serious injuries, except perhaps the moral injury of survivor's guilt, wondering did I do enough to right the wrongs I saw and learned about. Given the huge scale of these injustices and suffering, can we ever do enough? The reasons these conflicts and suffering are continuing is that too many are doing too little – standing idly by – while too many also are complicit or actively involved in crimes against humanity.

In human communications, words are of huge importance, in how they are used and misused, understood and misunderstood. My experiences and the experiences of most members of the Irish Defence Forces have been that our service has been far more oriented towards making peace than making war. Even the word peacemaker is a much-misused work. The Colt 45 revolver, used far too much in nineteenth-century USA, was cynically known as the Peacemaker, and in recent times several bogus so-called humanitarian missions in Afghanistan, Iraq, and Libya have also been called peace-making or humanitarian missions.

The opinions I present in this book have been informed by life experiences varying from a tough but idyllic childhood on a small farm on the west coast of Ireland, through service as a UN military peacekeeper, multiple election monitoring missions in almost twenty countries that have experienced serious conflicts, leading on to significant involvement with peace and environmental movements in Ireland and internationally. I have been deeply privileged to have met and shared time and experiences with so many wonderful people and cultures, to have experienced the kindness of strangers so many times in foreign lands and shared in their joys and traumas in times of peace and conflict. My belief in the goodness of humanity has been reinforced rather than shattered by the conflicts I have witnessed, and it is my firm belief that all such conflicts are avoidable and that now, more than ever, violent conflicts and destruction of our living environment must be prevented rather than stopped after they have occurred. Otherwise, humanity and much of our planet's living beings and organisms may become extinct due to our reckless behaviour.

My sheltered life changed rapidly when I joined the Irish Army as an eighteen-year-old. My foundational values came from my family, and I built on these foundations with my enquiring and ever-challenging mind. Questioning the status quo and the authorities often made life uncomfortable for me, and for the authorities being questioned, especially in my military days, As a young army officer, I seemed almost invulnerable heading off overseas in command of a troop of four armoured cars and a team of twelve soldiers, on our way as UN peacekeepers to form a buffer zone between the warring Greek and Turkish Cypriot forces on the beautiful island of Cyprus. I received a quick lesson on my own vulnerability and mortality on my twenty-first birthday, 12 June 1966. Our buffer zone was in a valley with a Turkish village on one side overlooked by Greek Cypriot forces in the foothills of the Troodos mountains. There had been some shooting earlier in the day that had resulted in a Greek Cypriot soldier being killed, and an uneasy calm in the meantime. At midnight, all hell broke loose as the Greek Cypriots opened fire on the Turkish positions around the village with mortars, machine guns, and rifles. The situation we were in has been described as 'the pig in the middle'. My job as duty officer of the day was to get all our soldiers out of their tents and into sandbagged bunkers. The noise from the machine guns and explosions was so loud that I failed to hear or recognise the sound of a heavy machine gun that was firing at the ground a few feet behind me. I made an easy target with our camp lights still on, but all the lights in the Turkish village were wisely extinguished. I survived unharmed, but on reflection the following day decided that since my life was likely to be short, I was going to live life to the full, and hopefully, to live a life worth living. In the meantime, that incident has proven to be only one of many such close encounters with death.

In 1973, an Irish battalion was sent to the Sinai Desert as peacekeepers with the United Nations Emergency Force (UNEF 2). I was battalion logistics officer close to the Suez Canal in a buffer zone separating the Yom Kippur War forces of Israel and Egypt, in an area littered with minefields from several recent and past wars. I was a front-seat passenger in a Land Rover that drove over the edge of a live anti-tank mine. Fortunately, it turned the live landmine on its edge and tossed it unexploded to one side. My guardian angel was working overtime. A short time later, our Irish battalion handed over one of our outposts in this area to a platoon of a newly arrived Peruvian battalion. They decided that the steel tent pegs needed to be hammered down more firmly into the sand. The steel peg hit mine like the one I had encountered, but that mine exploded, ₍r Peruvian soldiers.

Moı₍ ₍cently in May 2015 while observing the presidential elections in southeastern Turkey near the Syrian border with the Organisation for Peace and Security in Europe (OSCE) I had arranged to meet the officials and candidates of the Kurdish HDP party in the city of Adana. As we walked into the building, there was an explosion in the office that we were about to enter, seriously injuring the six people and causing a fire and structural damage. The Turkish Government blamed the explosion on ISIS terrorists, but the Kurdish HDP party said it was more likely to have been the work of the so-called 'deep state', meaning sources close to the government security services.

Routine army service at home in Ireland is often boring, performing normal garrison duties, so we try to make life more interesting at times by being creative in our training exercises. One such training course I embarked on was a parachuting course run by the Army Ranger Wing. The course was intended as adventure training for soldiers in the First Tank Squadron, of which I was the commanding officer. The aircraft we were jumping out of was a tiny single-engine propeller Cessna aircraft. It looked so frail it was a relief to exit into the sky. In order to complete the parachute jump, one had to climb out under the wing and precariously stand on a step near the wheel while holding on to the wing overhead. The pilot was meant to switch off the engine and glide while the parachutist was getting out. On my second jump, the sequence of moves went a bit wrong, and the pilot forgot to switch off the engine as I climbed out under the wing. I managed to get one foot on the step and one hand on the wing grip before the force of the wind from the propeller blew me away from the plane. I counted the required ten seconds before looking up to see if my parachute had opened properly and found that my hasty exit had resulted in the strings on the left side being tangled up, and the parachute less than half opened. Even though I had a second emergency parachute in front of me, this was not a good situation. I had been told in training that if the main chute is half-open, then when you deploy the emergency chute, it is likely to get tangled up in the partially open main chute. I was dropping rapidly toward Mother Earth. My options were to jettison my main chute and then deploy my emergency chute or to try to rectify the problem with the main chute. I opted for the latter, pulling down the tangled strings, shaking them briskly, and letting them go again. Thankfully, this resulted in my main parachute opening fully. By now Mother Earth was much closer, so I had to prepare for a hard landing, knees slightly bent, don't look down, look out parallel, and roll into the ground. It was a hard landing, but I survived with just a few bruises.

These were just some of my close encounters, so much so that I have always been somewhat surprised to reach the next decade. As a result of these events and having seen so many young people's lives cut all too short by avoidable and destructive conflicts, I like to remind people of my vintage that getting old is not a problem, it's a privilege.

Readers may find some contradictions in this book. Welcome to the real world. The world as I have experienced it so far, is full of contradictions. With the benefit of hindsight, I do not always agree with things I may have said and written in the past. Every day should be a learning experience, modifying what we may have thought was the truth yesterday. The truth does not change, but our imperfect perception of the truth should change as we learn more, and we must always strive to learn more each day. Those who are certain that their opinions are always right are dangerous people. Religion encouraged blind faith where we were expected to switch off our brains and do what our religious leaders told us to do or not to do. The power that this bestowed on religious leaders was inevitably abused. Political leaders on the left and right understood this route to power and followed in the abusive steps of abusive religious leaders. Religious leaders called this the gift of faith, political leaders call it loyalty to one's flag or country or towards Mein Fuhrer, and Marxists believed that those who failed to appreciate the benefits of communism were suffering from false consciousness.

My first scheme for this book was to include the letters in separate chapters dealing with different themes and topics in various regions of the world. I soon discovered that humanity refuses to divide up so conveniently, especially in this interconnected twenty-first century. An air attack in the Middle East that kills dozens of people carried out by NATO (the North Atlantic Treaty Organization) air forces or CIA (the US Central Intelligence Agency) killer drones may involve a small town called Shannon in the west of Ireland, just as the terrorist attacks in New York on 9/11 that killed almost 3,000 people, also included two Irish victims Ruth Clifford McCourt and her four-year-old daughter Juliana. I therefore decided to adopt a simpler structure and to include the letters and articles in chronological order, beginning with my first efforts at publication. Readers who might like to begin with the most recent letters may decide to begin at the end and work backwards. Just imagine you are reading a book in Arabic.

For the convenience of the readers, I have numbered the letters and articles and compiled a Table of Contents, which included these numbers with the title or subject matter of each letter. I have included as many of my letters as I could find as well as articles that I have had published. The main focus of my letters is on matters of war and peace, human rights and human wrongs, and the environment, as well as some general matters of political and current affairs interest.

Readers may notice that my opinions, especially on matters of war and peace, have changed or modified over time, influenced by changing circumstances and new information gained through my experiences and research. This applies particularly to my views on the United Nations. Human society and interaction at all levels are constantly evolving, especially at international level. However, in my view, the UN Charter was written in a manner that almost prohibits evolution and reform. I will return to this issue towards the end of the book.

I tend to read the newspapers in print or electronically most mornings. Since good news is no news and bad news is enhanced by 'alternative facts', by about 10 a.m. my blood pressure will have risen, like the Victor Meldrew TV character, except I don't have 'one foot in the grave' just yet. There are so many half-truths, post-truths, and damned lies in our mainstream and alternative media these days, I'm likely to feel obliged to respond to some injustice or incompetence with a letter to the papers. I cannot single-handedly change the world, but I'm energised enough to follow my motto 'in the face of evil and stupidity, whatever you do, don't do nothing'. However, words written or spoken are not enough of themselves to counter the various local, national, international, and global crises that seem to be accumulating and threatening to destroy our human society and the fragile environment we need for survival. The 'doing' aspect is outside the scope of this book, but words, however robust, must be accompanied by determined actions if vital human rights and human lives are to be protected.

The truism that 'the pen is mightier than the sword' may have been true at times in the past, but with modern warfare and violence, the capacity of the modern swords is such that we must combine our pens and words with very determined civil society non-violent activism. The temptation to embrace the so-called just war theory and fight violence with violence is what gave humanity the horrors of First World War trench warfare, recurring acts of genocide, war crimes such as Hiroshima and Dresden, and crimes against humanity of which the Holocaust was by far the worst. The actions of deranged superpower leaders with their fingers on nuclear warfare buttons are no joking matter, and it is irresponsible for each of us to ignore the real threats to human existence and to all life on this increasingly vulnerable Planet Earth.

This book consists of letters and articles published in various newspapers, mainly in Ireland. I have been surprised how many of my letters have made it into print, so I owe thanks to the editors for their editing and their decisions to print. Each day that passes, we experience a multitude of events, each competing with the others for attention and notoriety. In this age of instant communication and travel, there are also no clear dividing lines between the local and the global. A butterfly flapping its wings in the Amazon rain forests may not always cause a tsunami or a hurricane in Texas but a decision taken on a Tuesday morning by a US President, or by a military or paramilitary commander, can have devastating consequences for a village wedding party or a sleeping family in Afghanistan, Pakistan, Yemen, Somalia, or wherever some possibly incompetent 'intelligence' officials choose to send drones or special forces on targeted assassinations. The global becomes the local, and the political in the USA becomes the personal in an impoverished village, especially if a second drone strike hits the funeral procession caused by the first strike. This is cynically known as the 'double tap', given the likelihood that the funerals will be attended by the local leaders, who may have been the target of the first attack. Such murderous examples perpetrated by the US, NATO, and their allies are now also being perpetrated by Russia and by military and other dictators in Africa and elsewhere.

Military Articles 1977 to 1986

Comment: For the purposes of clarity, I include separate comments on my letters in italic script to differentiate them from the actual letters and articles. My first excursions into print began during my military service and entailed a number of articles I had published in An Cosantóir, the Irish Defence Forces monthly journal and were usually on topics related to the Cavalry or armoured corps in which I served for over twenty-two years. Blitzkrieg was the title of my first article, an attempt by me to emphasise the point that the World War I tactics and equipment we were using were outdated by the 1970s, and that we should at least accept that World War II had changed the reality of how wars are fought. I had experienced modern war first-hand, when I had served as a UN peacekeeper in the Sinai Desert in 1973/74 where I had witnessed the recent battlefields of the Yom Kippur or October War where whole armoured brigades had fought and been destroyed, and human bodies were being devoured by wild desert dogs. These early articles are from what could be termed my warmongering days!

No. 1.
An Cosantóir May 1977
BLITZKRIEG by Capt. E.J. Horgan

There are two popular misconceptions on the use of armour, which are still current in modern military thinking. One is that armour is merely a cavalry weapon to be used in supporting roles, and the second is that the tank is simply a mobile field artillery piece. Costly experiences have proved these theories wrong and armoured forces now form the main battle forces of all effective modern armies. The traditional roles of infantry, cavalry, and artillery are now giving way to the combined arms team concept.

In the 1914–18 war, the Allies tried to break the German forces by application of the principle of ATTRITION, i.e., sacrificing three Allied soldiers to eliminate two Germans and relying on numerical superiority to win. History shows that this strategy was never fully successful. The

Germans were beaten but not broken. Twenty-three years later, Germany completely destroyed Poland, whose total forces were over 3 million men at a cost of only 10,000 German casualties.

The explanation for this victory lies in the German use of a military technique developed in England by men such as Capt. LIDDLE HART. The practical application of these theories was called BLITZKRIEG.

CONCENTRATION OF FORCE is the basic element of this technique. It is much easier to destroy the enemy by cutting off his supplies and communications and by destroying his command-and-control structure than by attempting to batter him into submission. The development of armoured vehicles brought back mobility and surprise into the battlefield. The BLITZKRIEG technique involves a quick breakthrough on the main enemy defences at a number of chosen points, followed by rapid use of PINCER movements to encircle and fragment the enemy forces.

The ATTACK FORCE is made up as follows:
1. Air cover attack aircraft
2. An armoured spearhead with sappers and shock troops
3. Main armoured attack force
4. Mobile artillery and tank destroyers
5. Armoured infantry
6. Motorised and holding infantry on foot

The attack is divided into four phases:

Phase I: Holding troops keep defenders occupied along as wide a front as possible, while attacking forces are assembled secretly at a number of strategic points. Three or four attack points are normal. Dive bombers and long-range artillery isolate the immediate battleground, cut off reserves, and silence enemy guns. The armoured spearhead with sappers and shock troops advance to the first obstacle. Special bridges and boats are used to seize and hold strategic points and to disrupt enemy rear areas.

Phase II: Assault troops seize and widen the bridgehead, and demolition squads deal with strongpoints. The armoured spearhead moves up through the bridgehead and attacks forward, followed by the main attack force. Mobile artillery and armoured infantry follow the armour and clear up remaining opposition and secure the flanks of the bridgehead. Dive bombers clear the area in advance of the armour and attack communications and reserves.

Phase III: When the armoured spearhead has broken through the main defence, it spreads out and deals with the enemy with localised pincer movements. Every effort is made to encircle and cut off the enemy and not drive him back.

The main armoured attack force moves through, supported by mobile artillery and armoured infantry and attack key road and rail junctions. Large bodies of enemy troops and strongpoints are bypassed and encircled. Motorised and holding infantry move up to secure and expand the bridgehead.

Phase IV: Spearheads should now have broken through at several points along the front. Armoured attack forces now plunge deep into the enemy rear areas and the attack forces, where possible, combine to form huge pincer movements, trapping the main enemy force. Mobile artillery and armoured infantry follow closely to maintain communications and reduce strongpoints. Motorised infantry and infantry on foot move in to collect prisoners and surround difficult enemy pockets. Reserve troops move up to the original front to carry out supply and security tasks for the forward troops.

The German attack on Poland in 1939 was the classic example of the Blitzkrieg technique in use. At 0500hrs on Sept. 1, the German Air Force crossed the frontier and began the destruction of Polish airfields, aircraft, roads, railways, and anything that looked like a communications centre or HQ. Within two days, the Luftwaffe controlled the air and could concentrate on tactical support for the advancing armour. The attack was broken into four main columns. Each column carried out the first three phases of the Blitzkrieg attack, which is basically breaking through the frontier defences.

Column 1 attacked from the northwest and headed towards WARSAW.

Column 2 advanced from the southwest and blasted its way north to join up with Column 1 just west of WARSAW and thus closed the inner pincher movement.

Column 3 attacked from EAST PRUSSIA in the north and moved south for BREST LITOVSK, which was captured on 14 September.

Column 4 attacked from CZECHOSLOVAKIA in the south and moved north to join up with Column 3 near BREST LITOVSK. This completed the outer pincer movement and led to the total collapse of the Polish army.

The tactics used in this campaign were soon to be repeated in France and the Netherlands. The effects were just as devastating as the Allies had as yet no defence against this onslaught.

BLITZKRIEG, however, did not originate in 1939. Such tactics and the use of high-speed armoured forces can be traced back through history. If we study the campaign between Alexander the Great and Darius of Syria about 330BC, we see that the Syrian army had a strong striking force consisting of elephants, armoured chariots which mounted a long blade on each side, and horse cavalry. The elephants and chariots were used to smash their way through the enemy front formations and cause panic in the rear ranks. These were followed closely by the mass of cavalry and infantry whose job it was to turn panic into a rout.

However, every attack has its counter-attack and every tactic has its counter-tactic. The Blitzkrieg tactic of Darius was countered by the Greek PHALANX system of Alexander, which stood fast against attack and allowed the elephants and chariots to pass between them and be captured in the rear.

Likewise, in the Punic Wars about 200BC between Carthage and Rome, Hannibal used what could be described as a Blitzkrieg tactic in his efforts to destroy Rome. With Hannibal himself advancing from Southern Italy and his brother Hasdrubal from Spain having crossed the Alps with his elephants, they hoped to trap the Romans in a giant pincer movement. However, this idea was defeated by the Romans, who, instead of sending one army against each of the Africans, sent both armies against Hasdrubal and clobbered him at the battle of Meturus. Hannibal was now in trouble with one army facing two Roman armies. He was 'up BLITZKRIEG without a paddle' and was defeated at ZAMA.

In modern history, the Israelis have proven to be keen students of German warfare. Moshe DAYAN's SINAI campaign in 1956 was a brilliantly executed campaign.

The attack opened with a drop of 400 paratroopers at MITLA. Egyptian airfields were bombed, and most of the planes were caught on the ground. The main ground attack consisted of four armoured spearheads that broke through the frontier defences and blasted their way westward.

Column 1 crossed the border on 30 October and headed for MITLA, where they joined up with the paratroopers.

Colum 2 broke through the strong defences at ABU AGEILE and advanced to within twenty miles of ISMAILIA on the SUEZ Canal.

Column 3 captured EL ARISH having bypassed the GAZA STRIP and blasted their way along the coast road as far as ROMANI.

Column 4 left KUNTILA and headed south for Sharm el Sheikh. Part of Column 1 moved south from MITLA along the Gulf of Suez with the object of taking SHAREM-EL-SHEIKH in a pincer movement. It fell on 5 November.

When the Israeli forces withdrew from Sinai, one would have thought that the Egyptians would have learned something from so expensive a defeat. However, this was not so. In the Six Day War of June 1967, the Israeli forces once again advanced into the Sinai Peninsula, using basically the same tactics, similar formations and almost the same routes of advance, as they had used in 1956.

This time, the Egyptian defeat was even more complete. Israeli forces captured the whole of Sinai and held the east bank of the Suez Canal, and unlike the 1956 campaign, they did not withdraw.

The subsequent YOM KIPPUR War in October 1973 is still being studied by military experts to find out what went wrong on both sides. The Egyptian forces appear to have carried out Phases I, II, and III, of the BLITZKRIEG technique with remarkable precision and efficiency. They then hesitated and instead of attacking on a number of fronts, they decided to defend along a wide front. This allowed the Israelis, who had taken a heavy beating, to recover the initiative. Using the Blitzkrieg method, they attacked on a narrow front, and succeeded in reaching and crossing the Canal, while at the same time encircling and trapping the Egyptian 3rd Army east of Suez.

While this method of warfare may be further refined in the coming years, the basic principles of armoured combat are unlikely to change in the foreseeable future.

I conclude with a quotation from Capt. Liddle Hart: -

"Napoleon once said: force = mass X velocity. This is very true of armour in modern war. The real force in tanks is the product of mass, velocity, and surprise. They give the Commander a chance of fulfilling FORRESTER'S famous recipe for success: GETTIN THAR FUSTEST WITH THE MOSTEST – FIRE AND FEAR –"

Comment: This article above was important for me as my first publication but it was also an attempt to update tactics and thinking in the Defence Forces. The older generation of officers were not for turning, secure in their mistaken views that their out-of-date tactics had worked well in the

Congo in the 1960s. Twenty-six Irish soldiers died on the ONUC mission in the Congo, and many of their deaths were due to inadequate equipment and training and, in some cases, to inadequate leadership.

In 1983, I was appointed Officer Commanding the 1st Tank Squadron, an appointment that I held for three years, which proved to be the highlight of my military career. As 1984 was the 25th Anniversary of the establishment of the 1st Tank Sqn, we decided to celebrate this by having a special ceremonial parade at the Curragh Camp to which we invited retired Lieutenant General Sean Collins Powell, who had been involved in the purchase of the first tanks for the Defence Forces and was a nephew of Michael Collins who led the fight for Irish independence. We were anxious to honour this esteemed former cavalry officer while he was still alive. He died in 1991, aged 96. With the cooperation of the Editor of An Cosantóir, the January 1985 issue of An Cosantóir was dedicated to the 1st Tank Squadron, with a total of eight articles about the Squadron, two of which I helped write, as well as assisting with the editing of the issue.

No. 2.
An Cosantóir January 1985
Today's Tank Squadron and Tomorrow's

The 1 Tank Squadron is a mobile, flexible unit manned by young professional soldiers whose skills vary from technical and gunnery to parachuting. Its present equipment consists of twelve Scorpion Light Tanks (CVRT) in three troops of four tanks, and one troop of five Mark VI Timoney APCs. The Timoney wheeled APCs are a temporary allotment pending the purchase of tracked MICVs (Mechanised Infantry Combat Vehicles). The full Sqn organisation consists of Sqn HQ, three Tank Troops, one APC troop, and an Admin Troop, with a total of 145 personnel.

The full vehicle strength of the Sqn should be as follows:-

Sqn HQ:

2 Scorpion Tanks - 2 Sultan Command Vehicles - 1 FFR Land Rover

3 Tank Troops: 12 Scorpion Tanks - 3 FFRs

APC Troop: 3 APCs - 1 FFR

Admin Troop: 1 Samson ARV (recovery) - 5 FFRs - 10 Trucks (4x4) - 1 Tank Transporter - 1 Mobile Workshop - 1 Field Kitchen - 1 Fuel Tanker

EMPLOYMENT OF THE SCORPION SQUADRON
In an operation situation, the 1st Tank Sqn comes under the control of the Chief of Staff under the Director of Operations. However, it would frequently be employed in support of or under the Command to a brigade or other formation.

For independent operations, the Scorpion Sqn needs Infantry, Air, Artillery, and Engineer support and could carry out close and medium reconnaissance, and advance to contact objectives.

When operating with an Infantry Brigade, the Scorpion Sqn can be employed in all phases of operation, including Offensive, Defensive, and Retrograde operations.

In the offence, it can carry out Recce, Advance to Contact, give direct fire support, form part of a manoeuvre element, or assist with the reorganisation phase or pursue the enemy.

In defence, maximum use should always be made of the Scorpion's mobility for such tasks as Counter-Penetration, Counter-Attack, Anti-Tank Defence, and Brigade security.

The Tk Sqn is very well equipped for retrograde operations. The Scorpion was originally to fight covering force and retrograde operations against the threat of advancing forces. Because of its high-intensity profile, a Scorpion-equipped unit is considered unsuitable for current internal security operations. The Tk Sqn has no capability at present to operate in a nuclear or chemically contaminated area.

Finally, in peacetime, the 1st Tank Sqn is a demonstration unit for the Defence Forces as a whole and for the Military College in particular, for the purpose of demonstrating and practising commanders in mobile operations.

No. 3.

In April 1986 I had a further article in *An Cosantóir*:
Armour Developments in an Irish Context

Producing the best armoured vehicle has been the ambition of professional soldiers since the horse, the spear, and the chariot were assembled into the original armoured fighting vehicles. The current East/West arms race has produced a range of dinosaur-like main battle tanks weighing up to sixty tons and costing hundreds of thousands to manufacture. While each tank is a wonder of engineering in its own right, in Western countries the multiplicity of designs and national self-interests have pushed the cost of tanks beyond the cost-effective barrier.

The three main characteristics and requirements of Main Battle Tanks (MBTs) are FIREPOWER, MOBILITY, and PROTECTION. The priority of these factors varies with perceived national requirements. The Israeli Merkava reflects the importance of crew survivability to Israeli designers, while British MBTs favour firepower and protection, and the USA relies on its massive industrial base to produce large numbers of good workhorses such as the M 60 series.

The cost of the latest models of MBTs, such as the US Abrams M1, have put them beyond the reach of all but a few wealthy nations. Even these industrialised countries are now questioning the cost-effectiveness of 60-ton MBTs. A greater number of lighter less expensive tanks may eventually provide better security for less expenditure. Heavy expensive tanks may be necessary for aggressive offensive operations. However, for purely defensive or deterrent purposes, less expensive, tank-killer type AFVs are adequate and more cost-effective, especially if combined with mechanised dismountable troops equipped with hand-held and guided missile type of anti-tank weapons.

Most of the less industrialised countries are already moving in this direction, for example, Argentina (TAM MBT), Brazil (OSORIO MBT), and Italy (OT 40 MBT). Britain and the USA are also producing lighter tanks for export and for marine corps-type operations.

Sweden traditionally has been a leader and an innovator in the field of tank design. In the 1930s, Ireland purchased two light Landsverk tanks which were very advanced for their time and compare favourably with the present-day Scorpion CVR(T). The turretless S-Tank was built for the Swedish Army in 1960 and was regarded as a major breakthrough in tank design. In spite of some limitations, it worked well and is undergoing a mid-life improvement at present. Its imaginative concept may not yet have reached its full potential. In the 1970s, Sweden produced the IKV 91 light tank killer and more recently has been experimenting with new designs, including external gun mountings such as the UDES-19. It has avoided building or purchasing the latest types of heavy MBTs but has opted instead for mobile mechanised forces capable of inflicting heavy losses on any attacker.

Sweden's armoured strategy is worthy of closer study by us for several reasons. While the threat to Sweden may be more immediate due to its strategic location sandwiched between NATO and the Warsaw Pact, and astride the northern flank of Europe, in the event of an East/West conflict we face a similar if lesser threat due to our location on the Western flank astride the US supply route to NATO. Our neutral status, like Sweden, makes an offensive capability unnecessary, but like Sweden, we are obliged to defend our neutrality and our sovereignty. This can be achieved actively by having the ability to oppose hostile incursions on our territory, and passively by having a defence force which would be a deterrent to any potential attacker. If we cannot achieve either of these options, then our neutrality and our independence are at risk. Our country needs a defence capability as surely as a household needs an insurance policy.

In order to oppose or deter such hostile incursions, we need a modern mobile mechanised force. The size of this force will be limited by our resources and could only be introduced on a gradual phased basis between now and the end of the century. Our present Defence Forces would have to be tailored accordingly. The basic unit of such a force should be a mechanised regiment, which is a battalion-sized armoured unit. The long-term objective could be to have one mechanised regiment and at least two motorised infantry battalions per Command, supported at Army level by a combat support corps and a unified service support corp. The expenditure would not be excessive, as there would be economics due to the rationalisation of the existing corps structure of the Defence Forces.

The following is a possible organisation for such a proposed mechanised regiment.

The Tank Sqn should be equipped with 18 MBTs which should weigh under 35 tons, have a modern low recoil high velocity 105mm main armament, give protection up to 30mm cannon fire and have very good cross-country mobility. The medium recce sqn should be equipped with Scorpion-type AFVs with improved main armament and the addition of mounted ATGMs.

The Close Recce Sqn should be equipped with light, highly mobile missile-launching scout AFVs and multi-wheeled support AFVs.

The MICV Sqn should be equipped with tracked mechanised infantry combat vehicles and should include an integrated company-sized dismountable element, and a plentiful supply of ATGMs and light anti-tank weapons.

This organisation, in addition to the obvious National Defence benefits, would allow Defence Force units to specialise i.e., mechanised units could concentrate on training and readiness for conventional operations, while motorised units would train for and carry out internal security and aid to the civil power operations. This would eliminate ad hoc arrangements, which results in no units being adequately trained for either role. It would also provide better value for money.

For those unfamiliar with military jargon and abbreviations, the following are some explanations:

Scorpion CVRT – Combat Vehicle Reconnaissance Tracked

APC – Armoured Personnel Carrier

FFR Land Rover – Fitted For Radio

MBT – Main Battle Tank

ATGW – Anti-Tank Guided Missile

AFV – Armoured Fighting Vehicle

Comment: In 1985 I was appointed as senior instructor in armoured warfare at the Command and Staff College. I found myself obliged to teach the future senior commanders of the Irish Defence Forces military tactics and strategy based on military manuals from the British and US armed forces, which I knew were almost totally inappropriate towards defending the territory and people of the Irish Republic. Despite, or because of, what I had outlined in the previous article, I had concluded that Ireland did not have the resources to defend its territory by conventional military means and that it could only be defended, as our independence had been achieved, by guerrilla warfare. The counterargument was that if we had a squadron of fighter aircraft and a brigade of tanks and other associated military equipment, we could defend Ireland against any likely aggressor.

Saddam Hussein and Muammar Gaddafi were to discover to their cost that hundreds or even thousands of slightly out-of-date tanks and aircraft were useless against the conventional weapons of NATO. Their armies were obliterated in the first days of US/NATO-led attacks on their countries and their unfortunate conscript soldiers were slaughtered in their thousands.

Algeria and Vietnam had demonstrated the success of the guerrilla warfare alternative.

Our Military College experts got around this conundrum by the clever trick of designing all military exercises as if the invading forces always had a little less military power at their disposal than we had. No sensible military power would invade a country like Ireland without employing an attacking force about three times the strength of our defending forces. However, since we had a force of less than 10,000 soldiers and given that we had no combat aircraft or modern battle tanks, we tailored our imaginary enemies accordingly. When I suggested at exercises debriefs that guerrilla warfare was the only sane option, but that this needed to be planned carefully well in advance, I was told that this was neither army nor government policy and was told to teach the officially approved doctrines.

After six months in this appointment, I decided I had had enough of military life, so I opted for early retirement. I had enjoyed most of my twenty-two years of military service and did not want to spend a further twenty years cynically teaching or applying military training that I knew was fundamentally wrong. A further consideration was that at this time I had family commitments including three young children, and as a result I had decided that long periods on UN service overseas were inappropriate for me and my family situation. Leaving the Irish Defence Forces was the right decision for me at that time of my life and I went on to do many interesting things in the following years, and this interesting life is ongoing.

Letters and Article 1999 to 2023

Comment: I worked in security and safety management for over ten years, including as head of security at Trinity College Dublin, and Security Manager and Fire Chief at Aughinish Alumina Ltd, a large chemical plant in west Limerick. I did very little letter writing during this period. Following redundancy at Aughinish Alumina, and now that our children were young adults, I was free to undertake international peace work once again, particularly in the areas of democratisation and election observation and mainly in countries that had experienced serious conflicts.

Bosnia Herzegovina was my first assignment in 1996, helping to organise the first post-conflict elections in central Bosnia, where a vicious three-way civil war had been fought over the previous four years. For me, it was a steep but hugely informative learning curve. In addition to employment in a diverse variety of jobs, and because I had not so far gone on to third-level education apart from the military academy, I decided to go back to school to further my education and ended up doing three degrees: a BA in History, Politics, and Social Studies, an M.Phil. master's degree in Peace Studies, and a PhD in international relations and UN reform.

In 1999, I managed to combine completing my M.Phil. thesis on Bosnia with observing an outrageously corrupt election in Nigeria, with a European Union mission. I then spent twelve weeks in Indonesia, the world's fourth most populous country with another European Union election mission. There was a sharp contrast between my experiences with a very corrupt election in Nigeria, compared with what turned out to be a very successful EU election monitoring mission in Indonesia. The UN had imposed severe sanctions on Nigeria because of serious corruption and human rights abuses, as a result of which European oil companies were unable to import cheap Nigerian oil, and so needed the Nigerian elections to be declared free and fair, so that the UN sanctions could be removed. The elections were blatantly corrupt, unfree, and unfair, yet the UN sanctions on Nigeria were removed shortly afterwards. A few months later,

I served with a team of EU election monitors in Indonesia, and we were expecting similar problems with our mission in Indonesia. Suharto's military regime had collapsed, but it was widely expected that the Indonesian military would prevent a transition to democracy. A combination of a very effective EU election monitoring mission, and a very powerful election campaign led by Megawati Sukarnoputri, daughter of Indonesia's first president Sukarno who was ousted by Suharto with the US CIA's assistance in 1967, resulted in the opposition winning the election and a peaceful transition to democracy.

I served with over twenty election monitoring missions with international organisations such as the European Union, the Organisations for Security and Cooperation in Europe (OSCE), United Nations, the International Organisation for Migration (IOM), and the US-based Carter Center in the following countries: Bosnia, Croatia, Ukraine, Russia, Armenia, Turkey, Pakistan, Nepal, Indonesia, East Timor, Nigeria, Ghana, Zimbabwe, Tunisia, Libya, and the Democratic Republic of Congo. Such missions were always a privilege, often challenging, and sometimes dangerous.

These missions and my service as a United Nations Peacekeeper convinced me, first, of the importance of creating international peace by peaceful means and, second, of the importance of Irish neutrality towards this objective. Great power conflicts, including their proxy wars, resource wars, and colonial abuses, have been the greatest threat to international peace for several centuries. Throughout the Cold War, neutral or non-aligned states had played a major role in providing troops for peacekeeping missions because of their genuine altruistic role and their lack of national interest in the various conflicts. My research and my experiences in working in countries that had experienced conflicts, especially in the Balkans convinced me that abuses of power by NATO countries posed a serious threat to international peace, and I was concerned that the development of an unnecessary European Union army would endanger international peace rather than contribute to it.

No. 4.
The Irish Times 1 November 2000.
Committing Our Troops to EU Force Clear Breach of Neutrality

The expected decision by the Government to contribute a full battalion to the new EU Rapid Reaction Force spells the end of the road for Irish neutrality, argues Edward Horgan:

The moves to sacrifice our neutrality have been signalled by successive governments since Sean Lemass indicated that such a price might be necessary to secure our membership of the exclusive European first-division club.

The Irish people have never had the opportunity to express their view on the abandonment of Irish neutrality because all recent governments at election times have fraudulently assured the electorate that our neutrality was not at risk.

The Fianna Fáil leadership under Bertie Ahern publicly assured the electorate just before the last general election that no decision would be taken on neutrality without a referendum. That electoral promise has since been reneged on. This U-turn suggests that the government does not trust the people to support its commitment to a European army.

In the meantime, Irish neutrality has been eroded by stealth. In 1997, a small detachment of Irish troops was placed under the command of NATO in the Sfor force in Bosnia, even before Ireland had joined the NATO-led Partnership for Peace (PfP). We have since sent a further unit of Irish soldiers to serve under NATO command with Kfor in Kosovo. Further erosion of our neutrality came with our formal joining of the PfP in 1999, and now it would appear that Ireland is about to contribute a battalion of troops to the European rapid reaction force, thereby ending Irish neutrality.

At each stage of this neutrality-eroding process, the public has been assured that its neutrality was not being compromised. On each occasion, the public has been lied to. The government's decision to commit troops to what I believe is a military alliance is in clear breach of the norms of political and military neutrality. In spite of assurances to the contrary, this will be the end of the line for Ireland as a neutral country.

Since the case for Ireland maintaining its neutrality is too complex to develop fully here, this article will confine itself to outlining some of the possible consequences of our government's proposed abandonment of neutrality within the next month.

Decisions on hypothetical issues such as neutrality are easily arrived at in times of relative peace.

To our brave politicians, there may seem little prospect of Irish soldiers coming home in plastic body bags to Dublin Airport after losing their lives fighting a war to protect the economic best interests of the United States and its principal allies, Britain, Germany, and France.
Since the fall of communism in Eastern Europe, global hegemony rests almost exclusively with the main NATO powers, among which the US is dominant. Minor members of NATO, such as Belgium or Greece, have virtually no influence in key decisions on the use of war to extend the political power of NATO's big four. This was demonstrated when Greece failed to prevent the NATO bombing of its political and religious ally Serbia in 1999.

Ireland will have even less say within any European military alliance. The Irish people should also be aware that the norms of international law were breached by the NATO bombing of Yugoslavia and by the continuing bombing of Iraq by British and US forces. Ireland could be complicit in such questionable acts of war if we continue down this road of military alliances.

Far from benefiting Ireland financially, this new commitment will cost the taxpayer dearly. It should be remembered that the forty million pounds already committed for armoured personnel carriers was intended to support our UN peacekeeping commitments, and the type of vehicles being purchased are wheeled and suitable for peacekeeping rather than peace-making or crisis management operations, such as the war against Iraq.

The requirement for the European rapid reaction force is most likely to be for a mechanised infantry battalion, which implies tracked and heavily armoured vehicles. In other words, we are talking about spending in the region of an additional 100 million pounds of taxpayers' money just to equip such a mechanised battalion.

As a member of the Defence Forces for over twenty years I – like tens of thousands of other Irish soldiers – served with the United Nations, risking our lives for the cause of peace. In the thirty-year period from 1960 to 1990, seventy Irish soldiers died while serving with the UN.

The Irish people also very clearly indicated that they supported this peacekeeping role for the Irish soldiers.

A further trip back in history is needed to jog our memories of what could be in store for Irish soldiers. John Redmond, leader of the Irish Parliamentary Party, supported the British war effort in the First World War, on the basis that we were helping to defend small nations such as Belgium. It was a con trick by the Entente powers of the day.

The small nations of Europe, and indeed the world, were as much at risk from the Entente powers as they were from the German-led powers. Colonial Britain, France, and even little Belgium and Holland continued to exploit and abuse the freedom and democracy of dozens of small countries until they were forced out in the aftermath of the Second World War.

Up to 50,000 Irish soldiers died defending imperialism in the First World War. This was a dreadful, unnecessary waste of human resources. Most of the families of these soldiers never got to see their graves. Many were never buried, just lost in the mud.

These 50,000 dead was the most catastrophic disaster to afflict the Irish people since the Great Famine of the 1840s, yet it is almost forgotten today.

We are now about to allow our present-day John Redmonds to make decisions on our behalf that could send our sons and our daughters to their deaths defending very questionable US-UK- or Franco-German-directed economic objectives, under the guise of crisis management. The questions we must ask include: Whose crisis? Under whose management? Who is giving the government authority to send our children to die in the next global flashpoint?

In 1988, the Nobel Prize for Peace was awarded to the United Nations peacekeeping forces. One of my most cherished possessions is the United Nations Medal for Peace, which I and every Irish soldier who served as a United Nations Peacekeeper was awarded.

If Ireland, as is expected, loses its neutrality by committing Irish troops to the European rapid reaction force, then I intend, as an act of protest, to hand back my UN Peace Medal to the Government. In addition, I will be encouraging other Irish soldiers and ex-soldiers to do the same. Those Irish soldiers who died for peace must not be allowed to have died in vain.

*Edward J. Horgan is a retired commandant who served in the Defence Forces from 1963 to 1986, including assignments with United Nations peacekeeping forces in Cyprus and the Middle East in 1966, 1971, and 1973. He completed a postgraduate degree in Peace Studies at the Irish School of Ecumenics in 1999.

Comment: As a follow-on to this article on the issue of handing back my military medals, I did hand back my military medals and my Commissioning document as an officer in the Irish Defence Forces. My reasons for doing so are outlined in this article that I had published on indymedia.ie

No. 5.
Indymedia **27 September 2003.**
Irish Army Officer Returns Medals in Iraq Protest

Shannon Airport is still being used as a virtual US military base.

Edward Horgan, retired army commandant, and United Nations Peacekeeper will return his medals in protest at the use of Shannon Airport as a de facto US military base.

On November 1, 2000, Edward Horgan, retired army commandant, and United Nations Peacekeeper, wrote an article in *The Irish Times* on the risks to Irish neutrality in which he undertook to return to the Irish Government, his military medals awarded by the United Nations, and the Irish Defence Forces, if our government took a decision to end Irish neutrality. On the 20th of March 2003, the Irish Government ended Irish neutrality by participating in the war against Iraq.

Commandant Horgan now feels obliged to honour his commitment to hand back these medals and certain items associated with his military service, as a symbolic gesture, in protest against Ireland's participation in the war against Iraq, and the loss of Irish neutrality. The medals and other items of uniform will be handed back at Government Buildings, Merion St., Dublin, on Saturday 27 September during the peace demonstration, organised as part of the Global Day of Action against war. They include the UNFICYP medal awarded for UN peacekeeping services in Cyprus in 1966, the UNEF medal awarded for UN peacekeeping service in the Middle East (Sinai) in 1973, the Irish Defence Forces Service Medal with bar, awarded for twenty-two years' service, and most importantly, the United Nations special Medal for Peace awarded to all military peacekeepers on the occasion of the Nobel Peace Prize being awarded to the United Nations in 1988. The uniform emblems being returned include silver parachuting wings, awarded in recognition of paratrooper training completed in 1984, unit insignia for HQ Cavalry Corps, and the Military College, indicating his last posting as a lecturer at the Command and Staff College, Cavalry Corps officer's Glengarry cap, and United Nations Blue Beret, as well as ceremonial lanyards. Of more significance is the original Commissioning Scroll presented to Edward Horgan in September 1973, when being commissioned as a Second Lieutenant into the Irish Defence Forces. This document is signed Eamonn de Valera as President, Sean Lemass as Taoiseach, and Michael Hilliard as Minister for Defence.

The following statement has been issued by Commandant Horgan:

While I have held each of these items as treasured reminders of my service to the people of Ireland and to United Nations peacekeeping, I feel obliged in conscience to return them because of the dishonourable conduct of the Irish Government in abandoning Irish neutrality, contrary to international law, by participating in the war against Iraq in March 2003, thereby actively assisting in the commission of crimes against humanity. Today, 27 September 2003, the war is still in progress; Ireland is still participating in this war, by facilitating the passage of US troops and munitions through Ireland, and by providing a de facto US military base at Shannon Airport. Our participation in this war against Iraq, and this loss of Irish neutrality has not been approved by the Irish people and poses a very serious threat to international peace and global justice. Irish neutrality and our commitment to global justice must be restored. The smaller countries of the world must reform and improve the UN and support UN collective security. We must rein in the dogs of war let loose by terrorism, and by states operating beyond the control of international law. International is vital to protect the majority of the world's individuals against terrorists on the lunatic fringe, and against the abuse of power by super-states.

An Taoiseach announced in the US that Ireland is considering offering Irish troops to the UN mission in Iraq, where they would serve under US command. This would be the equivalent of sending Irish troops to the Lebanon in 1982 under Israeli command, after that army had committed crimes against humanity in Palestinian refugee camps. Irish troops should only be sent on genuine UN peacekeeping missions and not as cannon fodder for the US occupation force in Iraq. An Taoiseach also stated that Ireland is a neutral country. The Irish High Court found, in April 2003, that

Ireland had contravened the Hague Convention and customary international laws on neutrality by allowing US troops and munitions to pass through Ireland on their way to the Iraq War. Mr Ahern should either withdraw his statement that Ireland is a neutral country, or appeal the High Court case of Horgan v Ireland, et al., to the Supreme Court.

In his address to the UN on the 25th of September, Mr Ahern did an amazing U-turn when he stated that he condemned the principle of "pre-emptive" military strikes against potentially dangerous regimes. This statement contradicts the reality that, in March 2003, Ireland shamefully failed to support a United Nations approach to the crisis in Iraq and backed an illegal war by US-led forces against Iraq. Irish participation in this unlawful war helped to kill over 20,000 Iraqi conscript soldiers and about 10,000 innocent civilians. We helped to murder little children who were incinerated in front of their parents, and parents who were shredded by weapons of mass destruction in front of their children. These crimes against humanity cannot be obliterated by a few well-chosen words in front of the UN.

My action in returning my military emblems and medals is to highlight the shameful crimes committed in our names, in the so-called Irish national interest, and the fact that Shannon Airport is still being used as a virtual US military base.

(end of *Indymedia* article)

Comment: I have always been concerned about environmental matters and especially about issues such as nuclear weapons and nuclear power. During my military career, I did some training on what we called NBC warfare, meaning Nuclear, Chemical, and Biological warfare. It was not that Ireland intended to attack any other country with nuclear, chemical, or biological weapons, as we had none, but we were supposed to know what to do if we as a country were exposed to such an attack by others. With the Sellafield nuclear facilities just outside our back door, we should have had adequate procedures, emergency plans, and equipment to deal with such an emergency. The Irish Defence Forces would have been among the first responders to such an emergency, but most army officers knew that we had no adequate logistics, equipment, or even a credible plan for any such emergency. The issue came to a head just after the 9/11 terrorist attacks on the USA and concerns were raised about a possible terrorist attack on Sellafield or other nuclear facilities on the west coast of Britain, and the implications of such an attack for Ireland. The junior minister responsible for such planning Mr Joe Jacob TD was interviewed on RTE radio by Marian Finucane and his idiotic and incompetent performance caused a national uproar. I responded with the following article published in The Irish Times.

No. 6.
The Irish Times 2 Oct 2001
Time to Face the Nightmare Scenario

The joke is on us really. Joe Jacob is still a junior minister and we, the Irish people, are still, and have always been, without an adequate level of national planning or protection in the event of a serious national disaster.

While many good regional disaster plans exist and have been practised, Mr Jacob has demonstrated that, at national level, chaos prevails. There was an initial flurry of activity following the Cuban missile crisis in 1962, and some attempts to put minimal precautions in place after the Chernobyl disaster in 1986, when radioactive fallout fell on several locations in Ireland.

Mr Jacob has portrayed himself, and been portrayed by Mr Ahern, as an established expert on nuclear preparedness, even if he knows very little about the other ingredients in the nuclear, biological, and chemical warfare cocktail.

We are being assured that the biological and chemical threats to Ireland are minimal and that if we had a nuclear or radiation threat, well sure, how could anyone be expected to cope with that anyway. Just close your doors and windows and turn off your ventilation systems and wait for government help to arrive.

We are told there are special nuclear bunkers for the government (Mr Jacob and Mr Ahern) and for the emergency services in Athlone and thirty-two other centres. None of this is quite true.

The greatest threat to the Irish people does not come from terrorism, globally or within the island of Ireland. It comes from Sellafield, just across the Irish Sea, which is already the most radioactive sea in the world.

This danger is constant and growing and many people on both sides of the Irish Sea have probably already died because of a fire at Sellafield (then Windscale) in 1957, numerous leaks of radioactive material in the meantime, and the ongoing approved dumping of radioactive waste material into the sea by its waste-water outlets.

The terrorist threats to the Western world from some Islamic fundamentalists did raise the level of threat to Ireland somewhat, and there are reports that Sellafield may have been, and may still be, on their secondary target list. Our lack of preparedness for a nuclear disaster is much deeper than most people realise.

The Republic of Ireland has no air defence at all. Our Air Corps has no interceptor aircraft. Indeed, apart from the Government executive jet and the fishery patrol aircraft, we have no military aircraft.

As a result of this, it may have been necessary to invite the RAF to defend our airspace against possible terrorist attack, or the British government may have demanded this, due to the threat to Sellafield.

If either has been the case, then successive governments, but especially the present one, must shoulder the blame for virtually decommissioning the Defence Forces, thereby leaving the Irish people exposed to terrorism, from within as well as from without. Neutrality does impose a duty to defend the country's citizens, as well as not endangering neighbouring countries by our lack of defence.

There are also other serious aspects to our lack of preparedness for nuclear, biological, or chemical threats.

The thirty-two so-called nuclear bunkers/communications centres are not all they are cracked up to be. Many of them may actually be cracked up, for example, the government bunker in Athlone, which is located in the basement of a nineteenth-century building in Custume military barracks. These old buildings have been cosmetically modified, but in many cases are neither fireproof nor bombproof, and are vulnerable to attack by aircraft, military or civilian.

The first essential for a government emergency bunker is the secrecy of its location. Yet the dogs in the street know where Ireland's bunker is located. But then, the government may have no way of getting to Athlone, apart possibly from Mary O'Rourke. It is likely that there are no vehicles in the Republic of Ireland capable of moving safely through a contaminated area. In 1970, when the Defence Forces were purchasing twelve Scorpion reconnaissance vehicles (light tanks), they should have come equipped as standard with nuclear, biological, and chemical filtering kits, which would have enabled their crews to operate safely for considerable periods in contaminated zones.

However, a civil servant in the Department of Defence vetoed the inclusion of such filters, because of the word nuclear. People might think we were buying nuclear equipment! It actually cost an additional £48,000 to have the filters removed from these twelve vehicles before purchase.

In the early 1980s, about a year before the Chernobyl disaster, I, as officer commanding the First Tank Squadron, recommended that these filters should be purchased and retro-fitted. I cited the risk of an accident at Sellafield as one of the justifications. The recommendation was rejected.

Mr Jacob's recommendation that in the event of a Sellafield disaster people should stay in their homes is also flawed. The Chernobyl disaster in 1986 released over ten times the amount of radiation than that released by Hiroshima.

A major disaster at Sellafield could release much more than ten times the radiation released by Chernobyl. If the wind was from an easterly direction, serious fallout could be dumped on Ireland within hours.

The most urgent requirement would be to evacuate, in northerly and southerly directions, all town and villages in the immediate path of the fallout. Staying locked up in your home could be fatal.

If this is the best that Ireland, as a sovereign state, can do to protect its citizens, then perhaps we should be prepared to surrender both our sovereignty and our neutrality back to Britain.

*Edward Horgan served with the Defence Forces from 1963 to 1986 when he retired with the rank of Commandant. He is a member of the national executive of PANA, the Peace and Neutrality Alliance.

Comment: I played a very active part in the peace movement protests against Irish participation in the 2003 Iraq War, so not surprisingly this topic informed several of my letters to the papers. My peace activism included taking a High Court constitution case against the Irish Government over US military use of Shannon Airport, which has since become a landmark case of Irish constitutional law known as Horgan v Ireland et al. More on this later. In 2004, I was arrested in a small boat on the Shannon Estuary while attempting to arrest US President George W. Bush, who was attending a meeting of the EU Council, of which Ireland held the presidency at this time.

No. 7.
The Irish Times 26 Jun 2003
Aftermath of Iraq Invasion

In an RTÉ Prime Time interview with Brian Farrell on June 19, the Taoiseach was asked if he had been misled on the numbers of troops and weapons going through Shannon, and on the issue of weapons of mass destruction as justification for the war against Iraq. He answered evasively that there was "no great participation on our behalf" in the war (thereby appearing to admit for the first time that there was at least some participation) and agreed that there may not have been weapons of mass destruction in Iraq immediately before the war. He emphasised that it was right to "support our friends".

He failed to express any words of regret or sympathy for the innocent people killed in Iraq, just concern for "our friends" who had perpetrated these unlawful killings.

Mr Ahern, and perhaps a majority of the Irish public, seem to be satisfied that we were right to support the US Government in its unjust and unlawful war against the people of Iraq. On a purely short-term financial basis, it is probably correct to say that allowing the use of Shannon Airport was in our best economic interests. We are already reaping the benefits of cheap oil and continuing US investment. However, the destruction of Iraq, its pollution with large amounts of depleted uranium, and the unlawful killing and horrific maiming of thousands of innocent Iraqi people cannot ever be justified for Western or Irish economic interests, even if a majority of the Irish people think it was a good idea.

I seem to recall reading that in the late 1930s, the opinion was expressed that forty million Germans could not all be wrong in their support for Hitler. They were all wrong. Corporatism was one of the names given to the fascist movements that spawned Hitler, Mussolini, and Franco. Corporatism on a global scale, is also close to the reality of what we are now experiencing. There are dangerous parallels between the state of international affairs at present and those of the 1930s. It was not the minor dictators, the equivalent of Saddam Hussein today, who proved to be the threat to world peace in the 1930s. It was major powers – Germany, the USSR, and Japan – which placed themselves above and beyond international control, and fatally undermined the League of Nations.

Appeasement of these powers, who developed into rogue states, did not work in the 1930s and it will fail also at the beginning of the twenty-first century. It is ironic that Britain which, virtually alone at first, stood up to the corporatism and crimes against humanity of the mid-20th century, should be actively assisting the corporate raiders of today. Meanwhile Ireland, having asserted her neutrality in 1939, has shamefully abandoned it in 2003 when it could have made a difference by shining a light, if only a candlelight, on war and murder masquerading as peace.

No. 8.
The Irish Times 16 Jan 2004
State Not Neutral by Any Credible Definition

Neutrality of states such as Ireland is one way of keeping Europe from reverting to imperialism, writes Edward Horgan.

Deaglan de Breadun (*Irish Times*, January 12) says neutral Ireland will have a key role in implementing EU security strategy. In some respects, he is right, but on one key matter, his article is misleading. Ireland is no longer neutral by any credible definition of neutrality. This was a clear and definitive finding by Mr Justice Kearns in the High Court on April 28th, 2003, in Horgan v An Taoiseach et al. For the record, neutrality is a legal status and obligation in international law that applies only in times of war. In peacetime, a state that wishes to be considered neutral in future wars must establish credibility in order to have its neutrality respected by belligerents. Ireland established its credibility as a neutral state during the Second World War. It was arguably far more neutral than Sweden, Portugal, or Spain, and minor infringements, such as its treatment of captured British personnel, compare very favourably with much more serious infringements by Sweden and others. In the meantime, Ireland has maintained its credibility as a neutral by insisting on curtailing military transit through it even in times of peace. Ireland remained strictly neutral during the Korean, Vietnam, and Afghanistan/USSR wars.

The critical change in our neutrality status came during the Kosovo War when Ireland allowed US armaments, including cruise-type missiles, to pass through or over its territory while the US was engaged in an attack on Serbia, without UN Security Council approval. Further serious violations of Irish neutrality occurred during the US-led war against Afghanistan, even if the UN status of this war was less clear-cut. In the ongoing war against Iraq, the Government allowed the passage through Ireland of over 100,000 heavily armed US troops in preparation for and the conduct of the US-led war. The independent Medact report has confirmed that up to 30,000 people were killed in this war.

No definition of neutrality allows countries such as Ireland to facilitate military operations to that extent. Ireland is therefore not a neutral country under international law at present, and its credibility as a neutral country in the event of future wars can only be restored by including a clear neutrality clause in the Constitution. Deaglan de Breadun's assertion that fears for Irish neutrality have been "... allayed, to some extent, by the new constitutional provision that there will be no Irish participation in a common European Defence without a further referendum" is also misleading. This refers to the arguably bogus clause inserted in the Constitution (Article 29.4.9) in the second Nice referendum to mislead Irish voters that they were enshrining neutrality in the Constitution. Our participation in the Iraq War in the meantime proves the extent to which the Irish people were misled. Now we are being told that Ireland has a role to play in EU common security strategy. Notice the way the weasel words 'security strategy' have conveniently replaced 'common defence' to get around the new Article 29.4.9.

The Irish people should be alerted also that Mr Justice Kearns ruled that Article 29.1, 2, and 3 of the Constitution was purely 'aspirational' anyway, in his ruling last April 28th, thereby effectively rewriting our Constitution. The arguments for Ireland abandoning its neutrality in favour of joining a common EU defence (sorry, security strategy) are as bogus as Article 29.4.9 of the Constitution. UN collective security and support for the institutions of international law are now being replaced by 'multilateralism' in EU-speak and Irish Foreign Affairs lingo.

Let me remind readers that multilateralism means three or more countries deciding to attack another country, and killing thousands of people, innocent or otherwise. Tony Blair has used the term with this meaning repeatedly to justify British involvement in Iraq. All such talk of unilateralism and multilateral action has the effect, intended or otherwise, of undermining the UN and international law, and avoiding the necessary reform or transformation of the UN. Why waste time reforming the UN when we can trust the US instead? Indonesia, East Timor, Chile, Central America, Vietnam, and Cambodia could tell us why not to trust the US.

The European Union, as it drifts erratically towards becoming a super-state, now wishes to challenge the US superpower militarily as well as economically. This is the crazy logic of schoolyard bullies, and those that will suffer will be innocent victims of resource wars like that in Iraq, fought on the lies about weapons of mass destruction, against US erstwhile ally turned poacher, Saddam Hussein. Other collateral victims will be poorer-class Western conscripts fighting for the Clintons and Bushes who conveniently manage to avoid such war. Ireland lost some 50,000 men in the mud and blood fields such as the Somme, in that most useless of wars, the First World War.

Ireland has been playing its part in UN peacekeeping in important missions such as Lebanon, East Timor, and Liberia, and brave Irish soldiers have justifiably fallen in the cause of global peace and justice. Let those who want to fight energy/resource wars fight them themselves.

Ireland should harvest the wind and its renewable energy resources and stop participating in the exploitation of the poorer peoples of the world. The old truism *inter arma, silens leges*, 'in times of war, the law is silent', must be proved wrong. It is in times of war that law is needed most, as the people of Srebrenica, Rwanda, Iraq and elsewhere could tell us, if they were still alive.

Raphael Lemkin, who lost his family in the Holocaust, warned 'large countries can defend themselves by arms: small countries need the protection of the law'. *Caveat emptor*. Let the buyer of European security 'pigs in a poke' beware. The European Union is a great idea, but a militarised European super-state is not. Neutrality of small states such as

Ireland is one way of keeping Europe from reverting to imperialism and supporting UN reform against US multilateralism.

*Edward Horgan, international secretary of the Peace and Neutrality Alliance (PANA), is a retired Army commandant.

Comment: One of my most challenging yet interesting appointments during my military career was from 1975 to 1980, when I served as administrative office and deputy governor of the Curragh prison. This military prison, normally used for soldiers who committed offences against military laws, was converted to take civilian and paramilitary prisoners after the main wing of Mountjoy Prison in Dublin was severely damaged in prison riots in 1972 and the Curragh prison was used as a temporary emergency prison for paramilitary prisoners until more secure accommodation was provided in Portlaoise Prison. By 1980, most of the paramilitary prisoners had been transferred to Portlaoise Prison, but the Curragh prison continued to be used for some of the most disruptive and difficult ODCs as they were called (this term stood for ordinary decent criminals). They included some serving life for murder and other violent crimes and others who had serious drug problems. The Curragh prison continued to be staffed by military personnel, including myself, for the period 1975 to 1980. During this period, suicides of prisoners were a serious problem in prisons run by the civilian prison service. I make the point below that for various reasons over a ten-year period, there were no suicides of prisoners in the Curragh prison. In my view, this was due to the way the military staff of the Curragh prison implemented their duty of care.

No. 9.
The Irish Times 12 May 2004:
Heads Have to Roll at US Leadership Level

Prisoner abuse has roots in the contempt the coalition has shown for rule of law, writes Edward Horgan:

The depths of depravity reached by some US soldiers in Iraq seem more shocking because of the sexual perversion involved. Yet what has been happening in Iraq from the outset of this conflict amounts to a series of acts of depravity committed by a Western power and its compliant allies. The abuse of prisoners of war, while dreadful, has to be put in the context of the far greater war crimes resulting in the unlawful killing of up to 10,000 innocent civilians. Allegations of similar abuses by British soldiers at Basra are perhaps even more worrying for British politicians and military leaders. The British army does contain some units with a reputation for bad behaviour. The Queen's Lancashire Regiment (QLR) is not one of these. It is a 300-year-old respected infantry regiment, and I worked closely with them in central Bosnia for several months in 1996. I was very impressed with their behaviour and conduct. If soldiers of such a unit misbehaved, then the roots of the problem lie deeper. It indicates serious leadership failures. It may become another appalling vista. As a matter of honour, it may even lead to the resignation of the QLR commanding officer.

It is possible for soldiers to be given the unwelcome task of being placed in charge of difficult prisoners, without those soldiers committing gross misconduct.

Throughout the 1970s, the Curragh military prison, staffed by Irish Army personnel, was used to detain a wide variety of prisoners convicted of criminal and paramilitary offences, due to damage to Mountjoy Prison. I was one of the officers who had direct responsibility for those prisoners, and we took our responsibility very seriously. I recall being reminded by an old military police sergeant major that my safe-custody responsibilities included preventing the prisoners from harming themselves. Of course, there were daily problems with prisoners and staff cooped up in a small Victorian building. Unusually, however, during this ten-year-period, there were no suicides by any prisoners serving sentences at the Curragh, in spite of the fact that many had drug problems.

Officers in charge in such situations have an absolute responsibility to ensure that their subordinates do not abuse the prisoners in any way. They have a duty to know what is going on and not so much to punish any offenders but, more importantly, to prevent abuse taking place at all.

Clearly, this did not happen in Baghdad and Basra. The rules of law must be applied most strictly to those who have custody of powerless prisoners. The rules of law have been abused in the case of Iraq at the very highest levels. Low-ranking soldiers who will be punished for this abuse are already becoming victims – the real culprits at higher levels will escape.

The United Nations itself was in gross breach of its own UN Charter throughout the 1990s when it imposed genocidal sanctions on the people of Iraq, leading to the deaths of almost half a million children. The governments of the US and Britain broke the UN Charter by invading and occupying Iraq in March 2003. The Irish Government broke the UN Charter and the Hague Convention on Neutrality when it allowed the US military to use Shannon Airport for the transit of troops.

With this highest level of abuse of the rule of law, it was almost inevitable that some of the depravities now being revealed did occur. It seems clear from what has been revealed that many of those put in charge of the prisoners were unsuitable.

In such a case, the responsibility for the crimes rests with those who chose the guards and failed to supervise them. It would be wrong and unjust to claim that all US and British soldiers behave like this. Only a small minority do so. However, the responsibility lies with leadership at all levels to control this evil minority. The defence that some soldiers were only obeying orders may even have some validity.

From a US point of view, the scale of this disaster is immense. They were already in serious trouble in Iraq, but not yet as deeply bemired as they became in Vietnam. The prison scandal is likely to mean that the long-term damage to the US reputation in the world will be far greater than that caused by Vietnam. While the domino theory being cited as justification for the Vietnam War proved to be a myth, as did weapons of mass destruction in Iraq, the key difference between Vietnam and Iraq is that Vietnam was, and is, relatively peripheral. Iraq is central to the most volatile region in the world and the oil energy resources of the world. The

US's failure in Iraq, already a de facto failure, has very significant implications for the US and its small band of allies, including Ireland. They have abused international law, national laws, and the basic concepts of morality. There will be a price to be paid.

Unfortunately, the people of Iraq are being asked to bear most of the costs in human terms. Heads will have to roll at US leadership level. Donald Rumsfeld has presided over the pillage and attempted privatisation of Iraq, including the prisons, and has attempted to place American occupation forces beyond the rule of law. If, as seems likely, President Bush fails to fire Rumsfeld, then the people of the US will have the democratic opportunity to fire George Bush next November.

The US now has three stark options in Iraq: to cut and run at the end of June 2004, hang in until after presidential elections in November, or stay for over ten years as it did in Vietnam. At this point, it would be a courageous decision to admit defeat, admit the US was wrong, and pull out in June. With the dearth of courageous people in the US administration, this option is unlikely.

All other options will cost US soldiers' lives, and up to thirty times that number of Iraqi lives, if the Vietnam War and the Iraq War so far are indicative. If the US adopts the third option, it will become a prisoner of the Iraq War. It is already too late to say sorry. The dead cannot be brought back.

*Edward Horgan, a former Army commandant, served as deputy governor of the Curragh military prison in the 1970s. He is a peace activist.

Comment: There were many media reports arising from protests at Shannon Airport over US military and CIA use, or abuse, of Shannon Airport while the US was engaged in wars of aggression in the Middle East. In June 2004, US President George W. Bush visited Shannon Airport to attend a European Union Council meeting that was being chaired by the Irish Government. Edward Horgan got a few mentions in various newspapers during this US presidential visit on 24 June 2004 due to an attempt by three peace activists to arrest the US President on the basis that he was a war criminal. They were arrested after their small boat approached an exclusion zone on the Shannon Estuary near the airport. A naval vessel intercepted the boat approaching the exclusion zone around the airport and arrested the three occupants under the 1996 Harbours Act. They were taken to Foynes and their boat towed away by the naval vessel.

It took nine months for the case to come to trial, for trying to arrest US President George W. Bush. In reality, we never expected to get near the US President. Our objective was to publicise the fact that he was unwelcome in Ireland and to publicise the Irish Government's complicity in the Iraq War. We arrived in court on January 27, 2005. Ennis District Court is the lowest level of court in the Irish legal system and defendants normally just represent themselves or are represented by a solicitor. We arrived in court with three solicitors, four junior counsels, and three senior counsels, all dressed in their full legal regalia. After a few hours of legal submissions and debate, the three defendants including Edward Horgan were acquitted on all charges.

No. 10.
The Irish Times 28 Oct 2004
Battlegroup Bait Just Another Threat to Peace

Turning ploughshares into swords – the world needs peace groups, not battlegroups, writes Edward Horgan.

Most peoples' hopes for global peace rest with the UN in spite of its litany of failures, the worst of which was Rwanda. There are many calls for UN reform, but few indications that the necessary transformation will be forthcoming. The five permanent members of the Security Council use their vetoes to maintain the status quo to their own unfair advantage.

These five have refused to allow the UN to perform its collective security role, and to get around this, Secretary General Kofi Annan appears to be grasping at straws by looking for ways of contracting out its own failed collective security role.

On his visit to Ireland, Mr Annan canvassed support for use of EU battlegroups in peace enforcing missions around the world. This is an ill-conceived attempt to get around the abuse of the veto in the Security Council.

The UN's failure in Bosnia led to NATO intervention. NATO conducted the Kosovo War without UN approval and the US responded to the September 11th 2001 attacks with a unilateral retaliatory attack on Afghanistan without seeking UN approval.

In the Iraq War, UN approval was refused, but the illegal pre-emptive war and occupation went ahead anyway, causing the most serious damage to the UN since the Korean War in 1950. In Africa, attempts to use African regional security for peace enforcement, led to serious abuses in the Congo and West Africa throughout the 1990s.

Use of French forces in Rwanda in 1994 and the Congo in 2004, with questionable UN authorisation, has also proved problematic, although Mr Annan cited this as an example to justify the case for EU battlegroups for UN peace enforcement. The UN has been bypassed and international law flouted.

The EU has proposed the creation of so-called battlegroups for peace enforcement outside of Europe. The idea is that larger EU member states would each provide a battlegroup of 1,500 troops ready for immediate deployment to trouble spots.

Some smaller states, such as Sweden and Finland, have agreed to form one such battlegroup between them. The UN and Ireland appear to have swallowed the battlegroup bait, without realising there are hooks and lines, or strings, attached. The EU wants to project its economic interests abroad by use of military forces in order to compete with the US, which has been abusing its military power since the Second World War, as did Britain and

France. France and Germany want to recruit other EU member states towards achieving their objectives of projecting EU power. Britain wants a foothold in both camps. Continued exploitation of the majority world by the West is the goal. As with past empires, this will be done under the guise of bringing peace and civilisation to the world.

The alternative, as envisaged by the UN Charter, is that such peace enforcement forces should be provided to the UN, which would provide an independent and unbiased command structure, supported by international jurisprudence.

This system of collective security ran afoul of the veto system and superpower rivalry during the Korean War and has never been properly implemented.

This emphasis on peace enforcement at the expense of conflict prevention has always been at the core of the failures by the UN to achieve international peace. Conflict prevention was quickly abandoned by the five veto powers as soon as they realised that their vetoes allowed themselves the exclusive right to engage in military conflict in their national interests, without UN interference.

The proposal to set up a European army, or Rapid Reaction Force, and an EU peace enforcement capacity under the guise of battlegroups that might be made available to the UN, is taking root like Japanese knotweed. Its supporters have failed to specify, however, what controls will apply to the application of such large-scale lethal force. There are some important questions that are likely to remain unanswered. What will prevent the larger EU states from using their own components of these battlegroups to promote their own national interests, or to engage in military actions that are not approved by the UN or by the EU? Britain's involvement in the Iraq War is one example, and several EU states participated in the Kosovo War. Ireland's entanglement with such EU military forces will involve us directly with armies that possess and reserve the right to use nuclear weapons.

Will the UN and Ireland approve the use of such nuclear weapons as soon as we join in such alliances? The government says that a so-called triple lock will apply to protect Irish neutrality and the use of Irish troops. This means that approval by the UN, the government and the Oireachtas, will be required. No such locking system was applied to the loss of Irish neutrality resulting from the use of Shannon Airport by US troops engaged in the Iraq War.

Fifteen or twenty such battlegroups could exist within the EU, with or without a clear-cut command structure. Europe would then have a multitude of overlapping and possibly competing armies, including the armies of each state, NATO, EU Rapid Reaction Force/ Battlegroups, and the Russian army.

With a weak, ineffective UN, this anarchy of armies will be a threat to peace. Armies, once assembled, tend to find a use. The world needs additional armies like it needs a hole in its ozone layer. It behoves small countries such as Ireland to push for reform and reinforcement of the UN, rather than bypassing it. Stanley Kubrick reminded us that great nations act like gangsters; small nations like prostitutes. Ireland should be promoting a strong reformed UN rather than joining competing military structures. We cannot serve three military masters: the UN, the US, and the EU. We need to choose between peace and aggression. The UN, or its improved successor, should be the road towards peace. Ireland risks turning our peacekeeping UN ploughshares into EU swords. Our neighbour is no longer all mankind, just the rich people next door.

*Edward Horgan is a former UN peacekeeper in the Middle East, and has also worked in Southeast Asia, Africa, and the Balkans. He is completing a PhD on UN reform at the University of Limerick.

Comment: This next letter has an element of humour interspersed with more serious issues. Describing former UK PM as 'un gilipollas integral [a complete dickhead]' seems inadequate given his responsibility for so many deaths in Iraq and elsewhere in the Middle East. However, it is important to maintain one's sense of humour as a way of maintaining one's sanity in times of international madness.

No. 11.
Irish Examiner 19 March 2004
'un gilipollas integral'

Dear Editor,
A senior Spanish Socialist Party politician Jose Bono mistakenly blurted out live on Spanish television that Mr Blair was 'un gilipollas integral [a complete dickhead]', in connection with the Iraq War (see Daily Telegraph March 16). I have been unable to find the equivalent Irish language translation for this very appropriate phrase. 'Cheann Risteárd' just does not seem quite right. I appeal to *Irish Times* readers for some suggestions on this matter. Perhaps our own Bono could offer some help? A prize of a tour of Leinster House will be offered for the best suggestion.

No. 12.
The Irish Times 14 Apr 2005
Annan's UN 'Reforms' Fall Short of Needs –

The UN needs real, radical reform, not sticking plaster solutions for its problems, writes Edward Horgan.

Ireland's Minister for Foreign Affairs, Dermot Ahern, will be globe-trotting to support Kofi Annan's plans to 'un-reform' the UN Security Council. The UN has been crippled, almost since its foundation, by Charter provisions that give five states a stranglehold over all security actions undertaken by the UN. These five permanent members of the UN Security Council, China, France, Russia, the UK, and the US, effectively gave themselves the power of veto and special privileges when they virtually imposed the UN Charter on the world in 1945.

The idealism contained in the preamble to the Charter is undone by the 'realism' of the veto system. Not only does the veto give each of these five states the power to decide what the Security Council does, it also gives each the power to do what they like themselves with impunity, as the United States did in Vietnam, the USSR in Afghanistan, Britain/US in Iraq, and France in Rwanda and throughout Francophone Africa.

Mr Ahern justifies his stance in throwing in the towel on UN reform on the basis that 'obviously those who already have a veto are not going to play ball and allow a diminution of their powers'. There can be no real reform of the UN without first reforming the veto system.

The proposals for real UN reform have not just been watered down, they are already being abandoned. The only justification for special privileges at the UN should be on the basis of population – living people. India, with 18 per cent of the world's population, will probably be offered second-class permanent membership, while both Britain and France, each with 1 per cent of the world's population, will retain their first-class veto membership. British and French permanent memberships should be combined into one European Union membership.

Any proposals to expand Security Council membership should be based on limiting the existing powers of veto and ensuring that any expansion of membership is based only on the criteria of population. A 25-member EU still has less than half the population of India. Incomprehensibly, a third EU state, Germany (1.3 per cent of the world population) is also likely to be offered one of these second-class permanent memberships, as is Japan (2 per cent).

Token club membership may be offered also to Third World states such as Nigeria and Brazil. The fourth most populous country in the world, Indonesia, has not figured in any proposals. Britain, France, and the United States, the majority of the UN veto powers, account for only 6 per cent of the world's population.

The supposed justification for the predominance of Western economic powers in the UN is that they ostensibly pay for the UN. The reality is that the US has used its economic power to blackmail the UN and starve it of resources whenever it dares to challenge US global actions. Mary

Robinson, one of the UN's few effective leaders in recent decades, paid the price for challenging the veto powers on issues of human rights. A UN economic agency, the World Bank, will now be presided over by Paul Wolfowitz, one of the architects of the Iraq War. Democracy does not exist at the UN, oligarchy and oligopoly do.

The UN system is therefore inherently unjust and is being used to prevent a more equitable distribution of world resources. Ireland, by supporting these flawed proposals for reform of the UN, is hindering long overdue reform of the international system.

There is a further problem with UN reform that may mean that the UN is doomed in the long term. The veto system has a double-locking device. Any of the five veto powers can veto every attempt to remove this veto from their states, or to give it to another.

The Iraq War and occupation have been the ultimate abuse of the UN Charter by two of its veto powers. Why has Mr Ahern not challenged the participation of EU states in the Iraq War within the EU, and why has he not been promoting a Security Council seat for the EU? The unlawful killing of over 100,000 people in Iraq, for which Ireland abandoned its neutrality, was in direct contravention of the UN Charter.

Because the prospects for real reform of the UN are now so bleak, humanity should already be looking beyond the UN and towards the establishment of a more democratic system of global peace, justice, and governance.

The urgent need for UN transformation or replacement had already been clear from its catastrophic failures to prevent or stop genocides in Cambodia, Rwanda, and Bosnia, and the UN's culpability in the deaths of half a million children due to UN-imposed sanctions on Iraq. Each of the five veto powers played a role in these disasters by direct complicity or by neglect.

The altruistic and far-sighted foreign policies of Frank Aiken and others are being replaced with a short-term stratagem that can only damage Ireland's long-term interests. This could be a last chance for overdue UN reform. Ireland should be aligning itself with other small states and with developing states and the EU to ensure international law is not only respected, but undergoes constant updating and improvement.

The UN should be the kingpin of global jurisprudence. Instead, it is becoming the convenient scapegoat for an inherently unjust and unsound international system. The US has no wish to replace or reform the UN because it benefits most from the inequalities of the post-Second World War status quo, copper-fastened by the UN Charter.

If these latest UN reforms turn out to be sticking plaster solutions, as is likely, then the UN will be beyond reform. Humanity will then need to look beyond the present anarchic international society to a more interdependent global governance system that must supersede the UN.

*Edward Horgan is a Government of Ireland scholar, completing a PhD research programme on UN reform at the University of Limerick.

No. 13.

Article published in *The Irish Times* 25 May 2006

People Are Being Softened Up to Send Their Children to Fight for the West Against the Rest

Neuter the dogs of war and restore peace-promoting neutrality, writes Edward Horgan.

The debate on Irish neutrality has been gagged since March 20, 2003. Close to 900,000 armed US troops have marched through Shannon Airport to make war on Iraq in contravention of the UN Charter, and militarism is being promoted at the expense of peace and global sustainable development.

Minister for Defence Willie O'Dea continues to have problems with the fact that the EU battlegroups are actually called 'battlegroups'. Guns are made for killing people, individually, and armies and battlegroups are made for fighting wars, and killing people on an industrial scale. We could call the Irish battlegroup contingent the 'Fighting 51st' (given our virtual status as the 51st US state), as distinct from the 'Fighting 69th' eulogised in *The Irish Times* on May 13, and saluted by Minister for Transport Martin Cullen. There appears to be a propaganda campaign in progress to soften up Irish people towards sending their children to fight for the West against the Rest. International peace and justice and equitable distribution of the world's resources are a worthy cause for which Irish soldiers have given their lives with the UN, but participation in internationally divisive resource wars is not.

The Irish Times editorial of May 12 commends Willie O'Dea for 'bringing forward these new ideas', such as changing Irish legislation to make it easier to send Irish soldiers to their deaths on foreign battlefields. These ideas are not new. O'Dea and the present Government have plagiarised the ideas and practices of John Redmond. Calls for humanitarian military intervention are no more sincere than the 1914 call to 'defend small nations'. Fine Gael has called for the abandonment of all aspects of the so-called triple lock, and Irish neutrality.

O'Dea and his admirers repeatedly refer to the 'need to avoid other Srebrenicas or Rwandas'.

Ireland did nothing to avoid such atrocities in 1994/95 and is doing little to prevent crimes against humanity in Chechnya and Sudan, while facilitating atrocities in Iraq and Afghanistan. We are also planning on deporting asylum seekers to Afghanistan, having helped to destabilise it. One of the first EU battlegroups was deployed by France in Rwanda in 1994, with UN approval, not to prevent the Rwandan genocide, but to help the mass murderers escape into the Congo, sparking off civil wars that caused up to four million deaths in the Congo. Francophone interests were at stake because the Tutsi rebels, who stopped the genocide, spoke English. These are the type of battlegroups that Ireland is set to join, any day soon.

The Holocaust is often cited as a reason for abandoning Irish neutrality. Preventing wars that cause such acts of genocide is the strongest reason for promoting positive active neutrality. Wars to end wars, and wars on terror that become wars of terror are good for the arms business and hell for humanity.

Ireland is now proposing to join, or gate-crash, the Nordic battlegroup with an assortment of at least four other states that speak Norwegian, Swedish, Finnish, and Estonian, if they will have us. This is referred to as a 'coherent military force of 1,500 soldiers able to operate in a stand-alone fashion with full logistic and transport support', etc. Far more coherent English-speaking forces, such as the British and US armies, have suffered serious friendly fire casualties in all their recent joint actions.

The editorial states: 'Public opinion strongly supports Ireland's overseas military operations.' Ireland should never have 'overseas military operations'. We have rightly participated in many very worthwhile 'United Nations peacekeeping operations', but are now drifting dangerously into such Irish overseas military operations. Only minimal thought has been given to Ireland's almost complete lack of modern battlefield equipment. The costs of equipping such a battlegroup would pay for several Tallaght-size hospitals. Ireland's only armoured warfare equipment are the light Scorpion tanks whose main 76mm weapon has been removed from service in most other countries for safety reasons.

None of the battlegroups already in place have requirements for UN approval before being deployed. This is a breach of the UN Charter, which dictates that military force may only be used outside state borders in self-defence or with UN approval.

Britain and France, two UN veto powers, decided to set up their own single-state battlegroups, which will operate with minimal EU control as was the case with the French operation Turquoise in Rwanda and British Weapons of Mass Destruction (WMD) attack on Iraq in March 2003.

There will be no locks on any of these battlegroups. They are the dogs of war, not the doves of peace.

The Taoiseach stated in February 2003 that US military use of Shannon for a war against Iraq would require a UN Security Council Resolution. Within weeks, this 'lock' was shattered, along with tens of thousands of Iraqi lives.

Of course, Irish military officers welcome the opportunity to expand their professional opportunities. But let us not forget that Irish officers sent soldiers to their deaths in the Congo in Ford Armoured Cars that were not actually armoured, and sent troops on isolated unsupported patrols to places such as Niemba. In the Somme it was easy to shout 'Over the Top' from a bunker, well to the rear.

Ireland's priorities should be UN reform, yet this State, most of Europe, and the US are effectively abandoning the UN, and a multilateral approach to international peace and international law, in favour of what has become known as plurilateralism. This entails a few like-minded states pursuing their own national interests, such as the US and Britain in Iraq. The five UN permanent members placed themselves above the UN when they effectively wrote the UN Charter in 1945, and gave themselves the power of veto, and are now placing themselves 'beyond' the UN and beyond international law. Ireland, by joining in NATO PfP and EU battlegroups, both outside the UN framework, is rushing to join the equivalent of the global schoolyard bullies, or vigilantes, rather than supporting the rule of international law, and reinforcing and reforming the UN.

Neutrality and battlegroups are not vital issues per se, but the killing of innocent people is so appalling that ways must be found to curtail militarism, and promote peace and positive neutrality. About 46,000 children have died as a result of the Iraq War so far. The EU battlegroups will cause the deaths of many more children, as they did in Rwanda and the Congo, and are doing in Iraq and Afghanistan. Now is the time to neuter the dogs of war, and restore peace-promoting neutrality.

*Edward Horgan is international secretary of the Peace and Neutrality Alliance and a former UN peacekeeper.

No. 14.
Irish Examiner 13 December 2006
CIA Is Still Using Shannon for Torture Flights

According to a recent EU committee report, Ireland is the third worst offender in all of Europe, after Germany and the UK, in allowing torture flights to land and refuel, with 147 CIA flights identified at Shannon Airport. The report goes further by linking 14 CIA aircraft with Shannon refuelling stops and creating further linkages between these aircraft and actual transport of prisoners for torture and other landings in countries that habitually practise torture.

I have seen one of the most notorious renditions aircraft – N379P, known as the 'Guantanamo Express' – which was listed in the EU report, at Shannon in January 2003. Not only had the CIA been abusing Shannon Airport in the past, it is still doing so now. I photographed one of the CIA rendition aircraft listed in the EU report – N368CE – at Shannon as recently as July 8 last.

Claims by Department of Foreign Affairs spokesperson that at no stage has any prisoner been rendered through Shannon are clearly false given that it is confirmed that US military prisoners have been 'rendered' through Shannon and it is most likely to be proved in time that prisoners were rendered through Shannon to Guantanamo.

Foreign Minister Dermot Ahern's statement that assurances he had received from US authorities were 'factual and unqualified' is also likely to be proved false in time. This statement is not compatible with the contents of the EU committee report and is also contradicted by reports that Gardaí and workers at Shannon have witnessed prisoners on board CIA-operated aircraft.

Shannon was used extensively by US military Hercules C130 aircraft up to June 2006 when they appeared to have been 'warned off' by the government, possibly as a pre-election precaution. It is likely also that many of these military aircraft were used to transport prisoners to Guantanamo, from Afghanistan in 2002 and from Iraq in 2003.

Since the 147 CIA flights identified by the EU committee are unlikely to represent the total of such flights, and do not include any US military flights that are now known also to have been involved in the transport of prisoners, the number of rendition-related flights through Shannon is likely to be far greater.

Up to 50,000 prisoners were incarcerated in the US Gulag system that stretched from Guantanamo through Poland, Romania, Bosnia, across North Africa and the Middle East, and as far as Indonesia. Some of the most dreadful prisons existed, and are still in use, in Afghanistan. The abuse of prisoners in Abu Graib by US soldiers was just the tip of the iceberg. The number of these prisoners who have been tortured to varying degrees is likely to have exceeded 10,000, and an unknown number have died while in custody.

Ireland has failed in its duties under the UN Convention Against Torture, and this report puts Shannon and Dublin at further risk of retaliation for our complicity in the torture of prisoners and in unlawful war deaths in Afghanistan and Iraq.

No. 15.
Irish Examiner 29 January 2007
US Military Aircraft Opening a Second Front at Knock May Prove to Be No Apparition

Knock airport board has not ruled out allowing US troops to fly in there. Ulick McEvaddy has said he saw no reason why Knock should not benefit from the revenue of US military flights. He is one of the owners of Omega Air, a company with a fleet of converted Boeing aircraft that has gained lucrative contracts for mid-air refuelling of US military and air force warplanes. These warplanes have helped to destroy Iraq and Afghanistan in wars that have caused the deaths of over 660,000 people. The airport board, including the Archbishop of Tuam and the parish priest of Knock, acknowledged 'Mr McEvaddy's wealth of experience and integrity in the aviation and business world'. Mr McEvaddy's response to the board's announcement was: 'Never say never. I have huge connections with the US military, and if it came to using them, I would.'

Perhaps he could persuade B-52s to drop a few 'sticks' of white phosphorous near the Knock shrine if the Mayo clergy don't cooperate. Foreign Minister Dermot Ahern's remarks to the EU parliament that the CIA torture planes at Knock were apparitions may become prophetic.

I would like to make another prophecy: if they wish to use Knock to profit from unlawful US wars, they will need to look to their fences. The peace camps at Knock will be no apparitions.

The airport board's statement was very clear to those familiar with international law and international malpractice. 'Such flights would have to have the support of the Irish Government and the UN.' All the US troops and all the munitions and CIA torture planes that have passed through Shannon have had the support of the government, backed up by the Gardaí and the army. The fact that the government, Gardaí, and army are in breach of Irish and international laws is simply ignored.

The UN did initially oppose the Iraq War, but then caved into pressure and unlawfully approved the occupation post-facto, in contravention of a General Assembly resolution declaring it a 'Principle of the United Nations' that any such occupation cannot be legitimised post-facto. Effectively, the Knock board has already approved the use of their airport for US military misadventures. The first use may well be for the mid-air refuelling (by Omega Air?) of B-52s dropping nuclear-tipped bombs on Iranian nuclear facilities. Of course, this will only be done on 'humanitarian and ethical grounds'.

Comment: I was invited by Fintan O'Toole, The Irish Times correspondent to write the following article as part of a debate on US military use of Shannon Airport.

No. 16.
The Irish Times 26 Feb 2007
Should We Let US Troops Land at Shannon En Route to Iraq?

Head2Head: NO argues Edward Horgan, who says the role of Ireland and Shannon Airport in the Iraqi debacle has been shamefully selfish.

Like many Irish people, I am part American. My mother was a US citizen and my nephew served with the US Marines in Fallujah last year. But Irish/American friendship does not justify helping to attack our Iraqi neighbours. The US and UK launched an invasion of Iraq in contravention of the UN Charter. By allowing the passage of US troops on their way to this unlawful and unjustified war, Ireland was also in breach of international law, and complicit in unlawful killing. In the meantime, more than one million US troops have passed through Shannon Airport. It is now widely accepted that this war, and the consequential civil war, has caused, according to the Lancet study, the deaths of over 655,000 people, including about 262,000 children.

The Irish Government has argued that UN Security Council Resolution 1546 (June 8, 2004) approved the occupation of Iraq and that therefore the Irish Government is only complying with the UN in allowing US troops through Shannon. However, the UN General Assembly decreed in 1970 that it was as a principle of the UN that the occupation of territory by aggression cannot be legitimised post-facto. Therefore, the US is engaged in a continuing unlawful occupation of Iraq and UN approval of this occupation is in breach of its own charter.

However, such niceties of international law hold little sway on the bloody streets of Baghdad. If the US troops were in Iraq for humanitarian reasons, and if they were additionally succeeding in preventing crimes against humanity, pragmatists could argue that the occupation was justified, as was the case with the Vietnamese invasion of Cambodia that overthrew the genocidal Pol Pot regime in 1978. US troops are not succeeding in Iraq, and their presence is literally inflaming the situation. The primary reason for the US invasion and occupation of Iraq was to preserve US 'national-economic interests'. It did not invade oil-starved Rwanda in 1994, or Zimbabwe to date. Taoiseach Bertie Ahern has admitted (in the Dáil on March 20, 2003) that Ireland is supporting the US war efforts for reasons of 'our long-term national interests' and that to withdraw US military permission to refuel at Shannon 'would be a hostile act'. Was helping to kill 655,000 Iraqi people a friendly act? Local politicians have supported US military and CIA torture rendition use of Shannon because of the questionable economic benefits to Ireland and the mid-west. These actions make Ireland a 'rogue neutral state', and the Iraq War makes the US and UK 'rogue UN member states'. Peace, freedom, democracy, and the rule of law cannot be achieved by unlawful wars, internment and torture, imposing client governments, and gross breaches of international laws. The argument that we are helping our American friends raises the question: Who designated the people of Iraq as our enemies? The answer is that Dáil Éireann did, on March 20, 2003, when all Fianna Fáil and PD deputies voted to support the US in its war against the Iraqi people. Remember this on election day.

Bush administration supporters argue that violence would be worse if the US withdrew from Iraq. The present token surge of US troops amounts to little more than a US presidential face-saving device and is having the predictable effect of stirring a hornets' nest. Because the US has suffered its most embarrassing military defeat since Vietnam, it wishes to replace the type of panic-stricken withdrawal from Saigon by going out of Iraq with all guns blazing. Air attacks on Iranian nuclear facilities are also being planned (see Tom Clonan, *The Irish Times*, February 3), all regardless of the local and regional consequences. The mayhem in Iraq was predictable, predicted, avoidable, and caused by the US invasion and occupation. The beginning of the end of this mayhem can only happen when US forces withdraw. The use of Shannon Airport should be denied to US forces immediately because it is inherently wrong, and was never militarily necessary, as shown by the move of World Airways from Shannon to Leipzig. The solution now is to restore the UN as the only lawful international peacekeeper and interpose UN peacekeeping forces between the US and the various Iraqi factions, to facilitate a rapid US withdrawal, and help negotiate peaceful compromises between Shia, Sunni, and Kurdish factions. The troops for such a UN force should come from relatively neutral Islamic states such as Indonesia, Yemen, and Bangladesh.

I am deeply saddened by the unnecessary deaths of over 3,000 US soldiers, many of whom were Irish American. Almost one-third of the people of Iraq (over seven million) are now either refugees or displaced within Iraq. However, it is the children who have suffered the most. Some died when US bombs fell on their homes, but far more are dying of cancers caused by depleted uranium munitions, and from diseases because the water and sewerage plants were deliberately targeted by US warplanes. The role of Ireland and Shannon Airport in the Iraqi debacle has been shamefully selfish, and criminally irresponsible.

*Retired commandant Edward Horgan is a former UN peacekeeper and took a constitutional case against the Irish Government over US military use of Shannon Airport.

No. 17.
The Irish Times 13 June 2007
World War Commemorations

The colourful First World War commemoration ceremonies at Islandbridge in Dublin and at Messines in Belgium are truly sad when we examine the false heroism attributed to those who died in the most useless and wasteful of wars. President McAleese spoke of the Irishmen from different traditions 'who had a common cause . . . a goodness, a graciousness, a kindness, a love, a cherishing of one another . . . it is a shared memory and we need such shared memories'.

Balderdash. Most of the Irish soldiers who fought and died in that war were conned into joining up by Redmond, Carson, and the Lloyd Georges of this world. The 'shared memories' or myths that our President tells us we need would be better replaced by some home truths. The lies that fooled people into fighting in Flanders included fighting to 'defend small nations' such as Belgium (but don't mention the Congo). This was the 'war to end all wars', a war of liberty against tyranny. Such lies have reappeared in recent times to justify the Iraq War – weapons of mass destruction, a war against terror, bringing freedom, peace, and democracy to the Middle East. Tony Blair lied that the war in Afghanistan was partly to cut off the supply of drugs to the West. These wars, like the First World War, brought only death, more tyranny, torture of prisoners and crimes against humanity. Most of the Irish soldiers who were lost in the First World War died miserably, not honourably. They went, scared, 'over the top' because they would have been court-martialled and shot if they refused. The President fails to mention all the young German soldiers who were needlessly killed by young Irish soldiers. The youngest Irish 'soldier' recorded as killed in action was a twelve-year-old bandsman from Waterford. Surely that was child abuse, not heroism. Those who survived by deserting were the wise ones, and there were few heroes.

In order to get men in large numbers to do stupid and morally reprehensible things, you first have to find ways of getting them to switch off their minds. Imagined or invented shared memories, flags, bugles, pipers, and uniforms are essential parts of this process of turning men into military morons. When war memorials are being called 'peace parks', the dogs of war are being trained for unleashing. Lest we forget, again.

No. 18.
The Irish Examiner 12 October 2007
'Clinical' Killings Are Heinous Crimes

The drug-related killings in Dublin have been described as clinical gangland murders. Far from being 'clinical', many of the murders have been stupid acts carried out in a ham-fisted and brutal manner, costing the lives of their erstwhile friends as well as innocent bystanders. The reality is that many of these gang members are poorly educated and not very intelligent.

'General' Martin Cahill had also been given undue celebrity status by the media. At international level, we see a similar abuse of language. Murderous attacks that kill dozens of innocent civilians in places such as Baghdad, Basra, and Belgrade are described as 'surgical strikes' carried out with 'precision' using intelligent guided weapons. We should ask victims such as Ali Abbas how they and their families would describe these crimes against humanity.

The present war in Afghanistan is being fuelled by drugs on both sides, just as the violence in Dublin is drug-fuelled. The international and local thugs include generals in Burma and Baghdad as well as so-called generals in Dublin. Neocon leaders in plush Pentagon offices are backed up by mercenary contract killers, some of whom are Irish. Some of their actions on the streets of Baghdad are comparable with the Dublin gangland murders. The CIA uses torture methods previously used by the Gestapo, the KGB, and the Inquisition. 'Chemical Ali', Pol Pot and other mass murderers were covertly and overtly supported by Western governments during and after their heinous crimes. The drug gang murderers in Dublin are supported by drug users in poor housing estates and expensive nightclubs. It is time to stop glorifying local and international thugs. Unlawful killing is murder, and those responsible are murderers, not clinicians or Rambo-style heroes to be admired. The rule of law must be restored and respected, nationally and internationally.

No. 19.
Irish Examiner 10 December 2007
Why Irish Troops Are in The Wrong Part of Africa?

EU commissioner Charlie McCreevey has said the Irish public will be 'defying their commonsense' if they vote against the EU treaty, which is a constitution in all but name. What he and the host of other EU leaders being rallied to the cause really mean is that the Irish will be defying their local and European masters if they – as they should – reject this treaty in the referendum next year. Credibility is becoming a critically important issue in post-Celtic Tiger Ireland. Mr McCreevy talks of 'a strong and efficient Europe interacting with the rest of the world from a position of strength'. This is EU lingo for neo-colonial economic exploitation of the weaker 'bottom billion' of the world's population, using EU battle groups to project and protect European influence and unfair trade.

The proposed EU military mission to Chad, with 450 Irish soldiers, is one such example. It is portrayed as a humanitarian mission, yet inexplicably has a UN Charter, chapter VII mandate giving it powers to make war in the name of making peace. The hidden French intentions for this mission are to support the military dictatorship of Lt Gen Idriss Déby against insurgents who are seeking to overthrow him because of widespread human rights abuses. Chad, like Rwanda, is a border state dividing Anglophone Africa from Francophone Africa. Cultural imperialism is alive and well in Africa, and this EU treaty, by intensifying the militarisation of Europe, will deepen this problem.

The EU and Ireland should be working instead with the UN and with impoverished developing world states to create peace, justice, and sustainable development for the benefit of all humankind, not just working for what Mr McCreevy calls 'the only kind of Europe in which Ireland and its citizens can prosper' – that is a Europe of exploitation. The rogue elephant in the African room is the genocide in Darfur, and that is where Irish and UN soldiers should be. Given the European colonial abuses of Africa, no EU force should be allowed into Africa. By ostensibly 'protecting' the refugee camps in Chad, the EU military mission is helping to perpetuate the genocide in Darfur. This is only one complex example of reasons why the Irish people should reject the proposed EU treaty. This time, let's not obey our overpaid masters.

No. 20.
Irish Examiner 1 July 2008
FF Double Standard on Gay Marriage

I was dismayed to hear that a group of Fianna Fáil TDs and senators is seeking to reverse a government decision to allow gay and lesbian couples to register their relationships with the State. There are issues of equality, fairness, and human rights involved here that should transcend the personal opinions and biases of individual legislators. It is wrong in my view for the State to intervene or to continue to impose legislative restrictions on the legal rights of individuals in such matters as private morality or gender/sexual orientation. It is also indicative of flawed double standards that these same FF members seemed to have had very little problem with the level of financial corruption involving many of their TDs, councillors, and ministers, or with the very public extramarital affair of their former leaders. Morality within Fianna Fáil seems to be only focused on a particular aspect of sexuality. In 2003, all Fianna Fáil TDs and senators considered they were morally justified in approving the government's decision to support the Iraq War by allowing US troops to use Shannon Airport. To them, the deaths of more than one million Iraqi people in the meantime, and CIA torture, are not immoral, but official acknowledgement of gay relationships is.

Comment: The following was a somewhat angry article I wrote, and demanded right of reply from The Irish Times *due to what I considered to be significantly unjustified criticism directed partly at me and other peace activists.*

No. 21.

Article in *The Irish Times* 8 Aug 2008
Army Tied into Questionable Peace Missions

Our troops should be serving in Darfur, preventing genocide and taking justified risks, writes Edward Horgan

A leading article in *The Irish Times* on August 2 stated: 'It is wrong that the military side of [EU missions in Bosnia and Kosovo] is occasionally viewed in Ireland through a distorting and insular prism.' It also referred to Ireland's 'military neutrality'. The latter is a recent government invention intended to blur the damage done by the abandonment of Irish neutrality at Shannon Airport since 2003. Neutrality is a political decision by governments giving states international-law neutral status and protection, but also imposing obligations. On March 20, 2003, the Government invoked the status of neutrality by declaring Ireland a neutral state, but contravened the Hague Convention by allowing US troops to use Shannon Airport for its war on Iraq. An implied condition of neutrality is that states do not enter into military alliances, such as NATO, or an EU army if such develops.

The leading article incorrectly implies that I, and others who have been publicly critical of Ireland's abandonment of neutrality, are distorting the truth and viewing aspects of Ireland's international relations in an insular manner. My views are very much internationalist, not nationalist or insular. There appears to be a lack of comprehension, and resultant anger, in Irish political and media circles, at the decision by a mixed coalition of Irish civil society to reject the dictates of Irish politicians and Eurocrats during the Lisbon referendum. Instead of seeking to understand the message(s) that a majority of Irish people are trying to communicate to their political and European servants, it seems that discrediting the messengers is the preferred response. Those who are genuinely concerned about issues such as abortion are described as 'right-wing Catholics'. While I have not campaigned on the abortion issue, I have been publicly critical of the Catholic clergy's silence on the immorality of torture and crimes against humanity in the context of Shannon Airport. My campaigning has been on the related humanitarian issues – the right to life and bodily integrity of non-combatants, including prisoners, who become victims of conflicts. I consider that almost all wars are avoidable, if conflict prevention is given sufficient resource, and that the concept of just war is an oxymoron. Peace must be created by peaceful means, not warfare. In exceptional circumstances, peace must be enforced by legitimate UN authority, not by self-appointed vigilantes such as the US, the UK, or the North Atlantic Treaty Organisation. UN reform is needed to ensure that spurious enforcement mandates are not agreed, as occurred for example in the Korean War, the Rwandan Operation Turquoise, and arguably, in the case of EUfor in Chad. Peace should have been enforced by the UN in Bosnia in 1992, not in 1995, and in Rwanda in April 1994. My views are activist, therefore, not pacifist.

The neutrality I support is positive neutrality – if a country declares its intention to remain neutral in wars, it should use all practicable means to promote international peace. This goes further than the Hague Convention on Neutrality and is in keeping with past Irish policies of Éamon de Valera and Frank Aiken, who were active supporters of the League of Nations and the UN.

The Defence Forces have played a very honourable role as UN peacekeepers since 1958. As a small country, Ireland's international role should be confined to UN peace missions, including peace enforcement, where required. At present, Irish soldiers are over-committed on several questionable peace missions, such as Afghanistan and Kosovo. The Chad EUfor mission combines the flaws of French Operation Turquoise in Rwanda and the UNprofor mission in Bosnia that facilitated the continuation of those conflicts. I do not advocate only risk-free peacekeeping missions. East Timor and Liberia were examples of appropriate Irish-UN missions. Irish troops should be serving in Darfur, preventing genocide, and taking justified risks. The government should be insisting that the UN is properly reformed, resourced, and authorised to do this, as obligated under the Genocide Convention.

I speak from experience and expertise in these matters. Like very many Irish peacekeepers, I have risked my life on UN peacekeeping missions. I worked for nine months as a UN volunteer on election missions in Central Bosnia and in Vukovar, Croatia, in 1996/97, in heavily mined areas, subject to militia threats. I did not 'sit on the sidelines'. Yet, I seem to have aroused the anger of some who support deeper integration of Europe as a federal state.

Peter Murtagh's article, and the leading article (*The Irish Times*, August 2), represents unjustified criticism. Murtagh wrote: 'If I'm angry at anything, I am angry at some of the views back home in Ireland.' This criticism appears directed at a small number of people associated with the Peace and Neutrality Alliance ('These neuralgic and myopic arguments over neutrality.') By implication, he accuses me, and others, of being dishonest. I have always endeavoured to behave honestly, and I find this comment unjustified: 'It really is a gross and dishonest misrepresentation to suggest – as it was in the Lisbon referendum campaign – that by participating in the sort of EU or NATO military missions in the Balkans and in Chad, our country has somehow signed up to an "EU army" with imperialistic ambitions.' These criticisms appear specific because virtually the only criticisms of the Chad EUfor mission made during the Lisbon campaign were by me and Roger Cole, chairman of PANA. Murtagh wrote: 'What sort of morality is it to sit on the sidelines when others are trying to prevent war, impose peace, and help nations rebuild themselves?'

I, and many others in PANA, have not been sitting on the sidelines. We have campaigned for basic human rights on issues such as the unlawful killing of hundreds of thousands of people in Iraq and Afghanistan, and against the torture of prisoners, often at considerable personal cost. I call on the government to withdraw Irish troops from the French-dominated, inappropriate, EUfor Chad mission, and to send these troops to Darfur to join the United Nations/African Union peace mission and help prevent the ongoing genocide. As a civil society activist, I take inspiration from the late human rights activist Alexander Solzhenitsyn, who believed that 'we must not restrain our social consciousness within the [wretched dimension of politics]'. The gulags created by Stalin, Bush, and others will not be decommissioned by shooting the messengers.

*Retired Comdt Edward Horgan is international secretary of the Peace and Neutrality Alliance (PANA)

No. 22.
Irish Examiner 7 April 2009
No Mention of Neutrality in Constitution

FINE Gael leader Enda Kenny was questioned on the RTÉ Radio This Week programme on Sunday, April 5, by Gerard Barry on the statement by (Captain) Billy Timmins TD, that Ireland should abandon neutrality and join EU common defence arrangements. Kenny responded that: 'There is a constitutional prohibition on Ireland abandoning neutrality' and then proceeded to misinterpret and downplay what Timmins had said at the Fine Gael Árd Fheis. When further prompted by Gerard Barry that Billy Timmins had said that Ireland should be part of a common EU defence, Enda Kenny repeated his statement that: 'there is, as you know, a constitutional prohibition on ending neutrality and that ultimately is a matter for the Irish people'.

This is a false statement. Bunreacht na hÉireann, The Irish Constitution, contains no prohibition whatsoever on Ireland abandoning neutrality. There is no mention of neutrality in the Irish Constitution. Kenny's apparent ignorance of the Constitution on a matter of this importance is of grave concern, given that he aspires to be the next Taoiseach of Ireland. Some neutral states such as Austria, Finland, and Switzerland have neutrality enshrined in their respective constitutions. Ireland does not have any constitutional provision or article dealing with neutrality. In Ireland's case, neutrality is a declared policy of successive Irish Governments, since at least 1939, that Ireland will pursue a policy of neutrality. This commits the Irish Government to comply with international laws and treaties on neutrality, particularly The Hague Convention V 1907 on Neutrality, which forbids the passage of belligerent troops through a state such as Ireland that declares itself to be a neutral state. The High Court ruling by Judge Kearns in April 2003 in Horgan v Ireland confirmed this and found Ireland to be in breach of international laws on neutrality. The Irish people have consistently supported a continuation of neutrality, and the Irish Peace and Neutrality Alliance are campaigning to have positive neutrality enshrined as an article in the Irish Constitution. Before Enda Kenny and Capt. Billy Timmins send Irish soldiers off to another European war, as their 'forefathers' John Redmond and Major Willie Redmond did in 1914, the least they might do is read Bunreacht na hEIREANN. At least Willie Redmond went to fight and die in World War I.

However, history should warn us that politicians normally fight to the last drop of everyone else's blood.

No. 23.
Irish Examiner 18 July 2009
High Price of Corruption, Greed, And Incompetence

The spin doctors timed the publication of the McCarthy report while the Dáil was in recess, hoping that holiday amnesia would lessen the impact on Lisbon II, yet seeking falsely to imply the public service is the cause of the economic crisis. Unlike our politicians, public servants have a remarkable record for honesty and lack of corruption. It was political corruption, greed, and incompetence that fuelled the economic crisis. The unsustainable public service payroll costs were approved and encouraged by profligate and decadent squandering by successive governments led by Bertie Ahern and Brian Cowen. Let's not forget the decades of planning and other corruption involving mainly politicians and their client developers.

The €5bn expected to be saved by the public service cuts is probably less than the sum that will be given to just one of our failed banks. The eventual cost of the bailout of Irish financial institutions is likely to be more than ten times €5bn. The two main banks should have been nationalised, giving taxpayers some possibility of recovering their involuntary investment and the others should have been left to succumb to the bankruptcy system. The government has bailed out not just the failed banks but also many of the reckless builders and developers at taxpayers' expense, and in so doing has effectively corrupted the regulatory controls of the bankruptcy system. It provided inadequate protection for the taxpayer from corrupt developers and others who may have transferred assets offshore while abusing the bankruptcy system to evade their liabilities within Ireland. Those primarily responsible for the Irish financial crisis are, first, the Government and politicians who failed to govern in the people's interests; second, the financial institutions and regulators, and third, the developers and builders. This culpable Government is now in the process of inflicting impoverishment on the most vulnerable sections of society while bailing out their culpable partners and is seeking to lay the blame on the public service.

Comment: The vast majority of Irish citizens are allowed entry to the United States for tourism, business, and other reasons without the need to apply for a visa. However, as a result of my peace activism and opposition to US wars of aggression, and probably in particular to my failed attempt to arrest US President George W. Bush at Shannon Airport in 2004, not surprisingly perhaps, I found myself on a special list operated by US Homeland Security, of persons not allowed into the USA. When I did apply on two occasions, first in 2009, when I received an invitation to attend the inauguration of US President Barack Obama, and again in 2010, when I was to be a guest speaker at an anti-torture conference at Duke University in North Carolina, I was initially denied permission to enter the USA and denied a visa. On both occasions I did appeal this refusal decision, and with the help of high-level lobbying by Irish and US VIPs, I was allowed into the US, albeit with a very restricted visa.

No. 24.
Irish Examiner 3 April 2010
We Have All Become Passive Victims of Crimes

We have all become passive victims of crimes committed by politicians, bankers, developers, and so-called regulators with cuts and levies in services, salaries, pensions, and insurance.

Quinn insurance went into administration, regulators and bankers retired with lavish pensions and gratuities, Bertie Ahern is appointed professor emeritus at Maynooth – all fully legal, of course – while we got NAMA. The bankruptcy system that is meant to punish reckless trading has now been abandoned, protecting the reckless, but bankrupting the country and mortgaging our grandchildren. Let's not forget we zombie citizens are still paying for past scandals including PMPA, ICI, Goodman beef scandal, et al. Your house insurance is being loaded to pay for flooding of properties that should never have been built in flood plains. We pay exorbitant health insurance for the privilege of being left sitting on trolleys with our GP referrals unopened. It's time we kicked back.

First, we need to replace the current crop of politicians who contributed to this problem at every available electoral opportunity. Village idiots could not have performed worse, leading to the suspicion that many of these politicians are financially implicated in these scandals. We all need to evaluate whether we need to insure our properties and our health given the dreadful value we are now likely to get for insurance premiums. Large industries often carry their own insurances and minimise the risks by prudent loss prevention practices. Let's do the same with our homes and our health. Improve your home security, frost protection and fire prevention, and tell your insurance company to get stuffed. Over your lifetime you are more likely to be impoverished financially due to exorbitant insurance than by catastrophic house fires. If you have two expensive family cars, downsize to one cheap one, and if you are entitled to free travel, downsize to a bike. Likewise, with health insurance, those of us who try our best to live healthy and safe lives are paying for those couch potatoes who abuse drink, drugs, and behave recklessly. It is much better to carry your own health insurance, enjoy a daily two-mile walk, and eat proper food. We can also help and protect ourselves by family and community networking. This is just a beginning and when the powers-that-be start squealing, just tell them to go to hell.

Have a nice day.

No. 25.
Irish Examiner 18 June 2010
Paras' Leader Should Be Stripped of His OBE

On January 30, 1972, fourteen civilians were shot dead in Derry by soldiers from the First Parachute Battalion, under the command of Lt Col Derek Wilford. He was exonerated by the now-discredited Widgery tribunal and six months later he was awarded the OBE by Queen Elizabeth, probably on the advice of British Prime Minister Edward Heath. This was perhaps one of the greatest insults to the relatives of the victims of these shootings. There are many honourable units in the British army and many honourable soldiers also. The behaviour of members of the First Parachute Battalion in Derry in 1972, and elsewhere, indicates underlying behavioural and disciplinary problems. While it is unlikely that any of the soldiers involved in these shootings will be punished for these crimes, at the very least the decision to award the OBE to Lt Col Wilford should be rescinded. The Saville report found he disobeyed orders on Bloody Sunday, but he bears far more serious command responsibility for the deaths of fourteen innocent people.

No. 26.

Article in *Irish Daily Mail* 3 July 2010

Irish Defence Forces – We Must Defend Them –

He is a passionate supporter of the Defence Forces but in a denunciation of the way they are run, a former Army commandant says only sweeping cuts and a withdrawal from NATO will ensure their survival.

It was just an ordinary day on the job but I was in an extraordinary place – the Sinai Desert, more than thirty years ago. As a serving Irish soldier, I was part of the United Nations Emergency Force's 'buffer zone' operation, created there, in the wake of the Yom Kippur War, to maintain the ceasefire between the Israelis and the Egyptians. One afternoon, while driving across desert terrain, our vehicle drove over a live Israeli anti-tank mine. Fortunately, it failed to explode. I was blessed. In 1982, a similar thing happened to Commandant Michael Nestor in Beirut. This time, the device exploded, killing him and three other UN observers.

Opting for a career in the military brings many challenges – some of them life-threatening – but I always believed that the risks were justified in the interests of international peace. Indeed, it was that international dimension and the prospect of overseas service as a UN peacekeeper that prompted me to join the Defence Forces as a Cadet back in 1963. I served for twenty-two years, mainly in the Cavalry (armoured) Corps, but also saw service with the Infantry, Military Police, Engineer Corps, and the Military College. This range of service gave me a privileged vantage point to view the strengths and weaknesses of the Defence Forces and the structures that, I believe, hinder its efficiency and competence. My experiences as an Irish soldier were mainly very positive, particularly my UN peacekeeping service in Sinai and in Cyprus. The eighty-five soldiers who have died on UN missions were serving an honourable cause.

Traditionally, Irish foreign policy focused on supporting the United Nations diplomatically and providing peacekeeping troops for UN missions. Irish neutrality was a key factor in enabling Ireland to achieve a significant level of international influence and Irish soldiers participated only in genuine UN peacekeeping missions. However, since the 1990s Irish soldiers have also been serving with NATO and European Union military missions bringing into question Ireland's neutral status, and our foreign policy of opposing military aggression that is prohibited by Article 2.4 of the UN Charter, and Article 29 of Bunreacht na hEIREANN.

Of particular concern is the presence of seven Irish soldiers serving with the NATO occupation force in Afghanistan, where 102 NATO soldiers were killed in action last month. With the recent withdrawal of Irish troops from the Chad mission, there are now only 168 Irish soldiers serving overseas. However, they are serving in sixteen different missions, which is a scatter-gun approach for such a small army. In addition, the Northern Ireland peace process has removed the main internal security threat. So, now is a good time therefore to review the status, primary roles, structures, and costs of our Defence Forces. Our soldiers are held in high esteem at home and abroad – and justifiably so, but the Irish public are often unaware of the Defence Forces' shortcomings.

The UN 1960s Congo mission involved deploying poorly trained and badly equipped battalions of soldiers who were brave and dedicated individuals. The Niemba ambush and the surrender at Jadotville should not have happened. The Ford armoured cars sent to protect Irish soldiers were not bulletproof and senior Irish commanders knew this. This UN mission was a temporary success but a long-term failure. However, Irish soldiers adapted quickly and performance in subsequent UN peace missions was very good. The most successful UN missions with Irish troops were those in Sinai in 1973, and more recently in East Timor and Liberia. Back home in 1969, when the Irish Government ordered some units of the Defence Forces to deploy to the border area, their transport was so bad that they had to abandon their trucks and hire CIE buses.

Even though the Irish Defence Forces costs the Irish taxpayer far less in percentage of GDP than most other armies, much of this money is often misspent, especially in equipment procurement. The French Panhard armoured vehicles and Spanish Sandglass motorcycles are just two examples of wasted money in the past. At this point in the history of the Irish Defence Forces, and given the current economic constraints, fundamental questions need to be addressed. People may well ask if, in fact, we need the Defence Forces at all. Yes, I would say, we do. Just as a homeowner needs a home insurance policy, a State needs a defence force to protect its sovereignty and its citizens. The primary role of the Defence Forces is 'to defend the State against armed (external or internal) aggression'. All other roles assigned to it by government, including UN peace missions, are matters of optional government policy, and in these times of economic hardship the only one worth preserving is, in my view, that of UN peacekeeping.

So how can our Defence Forces' mission to defend us be best achieved? The Forces' website states that it is 'organised along conventional military lines'. This is a fundamental mistake that ignores the reality that a small country like ours cannot afford the modern military equipment that would enable it to repel a determined hostile invasion. Just one modern fighter aircraft can cost up to two billion dollars, while a main battle tank costs over five million dollars. Ireland did not win its War of Independence using a conventional army or tactics, and Ireland can be defended only by unconventional guerrilla warfare. If the Irish Defence Forces had crossed the border into Northern Ireland in 1969/70, as senior politicians proposed, one RAF aircraft based in Wales could have destroyed all our ammunition storage and most of the Curragh Camp and be back at base within an hour. To be cost-effective, changes are necessary. Not by cutting actual Defence personnel numbers, as the current level of just under 10,000 is, in my view, about right. (You would wonder, though, what the 357 civil servants currently employed by the Defence Forces actually do?) Rather, it is in structure and in overall organisation that sweeping changes are now required.

Back in the 1970s, the army went through a process that was jokingly called 'rank inflation'. The number of generals increased from two to about a dozen. While there has been some rationalisation since, the army still has too many chiefs, and yet has no overall Irish Army commander. The Chief of Staff has no direct operational command responsibility over the 'General Officers Commanding' the Eastern, Southern, and Western Commands. In addition, we have a system of Brigade Commanders, which means the army has three separate command structures. Then there's the Army Air Corps, which became an Air Force overnight with its own general in charge, even though it has no real combat aircraft – just some small trainer jets, a government taxi service, and an inadequate number of rescue helicopters. Not to be outdone, the Naval Service also got its own general level 'Flag Officer' or commanding officer. What we need is a common sense Defence Force that would be capable of putting up a credible defence on behalf of the Irish people, and also provide about 550 troops for UN missions which should be strictly peacekeeping.

This also makes economic sense because the UN pays most of the costs involved, while the Irish taxpayer pays all the costs of Irish soldiers serving with NATO and EU missions. There should be two generals only in the Defence Forces, one Army Commander, and a deputy who would be Army Chief of Staff. They should preside over a force of nine mechanised infantry battalions, and all other higher command structures at Brigade and Command levels should be removed. Meanwhile, the Air Force and the Naval Service should be reintegrated within the Irish Army and their 'generals' made redundant. All existing logistics and support units, including transport, engineering, and medical units, should also be disbanded or amalgamated with the exception of an ordinance support unit that would have responsibility for storage and maintenance of ammunition and weapons, and the provision of EOD bomb disposal teams. Decorative units such as army bands and the Army Equitation School should be dispensed with. The services provided by the Army Medical Corps can be better provided by public health services. The Air Corps should be relocated to Shannon Airport and given the primary task of search and rescue. A coordinated EU approach should be agreed whereby British rescue services would take responsibility for rescue off the northern coasts and the Irish Sea and the Irish Air Corps would be responsible for rescue off the west and southern coasts of Ireland. It should be adequately equipped with long-range and medium rescue helicopters, and it should absorb the existing coastguard and privatised air rescue services. These helicopters should be used for air-ambulance service when not on rescue duty. The government air-taxi service should be scrapped – let them use Ryanair – and Baldonnel Aerodrome should be sold. When it comes to the Naval Service, there is actually relatively little scope for financial savings. Their role in search and rescue, response to marine environmental disasters, and smuggling prevention needs to be improved, not cut back. They should be supplied with smaller, faster vessels, and their work should be more closely integrated with a relocated Air Corps. Overall, we need to run a tighter ship when it comes to Defence, a much tighter ship.

The financial savings involved if these changes were implemented would be substantial. More importantly, the charade that we have an army capable of defending Ireland would be replaced by a new reality and Ireland would have a credible, and cost-effective, defence strategy. Surely, we owe that to those who serve this State, to those who are prepared, if it comes to the crunch, to lay down their lives.

*Edward Horgan is International Secretary of the Irish Peace and Neutrality Alliance, and a retired Commandant of the Irish Defence Forces. In 2001 he was awarded a Government of Ireland Scholarship to complete a PhD thesis at the University of Limerick – 'The United Nations – Beyond Reform? The Collective Insecurity of the International System and the Prospects for Sustainable Global Peace and Justice.'

No. 27.
Irish Examiner 10 July 2010
Dáil's Tail End

In the Dáil on Thursday, former Ceann Comhairle John ('The Bull') O'Donohue described Labour Party leader Eamon Gilmore as a 'gadfly flying around the smelly tail of an old cow' (*Irish Examiner*, July 8). It was an apt description not of Mr Gilmore but of Mr O'Donoghue's own party,

Fianna Fáil. Mr Gilmore quite justifiably seeks to sting and provoke some signs of life from that old cow and its smelly old tail. It seems an appropriate comment to end a Dáil session presided over by a government that has the support of less than one-quarter of the electorate.

No. 28.
Irish Examiner 2 October 2010
Guess How Long It Takes to Pick Up €50bn?

Finance Minister Brian Lenihan repeatedly accuses the Irish media and political opposition of negativity and talking up the Irish financial crisis. So, should we muzzle the media, and create a one-party-state? When challenged on RTÉ's Morning Ireland that in 2008 he described the Irish bank bailout as 'the cheapest bank bailout in the world', he qualified this by saying – five times – the cheapest 'so far'. He also says we cannot penalise the senior bondholders because we need them to borrow more money to keep the economy afloat. This sounds like blackmail. They charge us exorbitant interest rates while demanding that we let them off the hook for their reckless financial gambling. The bankers, bondholders, and reckless developers who, with Fianna Fáil, got us into this economic disaster will for the most part keep their pensions, their bonuses and in some cases their offshore accounts while Irish taxpayers are forced to fork out up to €50bn. Lenihan also has the gall to state that the 'nightmare' of the banking crisis is coming to an end. Yes, it is coming to an end for the bankers, but it is just beginning for the taxpayers being penalised. Brian Cowen tells us, again several times on RTÉ that the economic crisis was a 'perfect storm'. We need an analogy to help us understand just what €50bn amounts to and to see through some of the Government's gobbledegook. If one person could pick up one euro every second, it would take that individual thirty-two years to pick up €1bn. It would take one individual twenty-five average lifetimes to pick up €50bn. It's time we created a perfect storm to blow them out of office.

No. 29.
The Irish Times 20 November 2010, *Indymedia*, 23 Nov 2010
National Strike

Expressions of anger, resignation, disgust, shame, and deep depression will achieve nothing in the present crisis. We must take positive action and do something. We do not have a real government at present, so we are in a state of virtual anarchy, and every extra day of such anarchy is causing further damage that will have to be paid for by our grandchildren. Our sham government is driving the country towards the edge of a cliff, so we the people need to stop the country and turn it around. The self-serving Fianna Fáil and Green hypocrites will not resign but will continue to the last possible day to maximise their ministerial and TD paycheques and pensions.

We need a national strike now to force a general election, before Christmas, and before any deal with the ECB/IMF is agreed upon. Any deals or national budgets brought in by the present regime will have no mandate from the people of Ireland. This national strike must be all-encompassing, and include public and private sectors, the young, the old, the Gardaí and the Defence Forces. Enough is enough; we need to re-establish our republic and take back our country.

We must do this now to restore the honour and self-respect of the Irish people, otherwise we will deserve the shame that has been forced upon us. We must do this peacefully but with firm determination, otherwise many people will be destitute and many will die because of lack of adequate medical care and essential support services.

No. 30.
Irish Examiner 23 December 2010
Complicit in Torture

Investigations by the European Parliament and the Council of Europe in 2006 have already revealed that the Irish Government facilitated the US Extraordinary Rendition program, which resulted in torture of many prisoners in Guantanamo and elsewhere, by allowing US military and CIA aircraft to refuel at Shannon Airport. The recent exposures by Wikileaks confirm that Dermot Ahern, in his capacity as Irish Foreign Minister, informed US Ambassador Foley that he was 'quite convinced' at least three such rendition flights had used Shannon. Irish Government ministers have repeatedly stated that there was no evidence of CIA planes using Shannon, and also stated that they fully accepted US Government assurances that the airport was not used to facilitate so-called extraordinary rendition. This indicates our ministers knowingly misinformed the Irish people, and more seriously, were complicit in torture in contravention of the UN Convention Against Torture.

No. 31.
Irish Examiner 4 January 2011
Incontrovertible

An Taoiseach, Brian Cowen TD, stated on December 7, 2010, that he was proud of the Government's achievements. Former Taoiseach, Bertie Ahern, said on December 30, 2010: 'I am proud of what I have achieved in politics.' Given the disastrous state of the country as a result of the performances of these two individuals, the only appropriate response is to borrow a quote from Dag Hammarskjöld's book, Markings. 'The madman shouted in the marketplace. No one stopped to answer him. Thus, it was confirmed that his thesis was incontrovertible.'

No. 32.
Irish Independent 1 April 2011
Pubs Going to The Wall Is a Positive Thing for Our Society

John Mallon wants to bring back smoking in pubs. He claims that 'our pub culture is one of the reasons why Ireland is a great place to live and visit, despite the tough economic times. Pubs bring people together. They are a great social glue where friendships are made.' The opposite is very often true. Irish pubs and our alcohol culture have destroyed many families. The time and money wasted in pubs would be much better spent on family and friends in a healthier way. Mallon bemoans the loss caused by 'more than a thousand pubs (that) have gone bust'. This is not a loss but a gain for our society. Why not consider a ban on alcohol in pubs also, and get rid of quite a few more, and initiate a major improvement in our physical and mental health?

Comment: It was a coincidence that this short letter was published on Fool's Day and some readers presumed it was a Fool's Day letter. It was not intended as such, but as a response to the dangerous attitude of Irish society to alcohol abuse.

No. 33.
Irish Examiner 13 March 2012
Irish Army Personnel Should Quit Afghanistan

The appalling killing of at least sixteen Afghan civilians, including nine children, by a thirty-eight-year-old US Army Staff Sergeant in Panjwai, Kandahar, Afghanistan, will have inevitable repercussions. US military spokespersons described the perpetrator as deranged, but arguably, this whole war waged by the US and NATO against Afghanistan was deranged and inappropriate from the beginning. Violent conflicts such as this do have the effect of destroying the lives of the victims, but also of deranging the minds of some of the perpetrating soldiers. The Mai Lai Massacre in Vietnam, the wanton destruction and killings in Fallujah, and the prisoner abuses in Abu Graib, Guantanamo, and Bagram are just some examples. There are always more appropriate ways of creating international peace than by inflicting wars on so many innocent people. As a result of this and other atrocities committed by NATO forces in Afghanistan, nowhere will now be safe for US and other foreign troops in Afghanistan. Up to eight Irish soldiers are serving with NATO there and they are now particularly vulnerable as a result of this latest incident. The Irish Government should immediately withdraw all Irish Army personnel from Afghanistan. They should never have been there in the first place.

Comment: The Irish Army personnel serving with NATO in Afghanistan were eventually withdrawn in March 2016.

No. 34.
Belfast Telegraph 17 September 2012
Is There Anyone Accountable for Sorry Mess?

Hillsborough, Birmingham Six, Guildford Four, child abuse scandals, banking and political scandals – all have resulted in apologies that came years and even decades too late. There has been far too little accountability so, one wonders, have only the wrong lessons been learnt? Those in authority who abuse that authority can avoid accountability by hiding the truth, delaying, and therefore denying justice and avoiding accountability. Independent oversight and investigative systems need to be in place to ensure prompt investigation of abuses by those in authority. Self-regulation is no regulation. By giving the appearance of regulation, it protects those in authority, rather than holding them to account. It is foolish to expect authorities to regulate themselves and politicians are on top of the pile. The starting point must be genuinely independent judicial and jurisprudence systems, accountable to the people, but not to the politicians.

No. 35.
Irish Examiner 31 October 2012
Shannon Transit Breach of International Law

A report in *The Guardian* on 25 Oct 2012 reveals that Britain has recently rejected US requests to use UK bases in its nuclear standoff with Iran because of secret legal advice that any pre-emptive strike could be in breach of international law. This raises the question as to whether the Irish Government has received a similar request to allow US military aircraft to use Shannon Airport in the event of a US/Israeli attack on Iran. This may have been one of the purposes of the visit by US General Martin Dempsey to Ireland last August, and his meetings with Lt General Sean McCann and Defence/Justice Minister Shatter. The question that must now be urgently asked is: has the Irish Government given assurances for continuing US military use of Shannon Airport?

The Irish High Court has already ruled (Judge Kearns in Horgan v Ireland, April 2003) that the transit of armed US troops through Shannon is in breach of international laws on neutrality. Allowing armed US troops and war materials through Shannon Airport in the event of an attack on Iran would be a further breach of international law.

No. 36.
Irish Examiner 28 January 2013
Committing Treason Against Our Grandchildren

Kicking the can down the road sounds like an amusing solution to Ireland's problems, but the reality is no joke. The Fianna Fáil/Green government committed acts of economic stupidity, equivalent to treason, by absolving the gambling debts of banks, builders, developers, and other scoundrels, and making Irish taxpayers liable. What the current Fine Gael/Labour Government is doing is even worse. Instead of cancelling the crazy bank guarantees and then dealing courageously with the resulting economic crisis, they adopted the cowardly option of just blaming the previous government and then continuing along the same crazy unsustainable road. Instead of marching a road of solidarity with our supposed EU allies, they are marching down a road to hell or to the fiscal Cliffs of Moher, doing as much damage along the way as Cromwell did a few centuries ago. Ireland now has the highest rates of emigration and suicide since the Famine. Government ministers are falsely claiming they will save billions of euro by extending the period of repayment into the distant future.

This is simpleton economics, treating the people of Ireland like simpletons hoping they won't understand that increasing the duration of our debt repayments will greatly increase the long-term Irish debt burden. However, the reality is even worse than this. Our present generation of mainly older, reckless, spendthrift leaders and gamblers are imposing this unjustified debt burden on our grandchildren and on to generations as yet unborn. Surely this is worse than treason.

Comment: This letter I had published in The Washington Post *came shortly after a major storm called Sandy had done huge damage and serious flooding in New York.*

No. 37.
The Washington Post **16 July 2013**
To Prepare New York For Next Sandy, Move to Higher Ground

The Washington Post reported on July 15 'New York works to be ready for the next Sandy,' [news] on New York authorities' plans to spend $19.5 billion on a blueprint for addressing climate change. Perhaps this money would be better spent moving peoples' homes back from vulnerable coastal areas.

Cities such as New York and New Orleans were understandably built on the coast in an era in which most travel and communications were conducted by sea and large rivers. A similar problem exists in Ireland for similar reasons, but this was compounded during Ireland's boom years, when far too much building occurred on coastal flood plains.

Mayor Michael R. Bloomberg is no more likely to be successful than King Canute of old in holding back the tide. Canute-type coastal barriers cannot hold back the rising sea levels. The solution in the United States and in all coastal regions is to move to higher, dryer ground and prevent all further building on coastal flood zones.

No. 38.
The Irish Times 24 July 2013
Neutrality and the Triple Lock

The so-called triple lock, referred to by Joe Ahern (*The Irish Times* 20 July), would be an important element of Irish positive neutrality and active support for the United Nations, if properly applied. However, this triple lock mechanism has already been 'picked' by the device of only applying it to units of Irish soldiers in excess of twelve individuals, thereby allowing the inappropriate sending of seven Irish soldiers to serve with the NATO International Security Assistance Force (ISAF) force in Afghanistan. Ahern argues that the 'triple lock procedure gives any one of the permanent members of the UN Security Council, ... a veto on when or where we deploy our troops on international missions'. This abuse of their veto by the UN permanent members does not justify the use of a scatter-gun approach by sending a small number of Irish troops to too many diverse missions with the UN, the EU, OSCE, and NATO. Other inappropriate missions were those organised at the behest of France for neo-colonial reasons in Chad and Mali. Such missions have more to do with keeping corrupt minority regimes in power rather than genuine peacekeeping. The decisions to send Irish troops to genuine UN peacekeeping missions such as UNDOF in Golan Heights and UNIFIL in Lebanon were justified. Joe Ahern calls for the 'redefinition or abandonment [of Irish neutrality] in the light of a hugely changed and volatile international security environment'. These international security changes are not changes for the better, but involve pre-emptive wars in breach of international laws in Afghanistan and Iraq, resource wars in Africa, and the use of torture and extra-judicial targeted assassinations. These crimes are facilitated by permitting US military use of Shannon Airport. Irish troops should only be sent on genuine UN peacekeeping missions and Irish neutrality must not be abandoned for Redmondite concepts of imperialist wars.

Comment: In the letter above, I referred to the Golan Heights UNDOF mission as a 'genuine UN peacekeeping mission'. This was a mistake.

UNDOF is indeed a UN mission but as I will discuss in subsequent letters, Irish soldiers should not be serving in this Golan Heights mission as what they are doing there is not genuine peacekeeping, because they are being used primarily to protect Israeli illegal occupation and attempted annexation of the Syrian Golan Heights.

No. 39.
Irish Examiner **28 August 2013**
Politicians Just Support the Elite

Ignoring elephants in the room and engaging in selective amnesia has become a national disease. The latest indications include the raised bogs dispute. Small-scale turf-cutters are being targeted by the EU and Irish Government for doing some environmental damage while everyone ignores the greatest environmental vandalism ever committed in Ireland, the destruction of over 90 per cent of all Irish bogland by Bord na Móna.

Instead of scaling back on this environmental disaster, a new mega peat-burning power station was built in Edenderry, funded by the EU and Irish Government, and consumes over one million tons of peat each year. In recent years, national gamblers including bankers, developers, builders, and corrupted politicians have been bailed out by their elite friends in power, while the bill for their collective madness has been imposed on the innocent 'small people' of Ireland. In the Beef Tribunal, only the whistleblower was punished, and the taxpayer paid the bills. We, the small people of Ireland, were forced to bail out PMPA insurance, Allied Irish Banks, ICI insurance, and pay for exorbitant tribunals that seemed designed to protect the guilty. Why is this continuing to happen? Perhaps it is because we the people have repeatedly allowed our republic to be hijacked by an elite cabal that includes business people, the Catholic Church, political dynasties, and crony politicians. The checks and balances that should have been in place to prevent such corruption failed because the regulators, the judiciary, police, trade unions, and senior civil servants were co-opted into the elite. Most of all, the legislators whose job it was to legislate on behalf of all the people, legislated mainly in their own interests and the interests of elites. It's time 'we the people' restored government of the people, by the people, for the people.

No. 40.
The Irish Times 2 October 2013
Abolition of Seanad Could Pose Increased Dangers for Peace and Neutrality Issues Say Campaigners

Sir, - We are appealing for a No vote (in the referendum proposal to abolish the Senate). We believe the abolition of the Seanad will make the adoption of EU decisions and legislation easier for a government that is determined to do so, even if those decisions are inconsistent with the stated views of the Irish people. Abolishing the Seanad will eliminate the chance of ever establishing a reformed institution that could scrutinise future EU military issues and will make it less problematic for Enda Kenny and his successors to pass controversial legislation.

With the EU pushing for more militarisation, there is a need to increase scrutiny and accountability, not support a decision that will allow for the easier passage of such decisions. Compared to Scandinavian countries, Germany, and many of the new member states, Ireland has one of the least effective scrutiny systems of EU legislation. A reformed Seanad could potentially correct this weakness in Ireland's oversight of EU policy-making, particularly on military issues.

The recent European Parliament session, which approved a report on EU's military structures, state of play and future prospects, demonstrates that the further erosion of Irish neutrality and the continued militarisation of the EU are on the EU and Government agenda and this will be made easier by removing the threat of a reformed Seanad.

This report, aimed at boosting efforts to further militarise the EU, calls for the creation of a fully-fledged EU military headquarters, for the strengthening of EU battle groups, for more money to be spent on arms production and research, and for a closer relationship with NATO.

While the report is non-binding, it sets the agenda for the EU Council meeting in December where further EU militarisation and increased support for arms production and research will be discussed. It is most disturbing to note that all Fine Gael MEPs – the party that wants the Seanad abolished instead of reformed – supported this report and only one Irish MEP, Paul Murphy, Socialist Party, voted against it.

Just because the Seanad has failed to promote peace and neutrality issues in the past is not a justifiable reason to support its permanent abolition. The failures of the Seanad are the direct result of the failure and refusal of the political parties to reform it.

It seems the government's strategy is to 'get rid of the Seanad quickly' before there is a chance to reform it in a way that would make any future government's task of passing controversial legislation more difficult.

While we all agree with the criticism of the current Seanad and the undemocratic procedure for allocating seats, if abolished, it can never be reinstated without a referendum, and the only body that can propose this is the government itself. Thus, it's unlikely that the institution that wants the Seanad abolished will ever propose its reinstatement. - Yours, etc,

Dr EDWARD HORGAN, Retd Army Commandant & UN Military peacekeeper;
Dr JOHN LANNON, UL & Shannonwatch coordinator;
CATHERINE CONNOLLY, Galway City Councillor;
NIALL FARRELL, Shannonwatch activist:
PATRICIA McKENNA, Former Green Party MEP and peace & neutrality activist;
Prof JOHN MAGUIRE, Prof of Sociology, UCC, C/o Iona Road, Glasnevin, Dublin 9.

No. 41.
Irish Examiner 25 October 2013
Irish Sea Coast at Risk of Nuclear Disaster

The Irish Sea is one of the most nuclear polluted, because of the number of nuclear power stations and facilities on its English, Welsh, and Scottish coastlines, and because its partial enclosure leads to a build-up of pollutants. Now, the British Government has approved another nuclear power station, at Hinkley Point in the Bristol Channel, risking further pollution into the Irish and Celtic Seas. There are proposals for additional nuclear power stations in Sellafield, Wylfa, Oldbury, and Heysham, all on the Irish Sea coastline. If approved, these will be in addition to the sixteen nuclear facilities (power stations, military, and research facilities) stretching from the Bristol Bay, in the south, up to Ayrshire, in Scotland, all of which are potential or actual pollutants of the Irish Sea. These are of no benefit to the people of Ireland, but are potential killers, a la Fukushima, in 2011, Chernobyl, in 1986, or Sellafield (Windscale), in 1957. There are safer, cheaper, and more environmentally sustainable forms of energy. Stop this nuclear madness.

No. 42.
The Irish Times 24 Jan 2014
A New Party's Policies

It's good to see a new political party 'The National Independent Party' being formed. However, one of its main policies 'it ... opposes economic migration' (Maria O'Halloran *The Irish Times* Jan 15) could cause some problems. In order not to be accused of hypocrisy, any such policy must apply to incoming and outgoing migration. While the number of incoming economic migrants to Ireland is relatively small, the number of Irish who migrated from Ireland is huge, with up to seventy million people internationally claiming Irish ancestry. A further complication is that during the last ice age, there were no humans living in Ireland. That means that the ancestors of all persons now living in Ireland were migrants into Ireland for mainly economic reasons. One of the party spokespersons, Mr

Martin Critten, is 'originally from the north of England'. Perhaps he is an economic migrant. Me thinks they will have to think it out again.

No. 43.
Examiner **25 January 2014**
Release Whistleblowers Like Margaretta D'Arcy

As the scandals unfold at the Central Remedial Clinic, and other top-up payments that look more like grand larceny, we learn that a seventy-nine-year-old Aosdána member and long-time human rights activist Margaretta Darcy has been jailed in Limerick prison for protesting against the use of Shannon Airport by torturers, human rights abusers, and US war criminals. The elite states of the world, such as the US, can do what they like internationally with apparent impunity, and our Irish 'elite' white-collar criminals appear to be able to do likewise with impunity in Ireland. It is the whistleblowers like Private Manning and Margaretta Darcy who are jailed and the most vulnerable in Irish society who are punished by having the funding for the vital services either withdrawn or stolen. In addition, we have to suffer the indignity of hearing the Fianna Fáil party seeking the high moral ground on such issues even though they were complicit in US military and CIA use of Shannon Airport and in the political and economic corruption that facilitated scandals such as that at the CRC. It's time to release the courageous whistleblowers and put the real criminals into their cells.

No. 44.
Irish Examiner **26 February 2014**
Gardaí Should Admit Mistakes and Resolve Them

There are thousands of excellent Gardaí, like Maurice McCabe and John Wilson. Too few of them have taken the courageous actions that Maurice and John have, because they fear the abuse to which they, and their families, may be subjected. In the interests of justice, they need to feel the fear and do it anyway. Mistakes are inevitable in human organisations.

Such mistakes are easily resolved, if quickly acknowledged and corrected. It is only when a culture of cover-up and false loyalty takes root that such mistakes lead to disasters, and crimes are committed that should have been prevented by the Gardaí. In the early decades of its history, the Gardaí, and its members, were noted for their dedication, unarmed bravery, and loyalty to the State and to the people. These recent difficulties, therefore, can and must be overcome. These difficulties and failures include a culture of denial, and complicity with the US misuse of Shannon Airport, including complicity with the CIA's Extraordinary Rendition program, which led to hundreds of prisoners being tortured in Abu Ghraib, Guantanamo, and elsewhere. Crime prevention must be re-established as the primary role of An Garda Síochána.

No. 45.

Irish Independent and *Irish Examiner* 22 March 2014
Moral and Physical Hazard in Unfair Imposition Of Levy

The proposed 1 per cent insurance levy to cover costs of flooding damage to homes that probably should never have been built in flood-prone areas is a levy too far. We have been forced against our will to bail out banks, builders, and irresponsible developers. In the past, our governments have forced us to bail out the PMPA, and AIB/ICI insurance, and we also pay for injuries caused by uninsured drivers. If this flood insurance levy goes ahead, then building in flood plains will also probably continue. Why not build a house too close to the sea or a river, if someone else will pay for any flood damage? It's far too easy for our politicians, who are among the highest-paid politicians in the world, to give away our money without our permission. Thousands of houses in the Shannon floodplain, and in low-lying areas of Cork and other coastal regions should never have been built, and exorbitantly expensive flood defences are like King Canute trying to hold back the tide.

No. 46.
Irish Examiner 7 July 2014
Gilmore Not Entitled to be EU Commissioner

Democracy still matters in Ireland, in spite of its imperfections and the damage done to people by recent Irish politicians. In our most recent democratic election, the people rejected Labour Party policies, leading to the resignation of party leader Eamon Gilmore. Over the past half-century, I have voted for Labour more often than not, and may do so again, given the dearth of better alternatives. However, I am deeply concerned by the arrogance of Gilmore, and of other senior Labour politicians, in seeking to have him nominated as Ireland's EU Commissioner. Education Minister Ruairi Quinn has had the sensitivity and common sense to bow out gracefully. Gilmore should do likewise, rather than claim 'entitlement' to such an important position as EU Commissioner. Public service is a privilege, not an entitlement. If Irish politicians continue to pursue such 'jobs-for-the-boys' attitudes, then even more serious damage will be done to Irish democracy. Mr Gilmore, the people have spoken, please accept their verdict.

No. 47.
Irish Examiner 5 September 2014
Ireland Should Be Humane and Offer a Home to Guantanamo Prisoners

The report 'Decaying Guantánamo Defies Closing Plans' (*The New York Times*, Sept 1) makes depressing reading. Not only is the prison camp decaying, so are its prisoners. Seventy-nine prisoners, considered low-level risk, have been awaiting release for several years, but Congress refuses to allow them to be released in the US, and the US has been unable to persuade other countries to take them. Seventy higher-risk prisoners should be transferred to prisons in the US, where they would be subject to constitutional laws, including habeas corpus proceedings, but this has also been blocked by Congress. Some prisoners have been in Guantanamo for twelve years without trial. The report, by Charlie Savage, refers to Guantanamo's 'decaying infrastructure and aging inmates' and cites the prison doctor that '20 to 25 prisoners have conditions… such as diabetes and high blood pressure. He expects other problems, like heart disease, strokes, and cancer, to arise in coming years'. Two prisoners from Guantanamo were resettled in Ireland in 2009. As a humanitarian gesture, Ireland should resettle more such prisoners, particularly given that the Irish Government facilitated the transfer of prisoners to Guantanamo by allowing CIA and US military aircraft, which were engaged in the so-called Extraordinary Rendition program, to be refuelled at Shannon Airport. Some prisoners on hunger strike are being force-fed, and at least nine prisoners have died in Guantanamo, including six by suspected suicide.

No. 48.

Edward Horgan @irishcentral 5 September 2014
Ireland Should Take More Guantanamo Prisoners

Most people, including the vast majority of US citizens, are firmly opposed to human rights abuses, including unlawful imprisonment and torture. Indeed, it was US governments in the post-World War II years that were foremost in developing and enhancing international laws and conventions, including the Geneva Conventions on War, the Nuremberg Principles, and the UN Convention Against Torture. Guantanamo prison is a contradiction of all the best elements of 'American values' and US constitutional democracy.

I got an insight into the damage that torture does when I worked for some time as manager of a torture care centre in Dublin, dealing with individuals who survived torture by dictators in Iraq, Zimbabwe, and elsewhere. There are clear indications that the treatment of some prisoners at Guantanamo amounted to cruel and inhuman treatment, if not torture, even if US Government legal advisors claimed otherwise. Long-term imprisonment without trial or access to constitutional rights such as habeas corpus contravenes US laws and best human rights practices. This is why

Guantanamo prison exists, attempting to place its inmates beyond the full protection of the US justice system.

A recent report, 'Decaying Guantánamo Defies Closing Plans' (*The New York Times*, Sep 1), makes depressing reading. Not only is the prison camp itself decaying but so are its prisoners. Seventy-nine prisoners, considered to be low-level risks, have been awaiting release for several years, but the US Congress refuses to allow them to be released in the US and the US Government has been unable to persuade other countries to take them. In addition, seventy higher-risk prisoners should be transferred to prisons in the US where they would be subject to US constitutional laws including habeas corpus proceedings, but this is also blocked by Congress. Some prisoners have been in Guantanamo for over twelve years without trial. The report by Charlie Savage refers to Guantanamo's 'decaying infrastructure and aging inmates' and cites the prison doctor that '20 to 25 prisoners have conditions ... such as diabetes and high blood pressure. He expects other problems, like heart disease, strokes, and cancer to arise in coming years.'

Two Uighur prisoners from Guantanamo were resettled in Ireland in 2009. As a humanitarian gesture, Ireland, and other countries, should offer to resettle more prisoners from Guantanamo. This would be particularly appropriate in Ireland's case, given that the Irish Government facilitated the transfer of prisoners to Guantanamo by allowing CIA and US military aircraft that were engaged in the so-called Extraordinary Rendition program to be refuelled at Shannon Airport. Some prisoners on hunger strike are still being force-fed, and at least nine prisoners have died in Guantanamo, including six by suspected suicide.

The recent horrific murder of Irish American James Foley in Iraq or Syria, while dressed for propaganda purposes in a Guantanamo-style orange jumpsuit, is an example of the blowback-type consequences that can result from democratic states behaving undemocratically, although this in no way justifies the horrific crimes being committed by extremists in the Middle East.

At the time of the Abu Ghraib controversy, several US military officers expressed grave concerns about the torture and abuse of enemy combatants and predicted that it could have consequences for captured US soldiers. President Obama must live up to his promise to close Guantanamo and thereby begin to restore the United States to its status as one of the leading protectors of human rights. Ireland and other countries should assist President Obama in this task by agreeing to take a quota of Guantanamo prisoners. Surely, if the US President has the authority to make war, then he also has a duty to make peace and protect human rights.

Dr Edward Horgan

*Edward Horgan is a human rights activist who served as an officer in the Irish Defence Forces and as a UN peacekeeper, and has worked extensively on democratisation programmes and election monitoring in post-conflict countries, including with The Carter Center. He is also a part-time lecturer in international relations at the University of Limerick.

No. 49.
Irish Examiner 20 September 2014
US Bomb Attacks in Iraq Contravene UN Charter

Bombing attacks by US warplanes and drones are already taking place in Iraq and are likely to be extended to bombing targets in Syria in the near future.

Regardless of whether the US Congress approves such acts of war, the US Government has not been given approval by the UN Security Council for such attacks and has not even sought such approval. Such attacks are therefore in breach of international law, particularly the UN Charter.

The US will no doubt claim justification for such attacks as it did for its war against Afghanistan, and quite falsely for its war against Iraq in 2003. These wars were in contravention of the UN Charter, and the resultant deaths of hundreds of thousands of Iraqi and Afghan people were disproportionate to any threats to the United States. Ireland is also in breach of the UN Charter by facilitating the transit of US warplanes and armed US troops through Shannon Airport.

No. 50.
Irish Examiner 7 October 2014
Junior Academic Staff Are Exploited at Universities

The latest Times Higher Education league table finds that most Irish universities have dropped down the league table. One of the causes for this downgrading is perhaps being overlooked. There are increasing levels of employee apartheid in many Irish universities. An elite group of staff and senior permanent academics enjoy remuneration and conditions that are in stark contrast with those of part-time, temporary, and hourly-paid staff. What probably began as a genuine effort to use postgraduate researchers as classroom assistants and tutors, thereby giving them important experience, has expanded over the past decade. Now complete modules and undergraduate courses are being taught by temporary hourly-paid employees, many of whom have PhDs, but who are being denied the permanent employment that their qualifications justify. The working conditions of many of them include no access to university office and computer facilities. In addition, they are expected to work many hours of unpaid work for each paid lecture hour, including lecture preparation, student guidance, the setting and correction of exams, and other administrative tasks. When it comes to the treatment of junior and temporary employees, most Irish universities are engaged in a race to the bottom. They are winning that race at the expense of unjust exploitation of employees and decreasing standards of third-level education.

Comment: While researching for my doctoral thesis on reform of the United Nations, I came to realise that acts of genocide are the most serious of war crimes and crimes against humanity and I found it necessary to research particular genocides including the Armenian, Cambodia, and Rwandan genocides with a view to evaluating the success or failure of the

UN towards achieving its primary purpose of maintaining international peace. I have also worked on election monitoring missions in Armenia on two occasions in 2008 and in 2013, which helped me to get a deeper understanding of present and past Armenian difficulties, including the trauma of the genocide. The people of Armenia suffered a horrific genocide perpetrated by the Ottoman government between 1915 and 1922, in which an estimated one and a half million Armenian people perished. It was my hope that this following letter might help to persuade the Irish parliament to officially recognise the Armenian genocide and I initiated discussions with a number of parliamentarians and political parties. However, my efforts so far have not been successful. Ireland does very little trade with Armenia, and quite a bit of trade with Turkey – money seems to count for more than human rights in present-day Ireland.

No. 51.
Irish Daily Mail **31 December 2014,** *Irish Examiner* **2 January 2015,** *The Irish Times* **5 Jan 2015**

Centenary of Armenian Genocide

2015 is the centenary of the Armenian genocide that cost the lives of up to a million Armenian men, women, and children. What makes the Armenian genocide so important is that because it was so 'successful' from an Ottoman Turk point of view, it became a sort of blueprint for further acts of genocide in the twentieth century. Infamously, Adolf Hitler, as he was preparing to attack Poland in 1939, is reported to have said: 'Who, after all, speaks today of the annihilation of the Armenians?' The relative success of the Armenian genocide encouraged others, including Hitler, Idi Amin, Pol Pot, and the Rwandan Government, to carry out further acts of genocide. Acknowledgement and recognition by the international community that the atrocities committed against the Armenian people between 1915 and 1922 amounted to genocide is vital in order to ensure justice and accountability for the Armenian people, and to strengthen global jurisprudence toward preventing further acts of genocide. France, Russia, the US Congress, and the European Parliament have already recognised the Armenian genocide but many other countries, including Ireland and the UK, have yet to do so. The present Turkish government must be pressured by the international community into accepting that its predecessors perpetrated genocide against the Armenian people. Turkey has aspirations to membership of the European Union, and Europe needs Turkey as a positive bridge toward the Middle East and toward Islamic communities. The European Union should make it clear that recognition of the Armenian genocide must be a prerequisite for EU membership and perhaps lead to EU membership for both Turkey and Armenia.

No. 52.
Irish Examiner 19 January 2015
Questions Remain About Shannon Stopovers

It's been revealed (Amy Goodman, Democracy Now) that a secret CIA 'Black Site' prison existed within Guantanamo in which prisoners may have been tortured and subjected to mind-altering drugs. A book by a former US sergeant at Guantanamo, Joseph Hickman, raises claims that three prisoners alleged to have committed suicide in 2006 may have died instead due to torture. Mani al-Utaybi, and Yasser al-Zahrani from Saudi Arabia were already approved for release. A review of Ali Abdullah Ahmed's case revealed 'no evidence of terrorist involvement'. In 2008, Murat Kurnaz, a former detainee, revealed in his memoir, that all the other prisoners at Guantanamo concluded the three detainees had been killed. I met Murat Kurnaz when he visited Ireland in 2008. His description of his 'rendition' journey from Afghanistan to Guantanamo in 2002 indicates that he was taken to Guantanamo by US military aircraft. He was bound, gagged, and drugged on the flight so he was unable to see which airports his plane landed at. These planes would have needed to refuel in locations such as Portugal, Spain, or Ireland. One of Kurnaz's refuelling airports may have been Shannon Airport.

No. 53.
Irish Examiner 4 March 2015
The Garda Síochána needs to downsize.

As of January 31, the Garda website reveals that there are 2,394 Garda officers at rank of sergeant or above, and 185 of these are superintendent level or above.

Incredibly, the Garda structure allows 15 officers with the title of commissioner including two deputy commissioners and no less than 12 assistant commissioners.

In a country of about 4 million, this defies logic.

No. 54.
Irish Examiner 10 March 2015
Irish Neutrality Is a Good Example for Europe

With EU Commission president, Jean-Claude Juncker, calling for a 'common European army' as a 'deterrent against further Russian aggression on the continent', the Lisbon Treaty hawks are coming home to roost. NATO's proposed expansion into Georgia and Ukraine sparked off conflicts and the Russian annexation of South Ossetia, Abkhazia, and Crimea. Likewise, the establishment of a European army, in addition to a NATO one that should have been made redundant after the end of the Soviet Union, will heighten tension with Russia. Vladimir Putin is not Adolf Hitler, and what is happening in eastern Ukraine is not a rerun of 1939 right-wing racist aggression. Such dangerous right-wing tendencies are resurfacing in Western political and military circles, not in the East. All European states have armies, and arguably too many armaments, and Britain, France, and Russia have nuclear weapons. Uniting all these into two super-armies would be a disaster, and would risk nuclear war. In matters of war and peace, there is far more strength and common sense in a diversity of views and of strategies. It was not appeasement that led to WWII, but European fascist doctrines of 'uno duce, una voce', combined with rampant militarism. The diversity of foreign policy that Europe needs includes positive neutrality by Ireland and other European states, combined with common sense. Common sense, however, is becoming uncommon in Europe.

No. 55.

Published on Clare Daly TD's website on 3 April 2015 (this was a copy of a post on my Facebook page)

A Powerful Easter Message from Edward Horgan of Shannonwatch

Hello all, Good Friday is celebrated by many in Ireland as the day Christ was crucified. Over the centuries, a corrupted version of Christianity perpetrated many crimes against humanity, including the Crusades and the Inquisition, just as a corrupted version of Islam is now perpetrating crimes against humanity in Kenya, Libya, Syria, and many countries across the Middle East. Ireland is continuing with its support for a corrupted version of the Crusades by allowing the US military to transport troops, war materials, and special forces on assassination missions through Shannon Airport. This Good Friday morning, there were two US warplanes at Shannon. One was an OMNI Air International aircraft chartered to carry US troops through Shannon Airport, and the other was a US NAVY Hercules C130T. These warplanes were being protected by an Irish Army patrol, arguably playing the role of Pontius Pilot's Roman Soldiers?

The United States is now involved in many unjustified conflicts, most of which have caused devastation, directly or indirectly, in Ukraine, Afghanistan, Iraq, Libya, Syria, Somalia, and most recently in Yemen through its proxy Saudi Arabia. Hope you have a nice and peaceful Easter. At the receiving end of such warplanes, many innocent civilians may be bombed and killed this Easter. May they rest in peace.

No. 56.
Irish Examiner 11 April 11 2015
Mary Lou McDonald is Acting in the Public Interest.

Deputy Mary Lou McDonald was correct to act in the public interest by using Dáil privilege to name politicians who were alleged in a civil servant's report to have been linked to offshore Ansbacher accounts. The Oireachtas Committee on Procedures and Privileges has concluded that she abused her parliamentary privilege. It said her utterances were 'in the nature of being defamatory' and she should not have named the politicians. There are still questions to be answered with regard to the manner in which the original civil servant's report was investigated but it now appears that these questions will not even be asked. If the politicians who were named were blameless, then their good names would be vindicated by a proper investigation of all the matters concerned. Any attempt to restrict the use of Dáil privilege to name individuals as Mary Lou McDonald has done will be contrary to the interests of the people.

No. 57.
Irish Examiner 22 April 2015
EU Should Face Court Over Its Cruel Policy on Mediterranean Refugees

In 2014, the European Union and its member state governments including Ireland decided to halt the Italian-led rescue operation in the Mediterranean called Mare Nostrum, which had successfully rescued about 140,000 refugees fleeing poverty, famine, conflicts, and human rights abuses in the Middle East and Africa. The EU and other Western governments have played a significant role in the destabilisation and overthrow of governments across the Middle East, thereby fuelling the refugee crisis. There are clear legal and human rights duties on all governments and international organisations to come to the aid and rescue of individuals in distress who are at immediate risk of death. The decision by the EU to end Mare Nostrum amounts to a breach of human rights obligations and could arguably be a crime against humanity. The EU should be brought before the European Court of Human Rights, and possibly before the International Criminal Court in The Hague to answer charges in these matters.

It brings shame on all EU citizens that our governments knowingly made a decision to stop rescuing people of our shared humanity just because they are considered to be 'them and not us' or 'insignificant others'. There are now indications that the so-called international community may exacerbate the situation by further military action in Libya in an arguably doomed attempt to stop this flow of desperate refugees.

No. 58.
Irish Examiner 28 April 2015
It Is Shameful the Government Failed to Commemorate Genocide

Yesterday I attended the commemoration in Dublin of the Armenian genocide. An Taoiseach Enda Kenny declined an invitation to attend. There were no Irish Government representatives. It seems the Irish Government does not want to upset the Turkish Government, who have been denying the Armenian genocide for 100 years. Ireland does far more trade with Turkey than with Armenia. Turkey is an important member of NATO, and our government does not want to offend the US, NATO's overlord. The failure to acknowledge genocide ensures other evil states and dictators will be encouraged to commit similar crimes, knowing the Armenian genocide was such a dreadful 'success' from the Ottoman Turkish Government's perspective. Hitler learned these lessons and went on to commit the Holocaust against the Jewish people. Germany had a previous record of 'successful' genocide in Southwest Africa between 1904 and 1907, killing up to 100,000 Herero and Namaqua people. Idi Amin in Uganda and Mengistu in Ethiopia both committed acts of genocide against their own people, but both died of old age in luxurious retirement in Saudi Arabia. Pol Pot died of old age surrounded by his family and supported by the Western powers, almost thirty years after he committed genocide against the Cambodian people. It is so important to publicly acknowledge such crimes of genocide and to bring the perpetrators to justice.

No. 59.
Irish Examiner **24 June 2015**
Irish Have Long Sought Refuge Overseas and So Must Offer Refuge

So far, the Irish navy has rescued 1,700 men, women, and children in the Mediterranean and deposited them in Italy. Not surprisingly, Italy is having great difficulty coping with the huge numbers of asylum seekers that are being forced upon it, estimated to have been 170,000 in 2014 and expected to be 200,000 in 2015. France has closed its borders to migrants travelling from Italy, and other European countries are also considering border restrictions. The international refugee system is at breaking point, especially in Italy, yet the Irish navy is landing hundreds of additional migrants in Italy each week. Ireland has clear obligations with regard to refugees and asylum seekers, under the UN Refugee Convention 1951 (and its subsequent protocols). Yet, instead of taking our fair share of asylum seekers, Ireland has been using another convention, known as the Dublin III regulation, to send asylum seekers back to the country where they first entered the EU, or to the other four countries (Iceland, Norway, Liechtenstein, and Switzerland) who are part of Dublin III regulations.

However, since the Irish naval ship, LÉ *Eithne*, is arguably the equivalent of Irish sovereign territory, when on the high seas, any asylum seekers who are taken on board should be entitled to apply for asylum in Ireland. Other states that have signed up to Dublin III should likewise be entitled to send these asylum seekers to Ireland. Irish people fleeing hunger, poverty and persecution have found refuge in many foreign countries, even in recent times.

It's time we lived up to our humanitarian obligations.

No. 60.
Irish Examiner 30 June 2015
Afghan and Iraqi Wars Exacerbate Conflicts in Middle East and Africa

Our deepest sympathy must go to the families and friends of the three Irish citizens, Laurence and Martina Hayes, and Lorna Carty, who were murdered in Sousse, Tunisia, last week. Nothing ever justifies murder, and nothing ever justifies mass murder. Yet, in order to prevent such atrocities in the future, it is important to begin the process of trying to understand what drives rational individuals to do such irrational deeds. There are media reports that the Tunisian gunman Seifeddine Rezgui deliberately chose Western tourists whose states supported US-led wars in the Middle East. A report in the *Limerick Post* (June 27) stated that 'Minister for Foreign Affairs Charlie Flanagan has defended the ongoing use Shannon Airport by the US military'. He reportedly told a recent meeting of An Oireachtas committee that the refuelling of US military arrangement 'does not flout Irish neutrality and that it does not pose a security risk. The Oireachtas Petitions Committee is investigating the use of Shannon Airport by US troops'. It seems clear the disastrous Afghan and Iraqi wars have initiated a conflagration of conflicts across the Middle East and North Africa. This recent atrocity in Tunisia is one of the outcomes of these conflicts and there will be more such incidents until we begin to address the root causes of these conflicts and focus our national and international attention on conflict prevention rather than fuelling conflicts.

No. 61.
Irish Examiner 8 July 2015
Unjustified Wars Cause Hatred, Further Violence, and Terrorism

I stand accused by Dr Frank Giles (Letters, *Irish Examiner*, July 2) of blaming the recent Tunisian mass murders on Western foreign policy and military interventions. My views are based on academic research on peace and conflict prevention, and practical experience on peace and democratisation programmes in countries such as Ukraine, Nigeria, Indonesia, Pakistan, Congo, Tunisia, Egypt, and Israel. In May this year, I narrowly escaped a terrorist attack while working in southeastern Turkey, so I have no sympathy with murderers of any type – right-wing or left-wing. Violence begets violence, and unjustified wars cause further wars, and inevitable blowback.

The establishment and growth of ISIS in the Middle East can be traced back to US support for the Mujahedeen in the 1980s against the USSR in Afghanistan. The USSR defeat brought the Taliban to power. The US overthrew the Taliban Government in 2001 without a UN mandate and failed to put an honest democratic government in its place. They then repeated these mistakes in Iraq with disastrous consequences for the Afghan and Iraqi peoples. Some of the Mujahedeen and Taliban helped spawn al-Qaeda. The chaos in Iraq, Yemen, and Libya, caused directly or indirectly by irresponsible military interventions by the US and its allies, further radicalised and enraged the more extreme Islamic fundamentalists who have gone on to create ISIS. While the conflicts in Nigeria and Syria are mainly internal, the Syrian civil war is being fuelled by regional and Western intervention also. If even a small fraction of the costs of militarisation and wars were spent on conflict prevention and making peace, and in making the United Nations the organisation for creating peace that it should be, then the blowback of terrorist attacks would not exist. Those who abuse the good name of Islam to perpetrate terrorist crimes are no better than those so-called Christians who perpetrated the Crusades, the Spanish Inquisition, burning witches, and more recently, the Catholic Church child abuse scandals. Understanding the causes of violence and terrorism is vital to preventing such atrocities. Peace and justice can be achieved, but not by labelling Muslims in general as fanatics who have been slaughtering fellow Muslims, and others, for many years.

Let's make peace, not war.

No. 62.
Irish Examiner **4 August 2015**
Austria Shows Us the Way with Show of Neutrality

On July 19, 2015, nine American marines were arrested in Vienna's airport for carrying assault rifles and handguns on board a commercial airliner without proper clearance. They were on their way to Ukraine to take part in the Exercise Saber Guardian that began July 20. The US soldiers involved were refused permission to travel on to Ukraine by the Austrian authorities and were put on a flight back to the USA. Like Ireland, Austria is a neutral country, except that unlike Ireland, Austria takes its neutrality seriously and complies with international laws and obligations on neutrality. Up to two and a half million US troops have transited through Shannon Airport since 2001, and most of them were carrying weapons with them, all in clear breach of Ireland's international neutrality obligations. The only occasion when any of these US troops were arrested in Ireland was on 22 June 2006 when a peace activist carried out a citizen's arrest on six uniformed US soldiers in Ennis, Co Clare, and handed them over to Gardaí, who released them. Irish neutrality, supported by the vast majority of the Irish people, needs to be applied and enforced at Shannon Airport.

No. 63.
Irish Examiner **31 August 2015**
Don't Damage Peace to Score Points on Sinn Féin

I am not a political supporter of Sinn Féin but I am a supporter of the peace process in Ireland. I fear that some political parties, north and south, are trying to achieve short-term political gain, at the expense of Sinn Féin, over the possible involvement of former or existing IRA or Sinn Féin members in recent murders. It would be irresponsible to damage the Irish peace process for such unjustified political reasons. Fianna Fáil and Fine Gael would do well to remember the crimes and human rights abuses committed by their own paramilitary predecessors during the war of independence and the civil war, including the execution without trial of prisoners of war. More recently, some former Irish Government ministers, and some opposition politicians, were convicted of various crimes, and perhaps several more should have joined them. However, this does not mean that the Irish Government as a whole, or any one political party, has been guilty of these crimes, or even complicit in them. I believe that Sinn Féin are now genuinely working towards peace and democracy. The crimes of a few members or ex-members should not be misused to damage the peace process, as this will damage the future of democracy in Ireland.

No. 64.
Irish Examiner 8 September 2015
Our Role in US Wars Helped Provoke Crisis

In 1624 John Donne wrote: 'No man is an iland, intire of it selfe; every man is a peece of the Continent, a part of the maine; if a clod bee washed away by the Sea, Europe is the lesse, as well as if a Promontorie were, as well as if a Mannor of thy friends or of thine owne were; any mans death diminishes me, because I am involved in Mankinde; And therefore never send to know for whom the bell tolls; It tolls for thee....'

Today's bells are not just tolling for Aylan Kurdi, washed away by the sea, they are tolling for us and Europe and humanity. The chaos that Aylan Kurdi and millions more were fleeing was substantially caused by unjustified wars waged by the US and European NATO states, shamefully fuelled by Ireland at Shannon Airport, for a few dollars more. We will ease our conscience by taking in 1,800 refugees, but will continue to allow US warplanes to refuel at Shannon.

No. 65.
Irish Examiner 21 September 2015
Conflict Resolution is Key to Solving Migrant Crisis

Up to 250,000 people have been killed in the Syrian civil war so far, and more than 11m Syrians have become refugees or displaced within Syria. That's the equivalent of twice the population of Cork City killed and twice the population of all of Ireland homeless. The suffering in the Middle East did not happen because of some unavoidable catastrophe like a tsunami. The chaos let loose by the US/NATO-led resource wars in Afghanistan, Iraq, and Libya have spawned reactionary forces such as ISIS, whose calculated violence and reign of terror is the equivalent of the German and Japanese reign of terror during the Second World War. The focus, therefore, must be to find immediate ways of stopping the slaughter and suffering and then examine what has caused these multiple but closely interconnected crises, and find effective ways of preventing such crises and suffering in the future.

The United Nations is the international organisation specifically set up seventy years ago for the purpose of maintaining international peace and dealing with refugee crises. In both respects, the UN has failed. The Palestinian refugee crisis and the Arab/Israeli conflicts in 1948 were among the UN's early challenges. Sixty-seven years later, these conflicts are unresolved and there are now more than 4.3m Palestinian refugees registered with UNRWA. The problem was, and is, that the UN Charter was drafted by the five Security Council permanent members, who placed themselves above the UN, and outside of its controls or sanctions, by virtue of their veto powers. They have abused their powers consistently, beginning with the Korean War and Cold War proxy wars.

Compromises must be made in the Middle East. In both Syria and Iraq, the keys to unlocking these conflicts are probably held by Russia and Iran. Russia played an important role in the disposal of most of the Assad regime's chemical weapons and the recent agreement on Iranian nuclear issues, combined with the important role that Iran is playing in confronting ISIS in Iraq, point towards Russia and Iran being key players in ending these conflicts. Razor wire and water cannons on Europe's borders will solve nothing.

Today is the UN International Day of Peace. One day of peace is pointless. The people who would avoid being killed by one day of peace would probably be killed anyway in the following few days as conflicts resume.

No. 66.
Irish Examiner **6 October 2015**
Ireland Should Recognise the Armenian Genocide

In a significant development in Turkey, the pro-Kurdish Peoples' Democratic Party (HDP) in their election manifesto for the November 1 parliamentary elections, has stated that if elected, it will recognise the Armenian genocide. HDP co-chairs Selahattin Demirtas and Figen Yüksekdağ said the state should issue state-level apologies for genocides and massacres committed against different groups over the years. Armenian genocide recognition refers to the formal acceptance that the massacre and forced deportation of Armenians committed by the Ottoman Empire in 1915–1923 constitutes genocide. So far, the governments of twenty-eight countries, including Russia, Brazil, France, Germany, and Canada, as well as forty-three states of the United States of America and the European Parliament, have recognised the events as 'genocide'. The Irish Government and Dáil Éireann have so far refused to recognise the Armenian genocide. Given the similarities between Irish and Armenian histories and cultures, it is very important that Ireland should formally recognise the Armenian massacres as genocide, especially in this centenary year of those tragic events.

No. 67.
Irish Examiner **7 October 2015**
Ireland Can't Distance Itself from the US Bombings Which Kill Children

The bombing of a Doctors Without Borders (MSF) hospital in Kunduz Afghanistan by US military aircraft caused the deaths of three children, seven other patients, and twelve MSF staff members. Reliable reports indicate that the bombing was carried out by a US AC-130W aircraft, which continued to bomb the hospital for thirty minutes after MSF had informed US military in Kabul that the hospital was under attack. Apart from the human tragedies involved in this horrific incident, why should we in Ireland care about an incident occurring over 8,000 km away? The US aircraft that carried out this bombing may well have travelled through Shannon Airport. Information received under FOI requests and Dáil questions clearly indicate that no proper oversight or searches are carried out into the transit of US military aircraft through Shannon, even though such activity is in clear breach of Ireland's obligations as a neutral state. On September 5, 2013, a US military AC-130W aircraft, landed and refuelled at Shannon Airport. There is an urgent need for an independent investigation [not only into bombings] but also into Irish Government's complicity in unjustified wars. Doctors Without Borders courageously provide vital medical care for all those injured in conflict zones. Unfortunately, reckless military operations also operate without borders or limitations.

No. 68.
Irish Examiner 22 October 2015
President and Taoiseach Absent from Funerals. Why?

President Michael D. Higgins and Taoiseach Enda Kenny quite correctly attended the funeral of Garda Tony Golden last week. However, at the funerals of five members of the traveller family in Bray on October 20, the President and Taoiseach were both represented by their respective aides-de-camp. Why did Mr Higgins and Mr Kenny not attend this very tragic funeral in person? Why do they not treat all the children of Ireland equally? May little Jodie and Kelsey and their parents Willie Lynch and Tara Gilbert, and Willie's brother Jimmy Lynch rest in peace. Perhaps Mr Higgins and Mr Kenny will find time to attend the funerals of Thomas and Sylvia Connors and their children, Jim, Christy, and Mary in Wexford on Friday.

May the Connors family also rest in peace.

No. 69.

Irish Examiner 4 November 2015

Having Fire Extinguishers in Cars is Dangerous

Recent proposals from Garda headquarters that legislation should be introduced to make it an offence not to carry a working torch, breakdown triangle, high-visibility vest, first-aid kit, and a fire extinguisher at all times while driving are to be welcomed, with one important exception. Carrying a fire extinguisher in a car is likely to be counterproductive and dangerous. Modern cars contain many materials that are highly inflammable, and in some cases very toxic. Recent videos of car fires demonstrate just how quickly fires in cars can spread. The only safe thing to do if your car goes on fire is to get all passengers out and abandon the car as quickly as possible. Attempting to fight the car fire with a small fire extinguisher is foolish and dangerous. It is therefore unwise even to carry a fire extinguisher in a car in case some drivers might be tempted to fight the fire. In a video of a recent car fire in Cork, one could see that the Cork fire brigade personnel who responded, wisely and professionally, did not attempt to fight the fire until after the fuel tank had exploded, and then approached the car wearing full breathing apparatus. In situations like this, it's best to save the people, not the car.

No. 70.

Irish Examiner 14 November 2015

Low Rank Arrest in Relation to Bloody Sunday Killings

On 30 January, 1972, soldiers of the 1st Battalion, Parachute Regiment, British army, shot dead fourteen unarmed civilians. Twelve others were wounded. Over forty-three years later, on November 10, 2015, one of the soldiers involved, known as Lance Corporal J, was arrested by detectives from the PSNI and questioned about his involvement in these killings. He has since been released on bail. The rank of lance corporal is the lowest military rank, just one step above that of private soldier. The commanding officer of the regiment was awarded the Order of the British Empire by HM Government in October of 1972.

No. 71.
The Irish Times 19 Nov 2015
Syria and Terror Attacks on Paris

Sir, – Our Minister for Defence, without Dáil approval, has backed the French decision to invoke Article 42.7 of the EU's Lisbon Treaty mutual defence obligation. Irish officials said that Irish neutrality will not be affected by the decision. Ministers have repeatedly stated that Ireland is still a neutral state, in spite of allowing over 2.5 million US troops to transit to wars through Shannon Airport. Ministers are afraid to acknowledge that Ireland's policy of neutrality has been abandoned since 2001, because they realise that up to 80 per cent of the Irish people strongly support a policy of positive neutrality that includes active involvement by the Defence Forces in maintaining international peace, and avoidance of becoming entangled in wars. Of course, we should be sympathetic and helpful toward the 129 people killed in Paris. Like many thousands of Irish people, I have immediate relatives, including three grandchildren, living in France. Ireland and the United Nations have serious obligations under the UN charter to maintain international peace in Syria. Yet the opposite is occurring. The so-called international community is now bombing Syria, contributing to the death toll of 250,000 people since 2011. That's well over 240 Syrian people killed each day. That means that up to 25,000 Syrian children have been killed. What Ireland must do is to promote peace in the Middle East and to oppose wars, and thereby to stop the killing of Syrian and other Middle Eastern children (and adults). This will eventually stop the sort of terrorist attacks that have killed children and adults in Paris, London, Madrid, and New York. The only justified 'mutual defence treaties' are those that respect the mutuality of humanity, including our friends and neighbours in Syria and Paris.

No. 72.
Irish Examiner **1 December 2015**
Ireland Must Make Peace and Not War

Fergus Finlay usually writes sensibly. His article 'Not helping when France is being terrorised is not neutrality' (*Irish Examiner*, Nov 27) departs from this rationality. He attacks Ruth Coppinger and Mary Lou McDonald because they dared to urge caution in responding to acts of terrorism. Of course, we must condemn terrorist attacks on the US, UK, Spain, and France, yet we seem to forget our 227 Russian friends killed in the Sinai terrorist attack and the hundreds of thousands killed in the Middle East. We must also condemn state terrorism, especially unjustified Western-led wars waged in clear breach of the UN charter. I have three precious grandchildren living in France, but I firmly believe that it would be racist of me to suggest that my grandchildren are more precious than the children who have been killed in Afghanistan, Iraq, and Syria, in wars substantially caused by our Western 'friends'. ISIS is just one of the evil by-products of these wars. Irish neutrality is not something to be ashamed of, which is why over two-thirds of the Irish people support neutrality. Positive neutrality, which includes active promotion of international peace and development, is the only practical foreign policy for Ireland, enabling us to achieve well beyond our size and economic weight. We can achieve virtually nothing by joining military alliances other than providing a target for terrorism.

Comment: During my service as an officer in the Irish Defence Forces, I was involved in an incident where one of the soldiers under my command experienced a mental breakdown or period of delusion while armed with a loaded sub-machine-gun and he was threatening to shoot his fellow soldiers, including myself. As the officer in charge at the scene, I had to resolve this incident by forcefully disarming the soldier, at considerable risk to myself, but it was my job to do so. That experience influenced what I wrote in this following letter.

No. 73.
The Irish Times 4 Dec 2015
Prepared For a Terrorist Attack?

The headline in Peter Murtagh's article 'Security expert urges public readiness in the event of any possible attack' is a good headline and wise advice. However, there is very little in the article itself to indicate readiness for such a possible attack either by the Irish Government, security services, or by the general public. Security expert Sadhbh McCarthy recommends that 'people needed to know how to stay safe and how to help themselves and help others'. This is true but of little value, unless such knowledge is provided.

One of the lessons that should have been learned from the Paris attacks is that the level of fatalities was unduly high, given the small number of attackers. The critical period in such an incident is the time between the beginning of the attack, and the counter-attack by well-armed security forces. In Ireland, this critical period could be catastrophically long. Given that the attackers will likely be both suicidal and murderous, those who have the opportunity to escape should do so, or barricade themselves in rooms or offices. This will not be an option for those who are too close to the gunmen. If in that situation, you are most likely about to die anyway, and your best and probably only chance is for a group of able-bodied people to charge down the attackers and subdue them. Some will die in the process, but their courage will probably save many lives. Such action must be taken in the initial seconds of any such atrocity in order to seize the element of surprise from the attackers, and any such counter-attack must be ruthless, using any available materials as weapons. If we have not thought this out beforehand, we will be too 'terrorised' to act if it actually happens.

The threat of a terrorist attack in Ireland is now a reality, even if it never happens. We do not have and can never have an armed SWAT team in every town, so we must be mentally prepared to act as individuals or small groups. We must also accept the reality that US- and NATO-led wars have caused the deaths of over one million people across the Middle East and that Ireland's unjustified complicity in these wars is the reason for Ireland being on the target list. Ending US military use of Shannon Airport will significantly reduce the likelihood of any such terrorist attack on Ireland.

No. 74.
Irish Examiner 12 December 2015
It's Shameful That We Can't Find Room at the Inn

So, refugees will not arrive in Ireland before 2016. That's great, isn't it?

There is no room in the inn over Christmas in our so-called Christian country. Some of the reasons cited for this delay would be funny if not so tragic, like 'problems on the ground where large numbers of refugees are arriving are affecting the relocation process'. So, it's the middle of winter, snow and storms in the Middle East and the Balkans, Britain has just joined at least nine other countries in bombing Syria, and Germany has just approved German military involvement in the Syrian civil war. Increasing numbers are fleeing the terror of war in Syria, and many who manage to escape from Syria will now die on the newly erected razor wire borders of Europe. Some people even have the cheek to refer to the European response to the Syrian crisis as 'defending European and Christian values'. Oh Jesus Christ, forgive us.

No. 75.
Irish Examiner 17 December 2015
Bankers Were Guilty of False Imprisonment

(Note: the editor's title only included Bankers as the alleged 'false imprisoners' but my letter included 'bankers, builders, developers, and politicians'.)

On the face of it, prima facie, the anti-austerity alliance protesters charged with 'false imprisonment' of An Tánaiste and her assistant should be found not guilty for several reasons. From the video evidence published in the media, it seems clear that both of the alleged victims were in the 'safe custody' of An Garda Síochána at all times, and if there was some risk to their freedom and safety, then An Garda Síochána must bear a significant share of responsibility, given that they knew that a public protest was taking place outside the building that the alleged victims had been in. The charges against these protesters seem to involve an unduly biased application of the law. How many very ill people have been 'falsely imprisoned' on hospital trolleys, due to the actions of corrupt and/or incompetent bankers, builders, developers, and politicians? None of these perpetrators have been charged with 'false imprisonment'. Our legal system and the courts are now being used to evict large numbers of people from their homes, through no fault of the homeowners, but due to the actions of corrupt and/or incompetent bankers, builders, developers, and politicians. Arguably, many of those being evicted are now being 'falsely imprisoned', by being denied access to their homes, and confined to unsuitable hotel rooms, or worse, forced to live rough on the streets of our towns and cities.

No. 76.
Irish Examiner 12 January 2016
Ireland Must Do More to Help Rid the World of the Nuclear Risk

Your editorial ('North Korea — Ticking Time-Bomb', January 7) raises important issues. The threat posed by North Korean Weapons of Mass Destruction (WMDs) is more of a regional threat than a global threat. Far more serious have been the crimes against humanity perpetrated by North Korean regimes against the people of North Korea. North Korea has possibly 10–16 crude WMDs, and only limited methods of delivery. This is just a tiny fraction of the estimate, by the International Campaign for Abolition of Nuclear Weapons, of well over 15,000 nuclear weapons possessed by other countries, including Russia 7,500, the US 7,200, France 300, China 260, Britain 216, Pakistan 130, India 120, and Israel 80. North Korea has never used nuclear weapons in a conflict, but the US has, and the US and Britain have used depleted uranium munitions in the Balkans,

Afghanistan, Iraq, Syria and elsewhere. Five of these countries probably have the capacity to make Planet Earth uninhabitable by humans and other living creatures. The threats to world peace from these other eight countries are far greater than that posed by North Korea. Four of these countries are bombing Syria at present. Your editorial states that 'mad men with military might have created global conflict. It could happen again'. Only with the benefit of hindsight were Hitler and Stalin considered to have been mad. History may well judge leaders of the other nuclear states to have been madmen. Ireland played a major role in the Nuclear Non-Proliferation Treaty signed in 1968. We have done too little in the meantime to rid the world of the madness of nuclear weapons.

No. 77.
Irish Examiner 13 January 2016
UN Forces Should Not Still Be in Golan Heights

Following the execution of forty-seven men in Saudi Arabia on January 2, the situation in the Middle East is deteriorating. Our relations with all countries in the Middle East need to be reviewed with the intention of promoting long-term human rights and human justice rather than short-term economic expediency. Ireland should also support proper UN peace-making initiatives in the region as well as challenging UN failures. Recent developments in the Golan Heights are of particular concern and call into question the rushed decision by the Irish Government to deploy 130 Irish soldiers with UNDOF after Austria withdrew its peacekeepers in 2013 when they were forced to abandon their positions in the UN buffer zone and redeploy to the Israeli-occupied part of Golan. The UNDOF Golan mission has existed since 1974 and was intended to supervise the return of Israeli-occupied Golan Heights to Syria. UNEF 11 in Sinai had a similar mission to supervise the return of Israeli-occupied Sinai to Egypt and this was achieved by 1982. UNDOF has failed to achieve its primary mission over the past forty-two years and is arguably now achieving the opposite, by helping to copper-fasten Israeli occupation and annexation of the Golan Heights. The illegal annexation of the Golan Heights by Israel is not just a matter of strategic security. Significant quantities of oil have been discovered in the Israeli-occupied part of the Syrian Golan Heights.

No. 78.
Irish Examiner January 21 2016
Israeli Illegal Annexation of the Syrian Golan Heights.

Martin D Stern (Letters, January 16) wrongly suggests that in my letter on January 13, I was trying to imply Israel was ultimately responsible for recent Saudi executions.

My reference to the Saudi executions was clearly intended to emphasise the deteriorating security situation in the wider Middle Eastern context. Stern goes on to state I am 'incorrect to claim the UNDOF Golan mission was intended to supervise the return of Israeli-occupied Golan Heights to Syria'. He is incorrect in this also. While UNDOF's immediate mission was 'to maintain the ceasefire until a negotiated settlement could be reached', its initiating UN Security Council (UNSC) resolution 350 of 1974 referred to UNSC Resolution 338 of 1973 that 'calls upon all parties concerned to start immediately after the ceasefire the implementation of Security Council Resolution 242 (1967) in all of its parts'.

UNSC Resolution 242, in turn, calls for the 'Termination of all claims or states of belligerency and respect for and acknowledgement of the sovereignty, territorial integrity and political independence of every State in the area'. I served as a UN peacekeeper in this region in 1973/74 and am familiar with the circumstances and provisions of both the Sinai UNEF 2 and the Golan Heights UNDOF missions set up at this time.

The subsequent Israeli annexation and continuing occupation of the Golan Heights is therefore in clear breach of international laws. The main point of my letter was that Irish troops serving in the Golan Heights are not peacekeeping but being used as human shields to protect Israeli illegal annexation of the Syrian Golan Heights.

No. 79.
Irish Examiner **19 January 2016**
We Need to Re-Address The Regional Imbalance

Peter O'Dwyer's article 'Proposed Cork-Limerick M20 motorway would pay off for State' simply states the obvious (*Irish Examiner*, January 16). Why, therefore, is our Dublin-based government side-lining this vital infrastructural project? The west coast of Ireland badly needs a government-supported strategy to counter the imbalanced planning that is sucking the lifeblood of the west into the greater Dublin region. One must suspect that because the bulk of our politicians and planners live and are based in the eastern region, they are prioritising eastern infrastructural projects. Our motorway system now looks like an outstretched hand with the fingers pointing from Dublin at Belfast, Galway, Limerick, Cork, and the southeast, with dangerously inadequate roads connecting these fingers. Lip service is being paid to the concept of an Atlantic corridor. The Atlantic Corridor Road project was announced as part of the Transport 21 project launch in 2005, and was due to be completed by 2015, eventually linking Waterford in the southeast to Letterkenny in the northwest by high-quality dual carriageway or motorway. The Cork/Limerick section of this project linking the country's second and third largest population centres is by far the most urgent section, and it needs to be made an election issue.

No. 80.
Irish Examiner **30 January 2016**
Permanent Members of the UN Security Council Are Above the Law

Barry Walsh (Letters, January 27) is correct to point out that 'Doublespeak around Putin shouldn't surprise.' However, the issues involved are deadly serious, not only in individual cases such as the murder of Litvinenko, but also in assassinations and war crimes committed by the governments of the five permanent members of the UN Security Council – Britain, China, France, Russia, and the USA. Since the foundation of the UN, a litany of crimes has been committed with impunity by these five states, in clear breach of the UN Charter and international laws. These include British crimes in Kenya and Malaya; Chinese crimes in Tibet and internally; French crimes in South East Asia and Algeria; USSR/Russian crimes in Eastern Europe and Afghanistan; and US crimes in Latin America, South East Asia, and the Middle East.

The UN and the international community have been powerless to take any punitive actions against these five states or their leaders, because the UN Charter is fundamentally flawed. This is due to the powers of veto that these five states gave to themselves in 1945, placing themselves above and beyond the rules of international laws. All this should be deeply worrying to the governments and citizens of small countries like Ireland. The five UN permanent members don't need the UN or international laws except to use and abuse them whenever it suits their perceived national interests. The rule of law should protect the powerless, not further empower the powerful. The Irish Government should be doing a lot more to reform the UN and international laws, instead of being complicit in the war crimes of our Western so-called allies.

No. 81.
Petitions Committee Publish Final Report on Irish Neutrality 1st Feb. 2016

https://www.oireachtas.ie/en/press-centre/press-releases/20160201-petitions-committee-publish-final-report-on-irish-neutrality/

The Oireachtas Joint Committee on Public Service Oversight and Petitions today published its 'Report on Petition P00072/12 "Investigation into US Military and CIA use of Shannon Airport and Irish Airspace" – Dr Edward Horgan and Shannonwatch'.

This report was conducted on foot of a public petition and allowed the Committee to address the broader issues of Irish neutrality.

Committee Chair Pádraig MacLochlainn TD said: 'This is an important report that raises a fundamental issue about Irish society – our neutrality. In compiling this report, the Committee travelled to Shannon Airport to discuss its operation with senior management; we engaged with the petitioner and held discussions with Minister Charlie Flanagan TD, Minister Paschal Donoghue and the Secretary General of the Department of Foreign Affairs and Trade.

'This report concludes that Ireland operates a policy of Military Neutrality, which is characterised by "non-participation in military alliances" and that neutrality is not reflected in Bunreacht na hÉireann, or elsewhere in domestic legislation. The Committee recommends that Dáil and Seanad Éireann debate the matter with a view to the holding of a Referendum so that the will of the people can be determined.

'This report is also an excellent example of how the public petitions process facilitates direct democracy and brings parliament closer to the people. In fact, we recently published a report on the learnings from our first term and how they can be carried forward by the next Government.'

The report can be accessed here.

ENDS/ Media Enquiries: Liam O'Brien,
http://www.oireachtas.ie/parliament/mediazone/pressreleases/2016/name-31582-en.html

No. 82.
Irish Examiner 3 February 2016
We Need to Ensure a Referendum on Neutrality Is an Election Issue

Over three years ago, I submitted a petition to the Oireachtas Joint Committee on Public Service Oversight and Petitions on behalf of civil society NGO Shannonwatch, on the issue of US military and CIA use of Shannon Airport. The committee issued its final report on St. Bridget's Day 2016. The committee, and its chairperson, Pádraig Mac Lochlainn TD, are to be complimented for doing a reasonably comprehensive investigation into this petition. However, given that the committee included members from FG, Labour, and Fianna Fáil parties, all complicit in the problems arising from US military and CIA use of Shannon since 2001, it is not surprising that the final report does not fully reflect the evidence and information presented to it by Shannonwatch and others, and does not comment at all on the serious human rights abuses, including hundreds of thousands of unjustified deaths that were facilitated by US military use of Shannon. The most significant part of the committee's findings is the following recommendation: 'The Joint committee recommends that the Dáil and Seanad debate the matter with a view to the holding of a referendum so that the will of the people can be determined.' The 'matter' to be debated and hopefully enshrined in Bunreacht na hÉireann is Irish neutrality. It is clear that our politicians cannot be trusted with the responsibility of Irish neutrality being only a matter of Government policy. While the proceedings of this committee did provide a small element of accountability in terms of the State's role in crimes against humanity, in the final analysis, the duty of holding our politicians to account rests with citizens. We as citizens have a duty to act on this in the forthcoming election.

No. 83.

Irish Examiner **22 February 2016**

Irish Politics Ignores Global Issues to Its Peril

The truism that all politics are local is being taken both too far and not far enough in the Irish election debates. We ignore important interconnected international matters at our peril, including climate change, refugee crises, conflicts in the Middle East, Palestine, and Africa, and the damaging militarisation of Europe and the world. In this era of state and non-state terrorism, instant communication, and erosion of borders, the whole world is now local.

US military use of Shannon Airport is both local and global and is contributing to the killing of innocents, as is Russian use of military bases in Syria. The gospels written 2,000 years ago tell us our neighbours are all humankind.

No. 84.
Irish Examiner 11 March 2016
The Refugee Crisis Has Shown Just How Much the EU Has Lost Its Way

The history of the European Union since its initial seeds were planted with the Coal and Steel Committee in 1951 has been mainly positive and helped promote peace and reconciliation within Europe. This changed with the Lisbon Treaty and clear moves towards a European super-state. The financial and euro crises and the unacceptable treatment of Ireland and Greece by our EU fellow member states were the beginning of a process of disintegration, whereby the better-off states ganged up on those in need, instead of showing genuine solidarity. The increasing militarisation of Europe and its ever-closer alignment with NATO, for the purposes of using military power to promote the economic interests of Europe at the expense of many impoverished peoples around the world, led to resource wars under the guise of humanitarian interventions. The resulting chaos and slaughter in the Middle East and North Africa seemed to have been acceptable as long as there was no blowback in Europe. The blowback came with the resulting refugee crisis. Far too many Europeans see this crisis as being a European refugee crisis, even if all its victims are of Middle Eastern and African origin. It is obscene that EU leaders, including our Taoiseach, are in the process of bribing a Turkish Government, guilty of serious human rights and anti-democratic abuses, to force Turkey to stem the flow of refugees and to take back refugees already in Greece. The Irish taxpayers' share of these bribes will be over €20 million, money badly needed for our own health services. Now, instead of using EU naval forces to rescue drowning refugees, they are going to be used to reinforce the new

Iron (or Razor Wire) Curtain. Sometimes the best-laid plans of mice and men go all awry and things fall apart.

If Brexit becomes a reality, should Ireland be far behind?

No. 85.
Irish Examiner 8 April 2016
Ireland Complicit in Irradiation of Iraq

A report, 'Irradiated Iraq', by Barbara Koeppel in *The Washington Spectator* (20 March 2016), makes for very disturbing reading. This report reveals that for the past twenty-five years, the US and its allies have been using radioactive weapons containing uranium that have been causing cancers in adults and very serious deformities and birth defects in children. These weapons have been used in the former Yugoslavia and the Middle East. Iraq has been the country most heavily polluted by depleted uranium munitions used in the wars in 1991 and since 2003, with areas near Basra and Fallujah very heavily polluted. The widespread use of such munitions amounts to a war crime, but because the five permanent members of the UN Security Council use their UN vetoes to claim immunity from war crimes prosecutions, we cannot expect to see the perpetrators of these crimes joining Radovan Karadžić in prison anytime soon. Ireland is complicit in these war crimes because Shannon Airport has been, and is still being used, to transport large quantities of US war materials to its Middle Eastern war zones.

No. 86.
Irish Examiner 11 April 2016
Irish Neutrality is Breached by NATO and US Military Aircraft at Shannon

Six NATO ships were berthed in Dublin over the first weekend in April, arriving on Fools' Day. This is no joking matter apart from the fact that the Irish people are being made fools of by our government. Information provided on these warships suggests an almost 'humanitarian' mission, including the disposal of munitions from two World Wars. A closer reading, however, includes the term 'area denial operations' in their mission, which means laying mines at sea. Perhaps they are checking out Dublin Port for future mining in case Ireland's neutrality becomes too problematic for NATO. This breach of Irish neutrality should not have been approved by the Department of Foreign Affairs at a time when we only have a caretaker government and no proper functioning Dáil to provide oversight.

Of even more concern is the ongoing refuelling of US military aircraft at Shannon on their way to and from combat operations in the Middle East. At 10 a.m. on Sunday, April 3, there were four US military aircraft at Shannon Airport, in breach of international laws on neutrality. The Irish taxpayer also has to pay all the landing and air-traffic control fees for these US military aircraft as well as paying for the security provided for them by the Irish Defence Forces and the Gardaí. Several opinion polls have clearly indicated that a large majority of the Irish people want Irish neutrality restored and respected. Our next government, whenever they get their act together, must respect the wishes of the people on neutrality.

No. 87.
Irish Examiner 8 June 2016
We Must Recognise Armenian Genocide

On June 2, the German parliament voted overwhelmingly to recognise the massacre of up to one and a half million Armenian people by the Ottoman Turkish Government between 1915 and 1922 as genocide. More than twenty other countries have now done likewise, but Ireland has yet to do so. Dáil Éireann and the Irish Government should now recognise the Armenian genocide.

No. 88.
Irish Examiner 28 June 2016
New States of Independence

The decision of the British people to exit the EU has created a whole range of problems. The people of Scotland may decide to exit the UK and remain or re-join the EU. That will leave the people of Northern Ireland in a critically disadvantageous position. In the short and medium terms, a united Ireland is unlikely and attempts to rush it could reignite conflict there. There is a case to be made for granting independence and EU membership to both Northern Ireland and Scotland. This would result in a block of three culturally and economically similar states within the EU.

No. 89.
Irish Examiner 8 July 2016
Charity Thieves Are Worse Than Robbers

On July 3rd, Judge McNulty jailed a thirty-nine-year-old woman in Bandon for ninety days for stealing food. She had fifty-nine previous convictions, so was not a very successful lawbreaker. While not attempting to justify such criminal activity sentences like this imposed on disadvantaged members of our society are in marked contrast with how our legal system deals with, or fails to deal with, much more serious crimes committed by so-called white-collar criminals. Of particular concern are crimes, or alleged crimes, committed by executives with responsibility for charitable or altruistic organisations. The recent scandals involving charities are just the tip of the rip-off iceberg and go back historically to include Irish Hospitals' Sweepstake and PMPA. It also includes the privatisation of many of our mutual companies, particularly building societies and cooperatives. The process is an invidious one, very often not covered, or inadequately regulated, by any of our regulatory or legal systems, whereby an organisation set up to provide altruistic services on a charitable or public interest basis, takes on paid employees as it grows. A cohort of these employees, including some of its founders, seize control of the organisation, and promote themselves to positions that enable them to legally, and sometimes illegally, rip off the organisations and the public or taxpayers who are providing their funding.

We need to invent special terminology to describe the much more serious evildoers who rip off charities.

No. 90.
Irish Independent 12 July 2016
New Threat of Militarisation

Commemorating the soldiers who died in World War I would be appropriate if it were done appropriately. In Ireland, we commemorate those Irish people who died in the Great Famine, and this is appropriate because the then government of the United Kingdom of Great Britain and Ireland bore significant responsibility for many of the famine deaths due to its negligence. The number of people killed in World War I on all sides was on a similar scale to the number who died in the Irish Great Famine and included up to 50,000 Irishmen. Their deaths were neither heroic nor justified. Even the term 'lions led by donkeys' is inaccurate on several counts. The soldiers who fought in World War I were more like sheep being led to their slaughter, and while there were some acts of heroism by soldiers attempting to save the lives of their comrades, the reality is that most soldiers fought or died in conditions of great misery and terror. The unjustified glorification and heroism that is now being applied to those who died in this useless war is part of a campaign of militarism that may well lead to irresponsible future European or World Wars that could make World War I seem like a minor skirmish.

No. 91.
Irish Examiner 16 July 2016
We Need Irish Version of Chilcot

During the month of June, while NATO exercises were taking place in Poland, I photographed a large number of US military aircraft at Shannon Airport, including mid-air refuelling aircraft, whose only purpose is to refuel other military aircraft in mid-air. On July 12, Minister for Foreign Affairs and Trade Charlie Flanagan TD gave a written reply to Clare Daly TD, who had asked the Minister 'to ascertain from the United States Government if any of the US military aircraft that transited through Shannon Airport during the month of June 2016, were involved in any capacity, in supporting military exercises in Poland or elsewhere.' Minister Flanagan replied as follows: 'The US Embassy has reconfirmed details which it had provided previously in relation to the aircraft that transited through Shannon Airport last month. The Embassy has reconfirmed that the aircraft were unarmed, carried no arms, ammunition, or explosives, and did not engage in intelligence gathering. The Embassy further reconfirmed that the aircraft were not part of a military operation or exercise. Permission for landings by these aircraft was granted subject to these conditions.' The information contained in this reply is incredible and unacceptable. There is no other possible explanation for the presence of such a large number of US military aircraft during the month of June, except that they were involved in military operations or military exercises. The Chilcot report in the UK demonstrates that diplomatic and government assurances cannot be relied on when matters of war and peace, life and death are concerned. It is now time that we had the equivalent of a Chilcot enquiry into Irish Government complicity in the US-led wars in the Middle East.

No. 92.
The Irish Times 28 July 2016
Sentencing for Child Rape

Gordon Deegan reports (July 26) that Judge Gerald Keys imposed a two-year suspended sentence on a seventy-seven-year-old man at Ennis Circuit Court after he was convicted of sexually abusing two of his nieces. Judge Keys cited the accused's guilty plea, his age, health, and remorse as mitigating factors. Yet the judge was quoted as saying: 'you suggested that both your nieces led you on and that they were promiscuous'. Since some of these offences took place when one of the victims was aged six or seven and other assaults when the victim was aged fourteen to fifteen years, these comments by the perpetrator may well have further traumatised the victims in this case. Age should also not be a mitigating circumstance in such cases because of the secrecy, deviousness, and difficulties in getting such cases into court. This arguably unduly lenient sentence should be appealed.

No. 93.
Interview with Russian media KATETON http://katehon.com/ on 22.08.2016

Americans are Insulting International Law on Irish Land

Since 2001 and the beginning of the war in Afghanistan, the US military has been using Shannon Airport in Western Ireland to send troops, ammunition, and other military items for deployment and dispersal in the Middle East and Europe.

I've been very actively involved in several demonstrations at Shannon Airport. In 2004, I attempted to arrest US President George Bush, who was visiting Shannon Airport. More recently, eighty-year-old lady Margaretta D'Arcy and other friends of mine went in and blocked the runway at the airport to prevent US military planes from taking off. I was also arrested at Shannon Airport on other occasions for attempting to search for US military aircraft on the way to the Middle East. Therefore we have been very active in protests against the American military misusing Irish airspace. Ireland is a neutral country, so we don't want to allow troops on their way to war to pass through our country.

On all these occasions, we are usually arrested and then we are charged and brought to the courts. In my case, I have been arrested six times at Shannon Airport, but I usually get a strong legal team to defend me. So far, on all occasions, I was eventually found not guilty. In some cases, like that of Margaretta D'Arcy, she was convicted of blocking the runway. She actually spent about four weeks in prison.

Ireland is a neutral country. Many Irish people are opposed to all that is happening in the Middle East, Iran, Iraq, Afghanistan, Libya, and Syria. We believe very strongly that Ireland should not be involved. We are also concerned that the United States has been creating tension in Eastern Europe and in Ukraine. The US is attempting to encircle Russia by encouraging the countries of the former Soviet Union to join NATO, which I believe is counterproductive.

The American base at Shannon Airport is not official. But at the same time, over 2.5 million US troops have passed through Shannon Airport since 2001. That is a huge number. So, effectively it is a US military base. In reality, they don't need to use it, because they have plenty of bases all around Europe. But the US Government likes to use Irish airbases in order to involve a neutral country in its unlawful and unnecessary wars. Americans don't have a real need to use Irish airports. But they are trying to involve us in their crimes. If everybody is involved, nobody can blame the USA. That makes us very angry both against the US and Irish Government that allows this to happen.

There are a small number of US soldiers based at the Shannon Airport, where our government allows the US military to fly through and refuel their planes. They don't have to be searched. American soldiers using our civil airport are a quite significant breach of international law on neutrality. A huge number of aircraft have been used by the CIA to take prisoners to Guantanamo. So, in addition to the military, the US torture program has used Ireland as a transition point. That is clearly a breach of international law.

NATO should have been dismissed in the 1990s after the Soviet Union collapsed. But the United States and some European countries wanted to keep NATO to fight a war for resources in the Middle East. This is a completely unjustified war. In more recent times, they've started to deepen conflict with Russia. This is very counterproductive from the European point of view. I believe most Russian leaders have been trying to develop good economic and political relationships with Eastern Europe, but NATO is interfering with that.

Based on my military experience, I think that there is a real danger of a Hot War. Some of the military and political leaders in the West presume that it won't happen, that the danger has gone away. There is a significant risk of mutual confrontation in Europe. The situation could move from a relative Cold War to a Hot War. The USA, Russia, Great Britain, and France might use tactical nuclear weapons and incite a serious clash which could escalate into an international nuclear war.

No. 94.

Irish Examiner 30 August 2016
Direct Provision Exacerbating Refugee Suffering

The death of a Korean asylum seeker, Youjung Han, at the Kinsale Road accommodation centre in Cork, is a tragedy. Her six-year-old son found her body. Is the Irish direct-provision system contributing to such tragedies, and is it inhumane? Does it impose further suffering on those who live in such unacceptable conditions? Ireland has one of the lowest rates in the European Union (EU) of permitting the entry of refugees and asylum seekers, and one of the highest rates of rejection of asylum applications. Our policy on refugees seems to be to make the system so difficult to enter, and so uncomfortable for those here, that others are deterred from seeking protection in Ireland. Given our own history of emigration, and the conflicts from which so many people are fleeing, we must live up to our obligations under the UN Convention on Refugees.

No. 95.

Irish Examiner 5 September 2016
Good Work at Shannon Airport?

It's good to hear that on October 10, Shannon Airport is being used for the transit of 1,500 animals being sent by Bothar to Rwanda for genuine humanitarian reasons. Well done Bothar and all concerned with this air shipment. Forty dairy cows, 260 pigs, 200 goats, and 1,000 chickens will be a significant boost to the many women in Rwanda who were made widows in that dreadful genocide in 1994, while the international community, especially the United States, stood idly by. Since 2001, about three million armed US troops and probably at least twice that number of weapons have been transported through Shannon Airport and Irish airspace on thousands of US military aircraft. Shannon Airport has received no real benefit from all this illegitimate military misuse that has probably seriously damaged the very good reputation that Shannon Airport had achieved over previous decades. It's overdue time to restore this good reputation to Shannon Airport and restore Irish neutrality, by ending the refuelling of US military aircraft at Shannon.

Comment: The following short letter of mine provoked a very considerable and arguably very biased series of responses from supporters of Israel. I include some of these letters below. My knowledge of Israel/Palestine and the history and conflicts in this region is also based on considerable research and practical experience in the region. I first visited the area in 1966 while working as a UN peacekeeper, and again in 1973 and '74 in the immediate aftermath of the Yom Kippur / October war. I also visited Bergen Belsen concentration camp in 1984 and helped to organise a series of seminars on the Holocaust at the University of Limerick in 1997. I have carried out extensive research into genocide and crimes against humanity. My view is that all of humanity is entitled to have their human rights protected and attempts to label those who criticise human rights abuses by the Israeli Government and Israeli security forces as being anti-Semitic are part of a propaganda campaign intended to enable the continuing efforts of the Israeli Government to annex most of the Palestinian West Bank and the Syrian Golan Heights.

No. 96.
Irish Examiner **22 September 2016**
Israeli Shoot to Kill Policy Designed to Terrorise

I spent seven days in the West Bank Palestine last week visiting areas that included Jerusalem, Bethlehem, Hebron, Jenin, Bil'in, and Ramallah. I was shocked at the deepening apartheid system I witnessed, especially the infamous wall, 20ft high in many places, which seemed more designed to intimidate, impoverish, colonise lands, and disrupt the lives of Palestinians rather than provide security. Equally shocking was the extent and location of Israeli Jewish settlements, which now seem to be designed to facilitate the eventual Israeli annexation of most, if not all, of the Palestinian West Bank. Up to half a million Jewish settlers are now living in lands that were Palestinian lands until 1967, and there is clear evidence that many of these settlements are in the process of being extended, as well as new settlements being constructed, all in clear breach of international laws.

No. 97.
Irish Examiner **27 September 2016**
700km Wall Will Be a Barrier to Peace

Karl Martin (*Irish Examiner*, September 24) takes me to task for my comments on the Israeli separation barrier in the occupied Palestinian territories and compares the wall to the peace walls in Belfast, and tries to minimise its significance.

The barrier consists of a mixture of concrete, fences, ditches, razor wire, electronic monitoring systems, patrol roads, and a buffer zone. Its length will be 700km, and it is almost 70 per cent complete. In rural areas, the barrier includes a two-metre-high, electrified, barbed-wire fence with vehicle-barrier trenches and a sixty-metre-wide exclusion zone on the Palestinian side. In urban areas, including Jerusalem and Bethlehem, the concrete wall is eight metres high. The International Court of Justice found the barrier to be a violation of international law.

In response to the comments of Desmond Fitzgerald (*Irish Examiner*, September 24), I refer to Jewish communities living in occupied Palestinian areas as 'Jewish settlements', because I consider that to be the legally correct terminology. In January 2015, the Israeli interior ministry gave figures of 389,250 Israeli settlers living in the West Bank, a further 375,000 Israelis living in East Jerusalem, and 20,000 in the Syrian Golan Heights. The International Court of Justice ruled, in 2004, that all these settlements are illegal. Mr Fitzgerald makes the incredible statement that: 'Before 1967, there were no Palestinian lands anywhere', in spite of the reality that Palestinian people have occupied, and owned, the vast majority of the lands in what was known as Palestine up until 1948, and have owned these lands for many centuries. The British Mandate population figures for Palestine in 1923 were 590,890 Palestinians, 83,794 Jews, and 82,498 Christians and others, yet Mr Fitzgerald seems to suggest that these 590,890 Palestinians did not exist in 1923, or, if they did, they did not own any land. He also attempts to belittle the Palestinian people by stating that 'Palestinians would prefer to see land go to waste' and 'certain Palestinians saw a means to steal from their own people to enrich themselves'. If a person made statements like that about Jewish people, they would be labelled anti-Semitic. Mr Fitzgerald denies the just cause of the Palestinian people. 'There was no such cause anywhere before 1967. The fantasy of a Palestinian homeland was dreamt up after 1967'.

The fact that the Palestinian people were betrayed by their neighbouring Arab states, who annexed Gaza and the West Bank after the 1948 Arab/Israeli war, in no way justifies Israeli efforts to annex East Jerusalem, the West Bank, and the Syrian Golan Heights. He also chooses to ignore the expulsion of large numbers of Palestinian people from their lands during the 1948 war, the destruction of many Palestinian villages, and the 'settlement' of these Palestinian lands by Jewish people, many of whom migrated from Europe. The Holocaust of almost six million Jewish people was the worst act of genocide ever committed, but it was committed by Europeans and not by Arabs or Palestinians.

There will be no lasting peace between the Jewish and Palestinian people in the Middle East, unless all involved prioritise matters of justice, human rights, and international laws.

No. 98.
The Irish Times 1 October 2016
John Kerry and Tipperary Peace Prize

I was surprised to hear that the Tipperary International Peace Prize is to be awarded to US Secretary of State John Kerry, given that I am not aware that he or the US State Department has achieved any peace-making over the past fifteen years. On the contrary, the US has initiated or participated in several wars of aggression in Afghanistan, Iraq, Libya, Syria, and Yemen, which resulted in the deaths of over two million people and innumerable others injured. The devastation that has resulted from these wars has led to millions of people fleeing for their lives, causing the greatest world refugee crisis since the Second World War. The US has made no real effort to undo the infrastructural and human damage caused by these wars, and far from making peace, it is still actively engaged in making or supporting wars right now in Syria, Iraq, and Yemen. Up to one million children have died as a result of these wars and unjustified Iraqi sanctions. If it were possible, the victims of these wars should first be asked if they think the US Secretary of State should be awarded a peace prize. Protests by peace activists are expected to greet Mr Kerry at Shannon Airport and Aherlow in Tipperary on Sunday, October 30.

No. 99.
Irish Independent 3 Oct. 2016, *Belfast Telegraph* on 5 Oct. 2016
Peace an Unattainable Goal in the Middle East

Comment: I disagree to the headline put on this letter. Peace in my view is always attainable if the necessary peace-making resources are applied. My argument in this letter is that deliberate wars of aggression and wars against peace are preventing peace being established in the Middle East and elsewhere.

On September 30, Shimon Peres was buried in Israel, hailed by many as a peacemaker, by others as a war criminal. Peace in the Middle East has never been so urgent, yet so far from reality. Afghanistan has been in chaos since the US-led invasion overthrew its government in 2001. Libya has been in chaos since the overthrow of President Gaddafi was assisted by NATO bombing in 2011. Russia's decision to annex the Crimea and become militarily involved in an effort to prevent the overthrow of the Assad government in Syria may have been prompted by President Putin's anger at being misled by the US over NATO plans to overthrow Gaddafi. The questionable ceasefire in Syria fell apart after the attack by US, Australian, British, and Danish warplanes, that killed up to ninety Syrian troops who were defending Deir ez-Zour military air base, enabling ISIS to capture the strategic Tharda mountain. In retaliation, the Syrian Government resumed its attacks to recapture Aleppo, supported by Russian warplanes, resulting in the deaths of many civilians. Iraq has been in chaos since the overthrow of its government in 2003. The misguided war on terror has been a fertile breeding ground for terrorists. In Egypt, in 2013, the democratically elected government of President Morsi was overthrown and a military dictatorship restored, supported by the US. The UN has been unable to create peace in the Middle East, partly because too many of its member states have failed to challenge those powerful governments who are abusing UN and international laws.

No. 100.

Irish Examiner 31 October 2016
Complicity to Refuel any Warship

Many Western media sources, including the *Irish Examiner* (October 27), carried the story of NATO protests over Russian warships refuelling at the Spanish-occupied port of Ceuta, in North Africa. British defence secretary, Michael Fallon, said, 'We would be extremely concerned, if any NATO member started to assist a Russian carrier group that ended up in the eastern Mediterranean bombing Syrian civilians.' His comments might be justified if the criteria of preventing the bombing of civilians in Syria were applied to all such refuelling of military forces involved in bombing. Figures released by the Irish Department of Foreign Affairs reveal that in 2014, 630 US military aircraft were given permission to land and refuel at Shannon Airport, most of them on their way to, or from, the Middle East. In addition, another 270 troop-carrier and cargo flights were given permits to take weapons/explosives through Shannon in 2014. It's likely that some of these aircraft and war materials, which refuelled at Shannon Airport, were involved in some of the incidents in which civilians were bombed and killed in Syria. The following countries have had some involvement in aerial attacks in Syria, Iraq, and Yemen over the past several years: USA, Russia, Britain, France, Belgium, Netherlands, Germany, Spain, Denmark, Turkey, Australia, Jordan, Saudi Arabia, Qatar, United Arab Emirates, Canada, Morocco, and Bahrain. This list, of nineteen UN members, includes seven EU states. Capital punishment is outlawed in all EU states, yet many of these EU members are helping to kill people almost daily in the Middle East, in clear breach of international laws, including the UN Charter.

It's time this killing madness was stopped, and especially Ireland's complicity in it.

No. 101.
Irish Examiner 10 November 2016
Ireland Needs to Help Reform UN

The excellent article by Dr Roy Fox (*Irish Examiner* Nov 8) on the topic of the largely unfettered freedom to kill is of great importance to the people of the United States, many of whom are of Irish descent. It deals only with the problems of gun violence in the US. There is, however, an even more important but related issue that affects all of humanity. This is 'the unfettered freedom to kill' by waging unjustified wars exercised by the US and the other four permanent members of the UN Security Council, although the US has been by far the greatest offender, causing huge numbers of deaths, injuries, and massive destruction across the Middle East. These wars are in breach of the UN Charter, the laws of war and in gross violation of the human rights of the millions of people killed and injured. This is allowed to happen because the UN power of veto gives the five permanent members of the UNSC unfettered freedom to kill. Ireland should be at the forefront of reforming the UN to end such crimes against humanity, but instead, our government is complicit in these crimes by allowing the refuelling of US military aircraft at Shannon Airport and refuelling of NATO warships at Cork port.

No. 102.
The Irish Times 10 November 2016
American Revolution – Coming to Terms with Donald Trump, the President-Elect of the United States

On May 30, Taoiseach Enda Kenny said in Dáil Éireann that: 'If Trump's comments are racist and dangerous, which they are, there is an alternative to vote for'. Minister for Social Protection Leo Varadkar made similar comments: 'I don't think there can be any doubt that many of the speeches he has made were racist and showed a very misogynistic attitude to women'. Given that Mr Trump is now president-elect of the United States, and that it is not appropriate for senior Irish politicians to intervene in the democratic process of foreign countries, then perhaps Mr Kenny should resign as Taoiseach sooner rather than later, in the national interest. His successor needs to be carefully chosen.

No. 103.
Irish Examiner 30 November 2016
Most Irish Would Agree with Higgins About Castro

President Michael D. Higgins has been unjustifiably criticised by the media and government politicians for what most Irish citizens consider to be his dignified and appropriate remarks on the death of former Cuban leader Fidel Castro. Higgins has been accused of failing to highlight the human rights abuses of the Cuban Government. There are appropriate times for offering condolences and for defending human rights, and Michael D. Higgins has done far more than most other Irish politicians in defending those rights, especially in Latin America. Our government's decision not to be represented at Castro's funeral, at ministerial level, or higher, contrasts with the flying at half-mast of the Irish flag on the death of King Abdullah of Saudi Arabia, and with the attendance of Foreign Affairs Minister, Charlie Flanagan, at the funeral of Shimon Peres, former president of Israel. Both countries have committed human rights abuses. No mention has been made in recent media reports of ongoing abuses of prisoners in Cuba, possibly amounting to torture, not by the Cuban government, but by the United States, in Guantanamo.

May Fidel Castro rest in peace.

No. 104.
Irish Examiner 15 December 2016
Visit of Naval Vessel Was Not Welcome

A lot of media attention was given recently to a Russian naval convoy that made a journey in late October from Russia via the English Channel and Gibraltar to Syria. Spain cancelled its permission for this fleet to refuel at the Spanish enclave of Ceuta in Morocco. Should Ireland, as a government-declared neutral state, agree to provide refuelling facilities for such Russian naval ships? It is most unlikely that our government would allow this, or that most Irish people would approve. Yet on November 5, a Netherlands navy submarine – HNLMS *Bruinvis* – was refuelled in Cork harbour, and was also being resupplied by a container truck that had travelled from the Netherlands for this purpose. The Netherlands has been actively involved in the conflicts in Syria and Iraq, and is carrying out bombing attacks with its F16 aircraft, which have resulted in civilian fatalities according to US military reports. Therefore Ireland, as a neutral state, should not be allowing military forces of a belligerent state such as the Netherlands to transit through its territory and to refuel at its ports.

No. 105.
Irish Examiner 19 December 2016
Only Democracy is the Answer

International media headlines report that Barack Obama promises to retaliate against Russia for its alleged interference in the election campaign. This implies that the highest-level authorities in the US, the most powerful country in the world, believe that Russia effectively decided who the next president of the US would be, and ensured that this person is a politically incompetent misogynist and racist who will likely do serious damage to the United States. This suggests that the US democratic and electoral systems are seriously flawed, and that its security agencies, including the CIA, failed to properly identify this threat, or to counter it. Reports from the US are also claiming that false information spread by Facebook, and other means, also contributed to the election of Donald Trump. Yet the reason the information released by hackers against Hillary Clinton was so effective was that most of it was factual, and most of the false information circulating on social media originated in the US. Here in Ireland, we have elected three very good presidents in succession, although the same does not always seem to apply to our ability to elect our legislators to Dáil Éireann, who go on to elect our prime minister. The saying that 'democracy is the least-worst system' is attributed to Winston Churchill, and it is wise. The US election, Brexit, and political turmoil across Europe and elsewhere all indicate that our various democratic systems are broken. The solution is not dictators like Vladimir Putin. The solution to the flaws of democracy is more, and better, democracy, not less.

No. 106.
Irish Examiner 28 December 2016
Why is Navy Taking Break from Med?

The sailors of the Irish Naval Service deserve full credit for the very difficult missions they have undertaken in the Mediterranean to rescue drowning and endangered migrants, many of whom are fleeing in fear for their lives from violent conflicts towards questionable safety in Europe, even if Europe, especially NATO, played a major role in fuelling these conflicts. When the LÉ *Samuel Beckett* returned to its base in Cobh, Co Cork, on December 16, to a well-deserved welcome, most people did not realise that its rescue mission had not been replaced for the coming months by another Irish Naval Service ship. This would be justified if it were the case that no migrants were crossing the Mediterranean at this most dangerous time of the year. However, UNHCR and the International Organization for Migration reported that on Thursday, December 22, up to 100 migrants were feared drowned when two boats capsized. The Irish Naval Service has rescued more than 10,000 migrants so far, but the question must be asked, why have they taken a break from their rescue missions over the winter months? Why are these winter migrants who are drowning less important than those rescued during the remainder of the year? Ireland has about 500 soldiers serving overseas at present, and these soldiers will be continuing their arduous duties right through the Christmas period. This is as it should be. The same should apply to the Irish Naval Service. The defence minister – Enda Kenny – needs to explain why this decision was taken to abandon the Irish Naval Service rescue mission in the Mediterranean over the most dangerous winter months.

No. 107.
Irish Independent 15 January 2017, *Irish Examiner* 17 January 2017
Migrant Deal with Libya a Non-Runner

Associated Press (January 12) reports that the current EU Presidency, Maltese Prime Minister Joseph Muscat, calls for an urgent migrant deal with Libya. 'He says that the EU should draw up an arrangement with

Libya, from where most migrants leave Africa for Europe. It would use European money and expand an agreement already in place between Italy and Libya.' Has nobody told the European Union that there has been no effective government in Libya since NATO helped to overthrow its Gaddafi-led government in 2011? The following European countries, led by France and Britain, were directly involved in the bombing of Libya: Belgium, Bulgaria, Denmark, Norway, Sweden (supposedly neutral), Greece, Netherlands, and Romania. Each of these countries bears direct responsibility for the refugee crisis that sees large numbers of refugees attempting to cross the Mediterranean to Europe, where thousands of them have drowned. United Nations Security Council Resolution 1973 only authorised NATO to enforce a no-fly zone but the intervention went way beyond this mandate and engaged in widespread bombing against the Libyan army ground forces, in breach of the UN Charter. Now, these same European countries are proposing to bribe a non-existent Libyan Government in a futile attempt to stem the flow of refugees. A similar refugee crisis exists in Syria, where several of these same European countries have been attempting to overthrow the Syrian Government, having succeeded in overthrowing the Afghan and Iraqi Governments, and are also paying Turkey in an effort to stem the flow of refugees through Turkey. International law has not been flouted to this extent since Hitler invaded Poland in 1939, and the UN Charter has been effectively destroyed by three of its veto-wielding powers: Britain, France, and the USA. There is now an urgent need for the United Nations to be rebuilt on new, more solid foundations and for the rule of international law to be restored and enhanced.

No. 108.
Belfast Telegraph **11 January 2017,** *Irish Examiner* **7 January 2017.**
Killing Other Human Beings Is Never Heroic and Irish Citizens Must Resist Joining Foreign Forces

A report in the *Belfast Telegraph* (News, January 4), headlined 'Recruitment for British Army soars in Republic of Ireland', should be of deep concern to all Irish people. Grave concerns have been justifiably expressed over Irish citizens who have gone to fight in the Middle East with certain groups, such as ISIS and al-Qaeda, but the opposite has been the case with other Irish individuals who admitted fighting with militia groups that are supported by NATO states, or those Irish citizens who join British forces. We must be clear that there is nothing heroic in helping to kill people in the Middle East in wars that are almost wholly unjustified and counterproductive, causing the worst refugee crisis since the Second World War and retaliatory terrorist attacks in Europe. For those who wish to pursue a military career, the Irish Defence Forces provide just and altruistic opportunities towards creating international peace, instead of creating wars by joining foreign armies for mercenary reasons. It's time we Irish matured sufficiently to put behind us our cap-in-hand colonial servitude attitude of fighting in every clime, for every cause but our own. Legislation should be introduced that would remove Irish citizenship from any Irish citizen who joins a foreign army, or who participates in military actions as a member of a foreign militia. Killing other human beings should never be considered an honourable career option, and the use of deadly military force should never be justified except in very clear and limited cases of justifiable self-defence, as specified in the (much-ignored and abused) United Nations Charter.

N. 109.
Irish Independent 21 January 2017, *Irish Examiner* 23 January 2017
Apologies For Growing Old - Turns Out I'm Ruining the Country

Let me begin by apologising for growing old. I am a septuagenarian and, therefore, a possible danger to humanity. Successive ministers for health, and their senior HSE officials, repeatedly blame their own incompetence on 'bed-blocking' old people, who allegedly refuse to leave hospital and go home to die in convenient obscurity. Ministers for transport, union officials, and radio talk-show phone callers all line up to accuse old people of contributing to the bankruptcy of Bus Eireann, because of their free travel pass. Iarnrod Eireann is also in financial trouble, because elderly people, who cannot afford cars, need rail travel, as they live in forgotten and neglected towns like Roscrea or Nenagh, way outside the Pale encompassed by the M50. We 'elderlies' are insulted daily by media ads. Hearing-aid providers bombard us with ads, telling us that we should spend thousands of euros on hearing aids, whether we need them or not. An insulting HSE-type ad tells us, probably without a shred of evidence, that we elderly are more likely to get food poisoning, because we are too stupid to wash our hands. A so-called fair deal wants to take our homes to pay for the healthcare that we need. I could go on, proposing euthanasia for all over-60s, but will finish, instead, with a quote from Father Ted: "FECK OFF."

Comment: My views in this letter above exaggerated somewhat the reality as experienced in Ireland in 2017, but arguable foreshadowed the dreadful reality that occurred in 2020 when an estimated 54 per cent of all fatalities in Ireland due to the Coronavirus COVID-19 were elderly people in Irish nursing homes.

No. 110.
Irish Examiner 25 January 2017
Smuggling Armies as Well as People

The success of An Garda Síochána in hopefully ending the misuse of Dublin Airport for the trafficking of illegal immigrants is to be welcomed. The seriousness of this breach of security at Dublin leaves a lot of questions to be answered by the Dublin Airport Authority and Aer Lingus. Reports that this security scandal may have been going on for several years are deeply worrying and damaging to the reputation of our country. The possibility exists that Dublin Airport was not the only Irish airport that was being used for the purpose of illegal migration. However, it's very unlikely that anyone died or was seriously injured as a result of this illegal migration scandal. At Shannon Airport, however, events are occurring, or being facilitated, which do lead to the deaths and serious injury of very many people, not in Ireland, but just a few hours' flight away in the Middle East. The duties and responsibilities of An Garda Síochána not only to investigate crime but also to prevent crime are arguably not being adequately applied at Shannon Airport. During 2016, at least 732 aircraft belonging to, or on contract to, the US military landed and refuelled at Shannon Airport, most of them en route to or from the Middle East. None of these aircraft were searched or investigated by Gardaí at Shannon, in spite of the virtual certainty that many of them are transporting soldiers and munitions that are used to kill many people in the Middle East in wars that are unjustified and in clear breach of international laws.

No. 111.
Irish Independent and *Irish Examiner* 30 January 2017
Torture Simply Does Not Work and Can Never Be Justified

Torture is back on the agenda in the USA and UK. US President Donald Trump has repeatedly said that he agrees with torture, even though interrogation experts in the CIA and FBI have confirmed that torturing prisoners to extract information does not work. The views expressed by a former British senior army officer, Colonel Bob Stewart, now a senior Conservative MP, that he 'was a torturer' when he served in Northern Ireland are unacceptable and offensive to all those who value human rights. The report (*Irish Independent*, January 27) quoted Mr Stewart as saying: 'Sometimes [torture] might work, and sometimes it might be justified.' He used the very flawed argument of the ticking bomb to justify torture in spite of its total prohibition by the UN Convention Against Torture. He outlined some of the methods he had used against prisoners in Northern Ireland. Based on his own admissions, Mr Stewart should be charged with a variety of offences against persons in custody. He also stated that: 'Of course, it was acceptable then – it's now unacceptable and now it's defined as torture.' Torture and human rights abuses were never acceptable, whether they were committed by Roman emperors, Genghis Khan, the Spanish Inquisition, the Gestapo, the British army in Northern Ireland, or the US in

Guantanamo Bay. Suspected CIA and US Special Forces aircraft are still being refuelled at Shannon Airport, making the Irish Government complicit in any crimes that may be committed in the torture 'black sites' that Mr Trump threatens to reopen.

No. 112.
Irish Independent 7 February 2017
Our 'Turning a Blind Eye' Policy

Should Taoiseach Enda Kenny invite US President Donald Trump to visit Ireland? Recent Irish foreign policy seems to be based on duplicity and turning a blind eye, for economic reasons, to human rights abuses and war crimes by various countries. However, in cases where Ireland is a direct participant in, or is complicit in, some of these crimes, we should not allow alleged economic interests to justify such wrongdoing. Speaking in 2003 in criticism of US military use of Shannon Airport in support of the US-led war in Iraq, Michael D. Higgins said: "We are lessened at home and abroad by allowing ourselves to be complicit in an outrageous action." This is even more relevant today in the Trump era. A report dated February 2, by human rights NGO Reprieve, reveals that an attack by drones and US Special Forces in Yemen on January 29 seriously wounded a pregnant mother and her baby boy, who died from his injuries two days after being born in such dreadful circumstances. The Reprieve report also cites Mr Trump's views on killing civilians: 'On the campaign trail, Mr Trump said he supported the killing of family members of individuals being targeted by the US.' Yes, at the risk of being accused of using doublespeak, perhaps Mr Trump should be invited to Ireland. I rest my case.

No. 113.
Irish Independent 4 April 2017, *Irish Examiner* 5 April 2017
RAF Has No Right to Irish Air Space

A newspaper report last week revealed that a secret bilateral agreement between Ireland and the UK exists that allows British RAF fighter aircraft to intercept and shoot down aircraft suspected of being hijacked by terrorists in Irish sovereign airspace. This is a deeply worrying development for several reasons. First, it could mean that a hijacked Aer Lingus or Ryanair plane with 200 or more passengers onboard could be destroyed in mid-air over populated areas of the Irish Republic. Second, 'Bunreacht na hÉIREANN' Article 29.5.1 states that 'Every International Agreement to which the State becomes a party shall be laid before Dáil Éireann.' This agreement was not laid before Dáil Éireann. Third, it's been reported that senior officers of the Irish Defence Forces were deliberately not informed about this. The question must be asked: Why did these senior officers not resign in protest when they became aware of this? The issue of the lack of interceptor fighters by the Irish Defence Forces is not a justified excuse for this agreement. If the RAF wants to shoot down aircraft hijacked by terrorists over the Atlantic or Irish Sea, or over UK territory that is the business of, and the decision of, the British Government. Under no circumstances should it be allowed to do so over Irish sovereign territory. This agreement is of benefit only to the UK, and poses very serious risks to Irish citizens. We could even argue that the reason that we might need a few interceptor fighter aircraft would be to prevent the RAF from shooting down planes over Irish territory. This agreement is reported to have been put in place about fifteen years ago, which means that it has been approved by Fianna Fáil, Fine Gael, Labour, and possibly even Green Party ministers.

No. 114.

The Irish Times 18 March 2017
Supporting the Air Corps in its Mission

Sir, – It would be easier not to write this letter, but these matters need to be discussed openly. An Taoiseach speaking in Washington DC in response to confirmation that a request for Air Corps support by the Coast Guard on Monday night was denied due to a lack of experienced personnel, said 'It's well known the Air Corps have lost personnel, air-traffic controllers.' No problem then? There is a very serious problem. Decisions taken by government ministers, and Department of Defence civil servants, not to provide adequate funding for the Army Air Corps have resulted in the Air Corps being indirectly implicated in the Irish Coast Guard tragedy off the coast of Mayo ('Staff shortage initially curbed Defence Forces' role in Blacksod emergency', March 16th). Ireland as a neutral state, does not need an expensive offensive air force. However, due to its geographic island location, Ireland does need a comprehensive air-sea rescue service and the Army Air Corps should play an important or even the primary role in this service. Up until the early 1990s, the Air Corps had primary responsibility for air-sea rescue, but this changed in questionable circumstances when this essential service was partly privatised, and the role of the Air Corps significantly downgraded. Recruitment and retention of essential personnel have been problematic in the Air Corps for many years, partly for reasons of inadequate financial resources, but also due to leadership problems in the Department of Defence, and in the Defence Forces itself. While it is necessary in a democracy that civilian control is exercised over the military, this has been taken to extreme levels in Ireland, where civil servants, with little knowledge of military affairs or requirements, exercise a stranglehold over all military matters, sometimes with dangerous consequences. If the problems in the Air Corps were 'well known', Taoiseach, then they should have been resolved.

No. 115.
The Irish Times 5 May 2017
The UN, Saudi Arabia, and Women's Rights

Of all the 193 UN member states, Saudi Arabia has one of the worst records with regard to the status of women. Human Rights Watch described Saudi Arabia's election to the UN women's rights body as an 'affront to the mission of the commission itself, and a rebuke to Saudi women'. While the Department of Foreign Affairs has refused to say which way Ireland voted, Ireland's Ambassador to the UN is the chair of the Commission on the Status of Women, which coordinates that body's work. The prime minister of Belgium has already been forced to apologise to the Belgian parliament because Belgium voted for Saudi Arabian membership of this UN commission. Members of the Oireachtas urgently need to make the Minister for Foreign Affairs accountable to Dáil Éireann on this important issue.

No. 116.
Sunday Independent **7 May 2017**
Peacekeepers and the Drones

Criticism of the decision by the Irish Defence Forces to buy sophisticated electronic and intelligence-gathering equipment from Israel is not just 'facetious nonsense' as described by former soldier Declan Power (*Sunday Independent*, April 30). From a military perspective, an important use for these drones will be monitoring both sides across ceasefire lines or border areas in UN peacekeeping missions in areas such as Lebanon and the Syrian Golan Heights, where Israeli forces are involved in frequent violations of sovereign territories. In such situations, it is vital that the forces being observed do not have access to the design and electronic components of such drone equipment. Given that almost 500 Irish soldiers are serving in Lebanon and the Golan Heights, it is most unwise to purchase such equipment from Israel, when similar equipment is available from other sources. Price alone should not be the deciding factor when the lives of Irish peacekeepers may be at stake. The Israeli price might have reflected the advantages that Israeli intelligence services might get from such a sale. These drones do not in my view provide the 'greatest possible force protection' to Irish troops. Irish soldiers have been killed and injured in the past by military actions by Israeli forces and its militia allies. It is likely that the Israeli forces would be able to disable or counter these drones if they were used to spy on Israeli forces. Declan Power's statements that 'The people who make those kinds of statements demonstrate their lack of knowledge about such matters. They are hugely politicised and know nothing about operational reality' are at best inappropriate and inaccurate. His question, 'Are we supposed to down tools because some group of political extremists and malcontents have an issue with that?', is particularly inappropriate.

No. 117.
The Irish Times 18 May 2017
Neutrality, 'Sacred Cows', and Brexit

Prof Brigid Laffan wants to shoot Ireland's sacred cow that she calls 'military neutrality'. First, let's put to bed the myth propagated by recent Irish governments that there is a lesser form of neutrality called 'military neutrality' that permits the Irish Government to participate in and support wars of aggression against other sovereign states. International law recognises only one form of neutrality, as defined in the Hague Convention on Neutrality, and that neutrality applies only to military affairs and military actions. Any country can be friendly and politically allied with any other country, and still be officially a neutral state, provided its military policies and actions comply with customary international laws on neutrality. The most basic aspect of neutrality is that it only comes into effect in time of war, and the neutral state must not participate in any such war, except in genuine self-defence, and must not assist the military forces of any belligerent in any war. The 'safety of Ireland's geographical location' is still an important factor that enables Irish neutrality and the 'world of Putin and Trump' increases rather than decreases the justification for neutrality. Ireland is already a potential target for terrorist attacks because of our support at Shannon Airport for US wars of aggression. If we accept the advice of Prof Laffan and others and join NATO or an EU military alliance, then we will additionally become a nuclear target in any war between the likes of Mr Trump and Mr Putin. Now is the time to value and protect our geographical island location and our valuable neutrality.

No. 118.
Irish Independent 19 May 2017
Britain Has Lost Its Way

UK Prime Minister Theresa May has stated that Brexit will define Britain's place in the world. She may well be correct for the wrong reasons. With Brexit, the likelihood is that Britain's place in the world will become that of a former empire that has lost its place in Europe, and lost its way in the wider world. The people of Britain will likely suffer the most from Brexit, but the cost in Ireland, and internationally, will also be significant. Brexit represents a retreat to damaging nationalism, and national self-interest at the expense of the increasing need for international and global cooperation, especially in matters of global governance, the rule of law, matters of international peace, and our very-threatened living environment. Also, since Britain no longer controls a vast empire, which in 1945 included India and Pakistan, its continuing status as a permanent veto-wielding member of the UN Security Council is no longer justified, especially when the second most populous country in the world, India, with about seventeen times the population of Britain, has only the same UN status as a tiny country such as Ireland. Brexit is an own goal that may collapse the international goalposts.

No. 119.
The Kerryman 26 May 2017
Manchester Terrorist Attack

The deliberate killing of children is the most heinous of crimes, and the atrocity carried out in Manchester on Monday night 22 May falls into this terrible category. The individuals who organised and carried out this crime are in the same category as the Moors murderers, Myra Hindley and Ian Brady, who committed their crimes also in and around Manchester. No war or no cause justifies the deliberate or reckless killing of children. Like so many Irish families, I have grandchildren and nieces and nephews living in this part of England, and I have enjoyed spending precious time with them in this very part of Manchester city. The outrage being widely expressed at this latest Manchester bombing is fully justified, and our thoughts and prayers are with the bereaved and injured. On 15 April 2017, up to eighty children were killed near Aleppo as they were lured to a car bomb while they were being evacuated from war-torn villages. These eighty Syrian children were no less precious or important than the children in Manchester, and no less important than my grandchildren. Ryan Tubridy, on RTÉ 1, speaking on this atrocity, said that 'children should be immune from war'. This is very true and desirable, but unfortunately is almost impossible in modern indiscriminate warfare. The solution towards ending such dreadful crimes is to end wars, and actively promote peace and reconciliation internationally, as we have succeeded in doing in Ireland. The pity is that we cannot seem to promote peace and reconciliation instead of wars, in Ireland and internationally, before such dreadful atrocities occur.

No. 120.
Irish Independent 2 June 2017, *Irish Examiner* 13 June 2017
The world, and Ireland, Must Wake Up to Genocide in Yemen.

Genocide is defined as 'Deliberately inflicting on the group conditions of life calculated to bring about its physical destruction in whole or in part.' What is happening in Yemen at present falls within this category, yet the international community is actively facilitating rather than preventing it. In the 1990s, when questioned by a reporter about up to half a million children who died as a result of UN and Western-imposed sanctions on Iraq, US Secretary of State Madeleine Albright replied: 'Yes I believe it was worth it.' Our Irish Government remained silent then. In 2017, a greater catastrophe is being perpetrated in Yemen actively supported by the United States and its allies. One branch of the United Nations, the UN Human Rights Committee, is condemning this situation, while the UN Security Council is the organisation that is imposing sanctions and a naval blockade that is preventing the importation of vital food supplies to Yemen, at the behest of its permanent members the US, supported by Britain and France.

They do this on behalf of Saudi Arabia, which is the leading aggressor in Yemen, while selling large amounts of arms to Saudi Arabia. Yemen is the oldest country in the Arabian Peninsula as all the others were hobbled together in the twentieth century by dying imperial powers Britain and France. Now Yemen is one of the poorest countries in the world. UN members such as Ireland are facilitating the ongoing atrocities in Yemen just by remaining silent, and additionally in Ireland's case by actively facilitating US wars of aggression through Shannon Airport. Ireland suffered a similarly imposed famine in the 1840s, so of all nations, we should be at the forefront in working to end this famine in Yemen that is killing tens of thousands of innocent children by deliberate starvation and diseases such as cholera spread by the bombing of water and sewerage treatment facilities and medical facilities. Yet our Irish Department of Foreign Affairs and Trade remains silent in the interests of trade and jobs at Shannon.

No. 121.
Irish Examiner 9 June 2017
Neutrality Must Mean Making Peace, Not War

Sean O'Riordan (June 6) asks 'Are we really as neutral as we think we are?' Three million armed US troops transiting through Shannon Airport on their way to wars in the Middle East ended Irish neutrality, unjustifiably and recklessly. Now we need to restore Irish positive neutrality and focus our efforts on promoting international peace rather than shattering it. O'Riordan suggests that 'the public seems largely not to care' about what the US military is transporting through Shannon. Repeated opinion polls show that up to three-quarters of Irish people support Irish neutrality. He raises the old chestnut of two Russian bombers flying down the middle of the Atlantic, which has nothing to do with neutrality. Let the RAF continue 'playing cat and mouse games with Russian bombers' if they want to. Our government's agreement inviting the RAF to carry out hostile operations over Irish territory is extremely unwise. Let the RAF shoot down hijacked planes over international waters or UK territory but not inflict the results of such carnage on Irish territory or over an Irish city. On the issue of the

Irish Navy operating in the Mediterranean, O'Riordan (Page 1, June 5) says that Ireland may take a more 'robust' role, by abandoning the rescue operation in favour of joining the EUNAVFOR. 'The Defence Forces have told the Government it is time to join the EUNAVFOR'. In a democracy, the Defence Forces should not tell the Government what to do. The Irish Naval Service should focus only on genuine rescue missions but should not abandon these rescue missions over the most dangerous winter months.

Positive neutrality means making peace, not war.

No. 122.
Irish Independent 15 June 2017
Varadkar Must Do Better for Our Unfortunate Asylum Seekers

A Government Press Release reveals that people living in Ireland's direct provision are to have their weekly welfare payments increased, in a move announced by Taoiseach-elect Leo Varadkar and Minister for Justice and Tánaiste Frances Fitzgerald. The rate for adults will rise from €19.10 to €21.60 per week from August. This is the first increase in this rate since 2000. This ridiculously tiny level of increase is insulting not only to the asylum seekers themselves, but it also insults the generosity of the people of Ireland, the vast majority of whom want refugees and asylum seekers in Ireland to be treated humanely and with dignity and in accordance with Ireland's obligations under international laws. Is this indicative of our new Taoiseach's leadership style?

No. 123.
Irish Independent 26 June 2017
UN Day In Support of Victims of Torture

Monday 26 June is designated as the UN day in support of victims of torture. The UN Convention Against Torture (UNCAT) was ratified on 26 June 1987. UNCAT was incorporated into Irish law by the Criminal Justice

(UNCAT) Act 2000. The heinous crime of torture has not been eliminated and the twenty-first century has seen an increase in torture by states, including the United States, with its so-called Extraordinary Rendition program, which saw torture inflicted on prisoners in Guantanamo and other prisons and so-called Black Sites, with the approval of officials of the US Government. Such torture programs are not confined to the United States. A recent Human Rights report dated 22 June 2017 states that: 'The UAE (United Arab Emirates) supports Yemeni forces that have arbitrarily detained, forcibly disappeared, tortured, and abused dozens of people during security operations.' Reports by the European Parliament and the Council of Europe also questioned the Irish Government's role in facilitating the US Extraordinary Rendition program by allowing CIA aircraft involved in this torture program to be refuelled at Shannon Airport. Under the UN Convention Against Torture and enabling Irish legislation, not only is it illegal to commit acts of torture, but it is illegal to facilitate such acts. This is specified in Article 4.1. of UNCAT, which states: 'Each State Party shall ensure that all acts of torture are offences under its criminal law. The same shall apply to an attempt to commit torture and to an act by any person which constitutes complicity or participation in torture.' As yet, there has been no accountability for Irish complicity in acts of torture, and our Irish Government has failed to adequately advocate against torture or in support of victims of torture.

No. 124.
Irish Daily Mail 28 June 2017
Leo's Shannon

An Taoiseach Mr Leo Varadkar TD has made significant statements on Irish foreign policy since he became Taoiseach. When asked in Brussels on June 22 if the time had come for a revision of our traditional neutrality, Mr Varadkar said: 'No. Ireland's position on neutrality is long-standing. We believe that by being a country that is neutral, but not being part of any military alliance, that it actually makes us stronger in the world. That we're more respected around the world, particularly beyond this continent, because we aren't members of NATO and we don't take part in a military alliance; our focus is on other things, like development for example.' This is the clearest statement on Irish neutrality since Éamon de Valera was Taoiseach. Speaking at a dinner for the Ireland Funds in Wicklow on June 23, Mr Varadkar said: 'I would like Ireland to secure a seat on the UN Security Council, so that we can play an even greater role in international affairs and achieving "a world of laws". The best way of responding to uncritical and seductive populist appeals is not to try and match them, or to ignore them, but to inspire people with something more truthful, more realistic, and more noble.' Hopefully, Mr Varadkar is drawing on the values of his Indian heritage in defending Irish neutrality – India, inspired by peace activist Mahatma Gandhi in the largest democracy in the world. The reality is that Irish neutrality has been suspended since 2001, due to US military use of Shannon Airport, as confirmed by High Court judge Nicholas Kearns on April 28, 2003. It's important that Mr Varadkar has the courage to match his important words by restoring Irish neutrality in full compliance with the 'world of laws' that he espouses. Such actions, including ending US military use of Shannon Airport, will be 'more truthful, more realistic, and more noble'.

No. 125.
The Irish Times 5 July 2017
An Erosion of Neutrality?

Your editorial (July 3rd) states that 'Ireland faces a big decision on EU military cooperation'. The Lisbon Treaty introduced 'Permanent Structured Cooperation' (PESCO) that allows member states to buy in or stay out of issues of enhanced cooperation in security and defence. This is now being used to justify setting up a more formal EU military alliance, led by Germany and France. We were assured that the Lisbon Treaty would be no threat to Irish neutrality, but PESCO represents the Lisbon chickens coming home to roost. We are once again being presented with government obfuscation on the meaning of neutrality. We are told that Irish military neutrality is a nuanced form of neutrality that enables Ireland to breach the most fundamental international law requirements for neutrality while still claiming to be a neutral state. Just to clarify, there is only one form of neutrality recognised in international law and that is 'military neutrality'. There is no international law concept or conventions relating to political, economic, or diplomatic neutrality. Just as the Irish High Court ruled in 2003 that allowing large numbers of armed US troops through Shannon Airport is a clear breach of international law on neutrality, likewise, Ireland participating in an EU military alliance will also breach international law on neutrality. Some experienced commentators, including former Irish ambassador to the UK Ray Bassett, are already suggesting that Ireland should reconsider its EU membership in the light of Brexit. While many who support Irish neutrality also support our EU membership, if neutrality is to be further eroded, our continued membership of the EU will be called into question.

No. 126.

The Irish Times and *Irish Independent* 11 Aug 2017
War of Words Between North Korea and US

The threats being issued by the leaders of the US and North Korean governments (*World News*, August 10) indicate that the risk of nuclear war is now possibly greater than during the Cuban missile crisis in 1962. At least in 1962 we had two intelligent pragmatic leaders, both of whom compromised to avert a nuclear war. Now we have the opposite, two national leaders who are behaving irrationally and recklessly. While it is impossible to predict accurately what will happen if the shouting war develops into a shooting war, a possible scenario is that the US will begin by attempting to shoot down any further North Korean missile launches and may also attack North Korean missile launch sites and other targets using sub-nuclear bunker bursting bombs. If this happens, a possible response may be massive artillery attacks by North Korea on South Korea. Since North Korea does already have some nuclear weapons, there is a very serious risk of these being used and possible US nuclear strikes in retaliation. The Irish Government has been silent on this threat to humanity and Irish preparations for a nuclear disaster, either civil or military, are almost non-existent.

Experts are already saying that most seafood in the Pacific is already unsafe for human consumption due to the Fukushima disaster. While it would be irresponsible for Ireland to be assisting North Korea at times like this, allowing Shannon Airport to be used by the US military is also irresponsible. Our government should now be restoring Irish neutrality and using its good offices towards creating international peace and avoiding nuclear war.

Comment: An article was published on 9 Sept 2017 by journalist Nina Hansen that had the following contribution from Edward Horgan based on my presentation in Copenhagen on 19th August to the Danish Peoples Movement on the Militarisation of Europe. The article is in Russian and below is a translation of my input.

No. 127.
Rossa Primavera 9 September 2017
http://rossaprimavera.ru/article/122e0291
(note: the complete article in Russian also has contributions from Jesper Morville from Norway, and Lave Broch from Denmark.)
EU Army an Alternative to the NATO-Led Army?

The opinion of Edward Horgan, the International Secretary of the Irish Peace and Neutrality Alliance, who by the invitation of the Danish Peoples Movement against the EU, participated in the debates on the militarisation of the European Union on August 26.

Edward Horgan notes that the EU army is an alternative to the NATO-led army, and not simply an extension or ally of NATO, for the realisation of the national-economic interests of the largest European countries such as Germany and France, for which small states such as Ireland and Denmark are 'useful idiots, ready to obey their dictatorships'. The southern European states such as Italy and Spain, which accept the economic benefits, also suffer from the Franco-German domination. Is an alternative possible? Yes, it could be, says Edward Horgan, and puts forward his own point of view, citing the parallel between Ireland and Denmark. Ireland is not a NATO member and theoretically has a neutral status, but has lost its neutral status by allowing Shannon Airport to be used by 3 million armed US soldiers on their way to US wars of aggression in the Middle East. Denmark is a member of NATO, but has opted out of European Defence arrangements, including the European Union Battlegroups which are in effect a European army. This reminds Edward Horgan of the famous prayer of St. Augustine: 'Oh, God, make me chaste, but not yet!'

The alternative for Ireland, according to E. Horgan, is the return to real neutrality, and Denmark must withdraw from NATO and not participate in the militarisation of Europe. The rest of Europe should also rebel against the domination of Germany and France. Here's how he sets out his point of view:

We need to study history more thoroughly, in order to prevent the recurrence of its worst times. The Corsican Napoleon had a French vision of the organisation of a united Europe, but he brought devastating disasters both to European territory and to areas of the Middle East and Russia. Hitler had a German vision of a united Europe, which brought terrible destruction and loss of life on European territory, and especially in Russia. So, it is no wonder why Russia is threatened by NATO and in connection with the expansion of the EU under the leadership of Germany and with the support of neo-Napoleonic France. The European Union should become a multinational union of sovereign states, contributing to the preservation of international peace, the development of economic relations, democracy, equality, human rights, and the rule of law. However, we see the return to exploitation of a huge part of the world instead of cooperation for the benefit of humanity. A clear example of this is the neo-colonial exploitation by France of its former African colonies. Perhaps from selfish and self-centred perspectives, this could be seen as a good idea. We, the privileged people of Europe, could work to maintain our levels of privilege, and to hell or to poverty with the rest of the world. This attitude was sustainable, even if morally repugnant, in the eras of slavery and colonisation, using brute military force to extract our undue share of the world's resources. Until 1945, mankind did not have the means to destroy all life on Earth, and we Europeans, perhaps, could continue to use force to achieve our unjustified goals. With the advent of nuclear weapons and the rapidly growing population of the planet, mankind has embarked on the path of its own self-destruction. The use of brute force, wars, growing militarisation, and gross violations of the rule of law cannot be considered rational.

Over the past month, two world leaders, Trump and Kim Jong-un, could have lit a nuclear fuse that would make our planet lifeless. In the coming months or years, Germany and France, the European Union or NATO and/or the US can also unleash a war with Russia. Of course, most of the immediate damage will be in Europe, or in the Far East well away from the United States, as it is US military policy to use what is known as the tethered goat strategy by always fighting US wars in someone else's country, and even provoking such wars. The people of Europe or the Korean Peninsula will be the equivalent of a tethered goat in a tiger hunt. The imperative of today is the search for an alternative to the management of our domestic and international affairs, as opposed to the policy of using force and brutal interference. Ensuring the rule of law is the only sensible and rational approach to moving forward.

After the devastating World War II, the UN Charter was to become the basis of international law, as stated in the preamble. However, after the end of the Cold War, three NATO member countries, which are also permanent members of the Security Council, repeatedly violated the provisions of the Charter, acting without the approval of the Security Council, committing acts of aggression. NATO and the US of course will claim that they have only bypassed the UN because the UN has been ineffective in maintaining international peace, and that they, NATO and the US, were therefore forced to step in to enforce international peace and wage so-called humanitarian wars. All this is nothing but lies, since these countries contribute to the collapse of the UN and all the wars they have waged since the Cold War have been wars for resources and are aimed at illegal regime change, which in itself is a war crime and a gross violation of human rights. This reality on the background of the weakening of the UN position means that the entire structure of international law should be reviewed, reformed and improved. The biggest obstacle to this is the UN itself, which has given enormous powers to the five permanent members of the Security Council, since their veto power can block any reform. None of these five will want to deprive themselves of this veto right, just as the US will not abandon its own special economic impact and control of the World Bank and the International Monetary Fund, and hence on the world economic system. It is urgent to create a new system of global jurisprudence. The existing system of international laws exists only or primarily as a system of laws and regulations between states and reached by agreement between those states, especially the most powerful states, and often with very little input from citizens of those states, or even from the majority of the world's least powerful states.

The non-aligned movement in the 1950s did attempt to overcome some of these problems by setting up an alternative system of states that were not aligned to either of the then two superpowers, the USA and USSR. President Sukarno of Indonesia even went as far as withdrawing Indonesia from the United Nations as part of this process, and this may have been one of the reasons that the US engineered his overthrow and his replacement by the military regime of Suharto. Europe must act in the interests of its citizens, to ensure that the EU does not fall prey to the same ailment that has broken the UN, while a small cohort of European states allows itself to rise above the majority and use its absolute power over it.

What can we, as tiny insignificant individuals, do to overcome these huge problems? Well firstly, we individuals are not as tiny and insignificant as our governments would like us to believe. There are lots of things we individuals can and must do. Standing idly by and doing nothing, hoping things will not get any worse, is no longer an option. Things are getting worse progressively and daily and will get catastrophically worse if allowed to continue. What we are doing here today meeting and discussing these issues is a start but is not nearly enough. Passive resistance is also not enough. We need to work as individuals and network together nationally and internationally to achieve the necessary change. Because positive change needs to happen urgently and quickly, we need to be creative and take direct actions, including challenging bad laws by acts of civil disobedience if necessary. Small-scale and even large-scale peaceful protests are no longer enough. In March 2003, millions of people marched against the Iraq War, but when the war went ahead regardless of these protests, most of these people went home and did nothing more. This was the point when military bases should have been occupied to prevent them being used for this and other illegal wars. While such actions will be described by governments as breaking the law, in my view, such actions are necessary to uphold and enhance the rule of law, and are therefore justified actions and any such peace activists should be acquitted in any subsequent trials on the basis of justifiable reasons for their actions. While we must avoid the temptation of exacerbating the situation by resorting to violent revolution or violent actions, we must be prepared to take all necessary non-violent actions to protect humanity from militarisation and wars of resources. The alternative to the militarisation of Europe is peace and cooperation with Russia.

No. 128.

Irish Examiner 18 September 2017
O'Loan Has Shown She's Up to the Task

I listened to Nuala O'Loan on RTÉ news on Sunday discussing Garda issues and the replacement of the Garda Commissioner. She spoke with considerable authority and integrity and made a lot of sense in what she said. Given her very excellent experience as Police Ombudsperson in Northern Ireland during an equally difficult transition process from policing under the old RUC to policing under the new PSNI, should consideration be given to asking Nuala O'Loan to take on the difficult task of being the next Garda Commissioner?

No. 129.
Irish Examiner **13 September 2017**
Square-Bashing Brainwashes Gardai

TV reports on the resignation of Garda Commissioner Noreen O'Sullivan included TV footage of Gárdaí training in Templemore doing 'square-bashing' and marching, and they were not doing this very well. One of the changes urgently needed to transform An Gárda Síochána, and end a culture of inappropriate omertá type loyalty, is to end such ridiculous type of military training for Gárdaí. Square-bashing and repetitive military drilling are designed to virtually brainwash soldiers into unquestionably obeying orders, regardless of how ridiculous and reckless such orders may be.

The litany of scandals that have almost destroyed the reputation and performance of An Gárda Síochána is probably due significantly to the training and culture Gárdaí are exposed to at their training in Templemore. Some Gárdaí have argued that the reason for the disasters such as the hugely exaggerated number of breathalyser tests was inadequate training and supervision. Yet, Gárdaí receive two years training in Templemore, and the education levels for entry for Gárdaí are also high. Therefore, the quality of the training received and the culture instilled in Templemore is likely a major part of the problem. Ending Gárda square-bashing and encouraging Gárdaí to think for themselves and behave ethically at all times is the way forward.

No. 130.
Irish Examiner **7 October 2017**
Legacy of Cosgraves is Multi-Faceted

The death of Liam T. Cosgrave is being greeted with genuine sadness by the vast majority of Irish people of all political persuasions. His contribution to democracy in Ireland is very considerable, as was the contribution of his father, William T. Cosgrave. One of the items shown on the RTÉ tribute to Liam T. Cosgrave (RTÉ News 9 p.m. October 4) showed him defending his father's decision to authorise the execution of republican prisoners during the Civil War in 1922. Lest we forget, these extracts from historian Diarmaid Ferriter's book *A Nation and Not a Rabble: The Irish Revolution 1913–23*, describe the reality of what arguably amount to war crimes committed with the approval of William T. Cosgrave. This quote is attributed to him: 'I am not going to hesitate and if the country is to live and if we have to exterminate 10,000 republicans, the three million of our people are bigger than the 10,000.' The National Army Council issued this order in February 1923: 'In every case of outrage in any battalion area, three men will be executed... No clemency will be shown in any case.'

Ferriter writes: 'By the end of the Civil War the government had authorised the execution of 77.' Many of these 'executions' were perpetrated without a proper trial. In spite of William T. Cosgrave's substantial contribution to Irish democracy, it is wrong to gloss over these very serious crimes unjustifiably committed in the name of the Irish people.

Ar dheis Dé go raibh anam Liam T. Cosgrave agus a athair William T. Cosgrave.

No. 131.
Irish Examiner 19 October 2017
Irish Naval Service Purchase of Ships

Sean O'Riordan (October 12) reveals Irish Naval Service (INS) ambitions to purchase a new multi-role vessel (MRV). In recent years, the INS has purchased three new ships with a fourth ship on order, for a total of over €250,000,000. This additional MRV-type ship is likely to cost over €200,000,000, bringing the cost of five new ships to almost half a billion euro. Yet, the INS is selling off its older ships for a pittance. The LÉ *Emer*, LÉ *Deirdre,* and LÉ *Aisling* were sold for €320,000, €240,000, and €110,000 respectively. These ships could have been refurbished for a fraction of the costs of these unnecessary new warships. Ireland only needs naval vessels for fishery protection, emergency rescue, and prevention of smuggling. As a neutral state, we have no requirement for aggressive warships. The misuse of the INS was highlighted when LÉ *William Butler Yeats* replaced the LÉ *Eithne* in the Mediterranean. 'Transferring to Operation Sophia will result in the redeployment of Irish Naval Service vessels from primarily humanitarian search and rescue operation to primarily security and interception operations' (*Irish Examiner* July 13). This has been condemned by MSF and others and is highly inappropriate for a neutral country. Taxpayer funding for the Defence Forces is necessarily limited when 700,000 are on hospital waiting lists and 8,000 homeless. This unjustifiably large expenditure on the Naval Service has resulted in expenditure on the Irish Army and Air Corps being severely curtailed with damaging consequences for the Air Corps search and rescue capabilities and for pay and conditions for soldiers. It's time to call a halt to this irrational policy change whereby our naval service is being transformed into a neo-colonial version of gunboat diplomacy that includes forcing fleeing asylum seekers back into inhuman and dangerous conditions in Libya.

No. 132.
Irish Daily Mail 20 October 2017, *The Irish Times* 23 October 2017
Exposing the Truth with Regard to Wrongdoing Often Imposes Costs on the Whistleblower

Exposing the truth with regard to wrongdoing often imposes costs on the whistleblower and can be dangerous. The other side of the coin is that staying silent and failing to expose wrongdoing allows the wrongdoing to continue and may put many others in danger. The child abuse scandals in Ireland continued for so long because many people who knew about these abuses remained silent. The recent exposure of widespread sexual abuse of women is to be welcomed, but we must also condemn the failures by far too many to expose the abusers. This criticism applies especially to men, because women who were abused were usually in a position of disempowerment. Many women have also been killed by their abusers and the failure to expose these abusers has been a factor in these murders. During the Beef Tribunal scandal in the 1990s, the only person prosecuted was the journalist Susan O'Keefe who exposed this scandal. In the Newstalk debacle, it would seem that there has been a closing of ranks, involving Dil Wickremasinghe's 'Global Village' show being cancelled because she dared to criticise her station masters. The appalling murder of Maltese journalist Daphne Caruana Galizia is a reminder of the ultimate price that some whistleblowers have to pay for exposing very serious corruption and abuses of power. Veronica Guerin suffered a similar appalling fate in Ireland. Those of us who become aware of abuses of power must be prepared for the reality that exposing these abuses will likely have costs for us, and we must expose these abuses regardless of these costs, otherwise far greater costs will be inflicted on others by our silence.

No. 133.
Limerick Leader 17 November 2017
Commemorating Wars

RTÉ news reports that An Taoiseach Leo Varadkar wore a Shamrock Poppy in the Dáil, on 7 November. The wearing of the Poppy is associated with British military imperial involvement in World War I in which over 18 million people were killed and 23 million wounded. This was the most unjustified war in human history but was justified at the time as 'the war to end all wars'. Far from achieving this, WWI was the root cause of World War II, which exceeded even the depravity of WWI. All the Irish men who died in WWI died needlessly, and many of the Irish soldiers who fought in WWI killed many German soldiers whose deaths were also tragic and needless. In reality, the wearing of the red poppy tends to celebrate militarism, rather than commemorate those who needlessly died. Ireland is once again being surreptitiously dragged into military alliances, including the NATO so-called Partnership for Peace, European Battlegroups, and the EU naval Operation Sophia. Like the period prior to WWI, imaginary enemies are being created in Eastern Europe to justify the militarisation of Europe, regardless of the reality that Russia is no longer the expansionist Soviet Union. Ireland should be reinforcing its positive neutrality and promoting international peace, rather than helping to threaten international peace. It would be far more appropriate for An Taoiseach to wear the White Poppy of peace rather than wear the divisive and militaristic British Red Poppy.

No. 134.
Irish Daily Mail 23 November 2017
All Citizens of the World Should Be Equal Before the Law, Including War Criminals

Bosnian Serbian military leader Ratko Mladić has been very justifiably sentenced to life in prison for crimes including Genocide in Bosnia. In March 2016, Mladić's political boss Radovan Karadžić was also convicted of similar charges and is already serving forty years in prison, and once again, his sentence was fully justified. What is not widely known because it received very little Western media coverage is that the tribunal that sentenced Radovan Karadžić also found that similar charges against former Serbian President Slobodan Milošević were not substantiated. Para 3460 of the tribunal's report found that: 'based on the evidence before the Chamber ... the Chamber is not satisfied that there was sufficient evidence presented in this case to find that Slobodan Milošević agreed with the common plan'. Milošević died in prison in suspicious circumstances before his trial concluded. War crimes tribunals provide a very important function in bringing war criminals to justice. Sadly, however, far too few war criminals are tried before such courts, and the leaders of the most powerful states in the world have given themselves immunity from prosecution at such trials through blatant abuses of international laws and the UN Charter. All citizens of the world should be equal before the law, including war criminals.

No. 135.
Irish Examiner **5 Dec 2017**
No Security for Us Without Neutrality

The debate in Dáil Éireann on November 30 on Ireland's participation in two European Defence Agency Projects should worry Irish citizens. Irish governments since 1939 maintained neutrality until the US military was allowed to use Shannon Airport for its Middle East wars from 2001. This debate is a precursor to the government seeking approval to join the EU Permanent Structured Cooperation (PESCO) which our EU overlords say is 'towards more security for the EU and its citizens'. PESCO will drag Ireland ever closer into an EU military alliance, and eventually into NATO. We have become used to the cynicism of parties in opposition supporting neutrality but quickly abandoning it when in government. Labour abandoned neutrality in favour of ministerial pensions when they joined Fine Gael in government. The Green Party did likewise when they got Ministries with the Fianna Fáil government, but now back in opposition and depleted, they are claiming once again to be supporting neutrality. Labour and Fianna Fáil voted with the government in this motion. Sinn Féin, who claim to be strong supporters of neutrality inexplicably abstained in the vote leaving the motion carried. Since Hitler and Stalin no longer exist, no one explains who it is we need to defend against. The security of the Irish people will not be guaranteed by dragging us into European wars, as we were in World War I, but by active neutrality promoting world peace and justice.

No. 136.
Irish Examiner, *Irish Independent*, **and** *Irish Daily Mail* **21 December 2017**
The Plight of The Homeless Is A National Concern

President Michael D. Higgins has said the 'burden of homelessness will overshadow the festive season for those deprived of a secure and permanent shelter'. He is correct but the burden of homelessness should overshadow the festive season not just for the homeless, but for all the citizens of Ireland. It is a matter of national shame that at a time of relative prosperity, we are unable to provide homes for our most vulnerable citizens, especially children. Our governing system has failed in several vital respects, and is our responsibility as citizens, to ensure that our government is governing. President Higgins also highlighted the problems facing refugees and asylum seekers internationally. Our government is also failing in its, and our, obligations to help and provide refuge for such people. Those who say that 'charity begins at home', implying that we should ignore the plight of refugees, are wrong. It is an insult for us to offer charity to our families, and it's an insult for our government to be offering charity to our vulnerable citizens. Our families and citizens have entitlements to important basic services. Charity is what we do for, and give to, strangers in need, in our communities and internationally. We as citizens, and our government are failing in our respective duties to provide basic services such as housing and health services, and also failing in our charity towards foreign strangers in need.

Happy Christmas – for some.

No. 137.
Irish Independent 24 December 2017
The Slaughter of So Many Innocents

One of the stories associated with Christmas is that of King Herod and the slaughter of 2,000 innocent children. In his first days in office, President Trump authorised an attack on the village of Yakla in Yemen that reportedly killed twenty-five civilians, including nine children. Nawar Anwar Awlaki aged eight, was one of those killed in 'collateral damage'. Since the first Gulf War in 1991, up to one million children have died due to wars in the Middle East. One was an Irish child, Juliana Clifford McCourt who was on one of the aircraft that was crashed into the Twin Towers in New York. Up to half a million children died as a result of UN sanctions on Iraq during the 1990s. Madeleine Albright, US Secretary of State, said 'yes it was worth it'. Over the twelve days of this Christmas, hundreds of children will e of disease, hunger, and bombs in Yemen. 'All across the lands' of the Middle East perhaps as many as 2,000 children will die over this Christmas. That star shining from the east may be a drone firing hellfire missiles. Perhaps King Herod was not so bad after all. We are not doing nearly enough to stop the slaughter of the innocents.

No. 138.

Irish Examiner 3 January 2018.
Police Adding Jam to the Cake

The report 'MP was told Birmingham Six evidence was "enhanced"' (Brian Hutton, Jan 1) is not surprising but shocking, nonetheless. It seems clear that the Chief Constable of Liverpool and a Tory MP had information in 1987 that the conviction of the Birmingham Six was based on unsound evidence, obtained by unlawful means. This crime was euphemistically described as 'Police adding jam to the cake.' If this information had been properly acted on in 1987, then the Birmingham Six could have been spared the last four years of their seventeen-year unjustified imprisonment. Failure to act on such information could amount to perversion of the course of justice. Such an event, of course, could never happen in Ireland, could it? Well, experiences in the Irish justice system in recent years might indicate that, yes, it could happen in Ireland.

No. 139.

The Irish Times 3 January 2018
UN Peacekeeping Missions

The Democratic Republic of Congo is drifting once again into increasing levels of dictatorship and violence and the UN peacekeeping forces are failing in their responsibilities to maintain peace there for a variety of reasons, including the poor quality of some of the peacekeeping forces. On December 7, rebels killed fourteen UN Tanzanian peacekeepers and wounded fifty-three others in North Kivu province (World News, December 8). On December 30, seven people were killed by police in

Kinshasa while protesting at Joseph Kabila's refusal to vacate the presidency. Mr Kabila completed his second term in 2016 and is constitutionally debarred from serving for a third term, yet elections have been repeatedly postponed. The Congo is one of the richest countries in the world in resources, but due to abusive colonisation and exploitation and indigenous corruption, its people are impoverished and continue to suffer far greater numbers of casualties than in the much more publicised conflicts in the Middle East. Good-quality peacekeepers are urgently needed in the Congo, and this is where Ireland's main peacekeeping efforts should be focused. Irish peacekeepers should be withdrawn in particular from the Israeli-occupied Syrian Golan Heights where all they are achieving is protecting Israeli occupation. It may also be time for Ireland to consider winding down its commitments to UNIFIL in Lebanon, so as to focus more on African conflicts where they are most needed.

(BLACK LIVES MATTER TOO.)

No. 140.
Sunday Times 7 Jan 2018
Neutral Stance a Positive Move

Leo Varadkar has changed his mind about neutrality and now does not expect Ireland to ever join NATO. This is the most significant statement by any Irish Taoiseach on neutrality since Éamon de Valera ('Ireland must stay neutral, says Leo', News December 24). Varadkar says neutrality meant 'something different' now from what it did during the Second World War and that Ireland was not neutral when it came to human trafficking, the management of mass migration, and cyber-attacks. However, such matters should have nothing to do with military affairs, being primarily matters for good international policing. They cannot be solved with tanks and missiles, which are more often the causes of such problems. This mixture of pragmatism and idealism makes Irish neutrality right and justifiable. So, thank you Mr Varadkar for walking with us halfway along the road towards positive neutrality. Let's walk together a few more steps into the New Year.

No. 141.
Sunday Independent 7 Jan 2018, *Irish Examiner* 9 January 2018
Human Rights Abuses Began Before the Holocaust

Corralling people into concentration camps and abusing their human rights neither began nor ended with the Holocaust. Britain was guilty of this during the Boer War, the Mau Mau rebellion in Kenya, internment in Northern Ireland and elsewhere, and many of the most powerful states in the world have done likewise, before, during and after the Second World War. The Holocaust perpetrated against European Jews was by far the most serious and most unjustified crime against humanity so far. This makes it difficult to understand how the Israeli Government could even consider, let alone perpetrate, the human rights abuses that are now occurring almost daily against Palestinians. The colonisation of large portions of Palestine, including the forceful expulsion of Palestinians from their lands and villages, resulting in the establishment of an apartheid state of Israel, is also one of the root causes of the catastrophe. Gaza is now the largest concentration camp in the world and this is absolutely unacceptable. The white racist South African apartheid government was perpetrating similar abuses against the majority of its people until international sanctions forced it to abandon apartheid. It's now time that the international community, especially Ireland and the EU, took effective actions to end the suffering of the Palestinian people.

Comment: I had the following short letter published in the Irish Examiner *in response to some of the very critical letters that the* Examiner *and the* Independent *received in response to my letter in the previous week on Israeli human rights abuses against Palestinians.*

No. 142.
Irish Examiner 20 Jan 2018
It Is Not Good Enough for Witnesses to Be Silent

It is always easier to remain silent on issues such as the Palestine/Israeli conflict, knowing that regardless of the truth in what we say, we will be severely criticised. It is always wrong to remain silent when human rights are being very seriously abused. It is not good enough for witnesses to be silent. Let us not forget the words of Pastor Martin Niemöller '… then they came for me – and there was no one left to speak for me.'

No. 143.
Irish Independent 11 January 2018
Our Troops Are Being Put at Risk

On Tuesday morning, Israeli military forces are reported to have fired several missiles and rockets at Syrian army positions near Damascus, in unprovoked attacks. The reports indicate that some of these missiles were fired from Israeli-occupied Syrian Golan Heights, where Irish peacekeeping troops are stationed. Given that under international laws Syria would be entitled to respond by attacking the launch sites of such missiles, this could put Irish peacekeeping soldiers in serious danger. Some of the Israeli missiles were also reportedly fired from Israeli aircraft flying in Lebanese airspace, where a further contingent of Irish peacekeepers is based. The Irish Government should contact United Nations headquarters about these reports and should also ask the UN Security Council to investigate these reported very serious breaches of international peace.

No. 144.
Irish Daily Mail 27 January 2018
Neutrality and Unlawful Orders

There are many reasons why Ireland should remain a neutral state, and avoid joining a European army, or signing up to PESCO, and why we should not allow the US military to use Shannon Airport to wage wars of aggression in the Middle East. One important reason is that abandoning neutrality curtails Ireland's ability to promote international peace and justice. The very good reputation of Irish soldiers on UN peace missions is not accidental. One of the reasons for this good reputation is contained in the oath Irish soldiers take on enlistment. Unusually, the Irish Defence

Forces oath contains the very important word LAWFUL: 'I, __, do solemnly swear (or declare) that I will be faithful to Ireland and loyal to the Constitution and that while I am a member of the Permanent Defence Force, I will obey all lawful orders issued to me by my superior officers …' US and British soldiers, and the soldiers of many other armies, take an oath to 'OBEY ALL ORDERS' of their superiors. During our military training, we were given a legal lecture by the late Colonel Pat Jordan who told us that, 'it is unlawful for you as a soldier to obey an unlawful order, and as an officer, it is unlawful for you to give an unlawful order'. If other armies inserted the word LAWFUL into their oaths, fewer war crimes would be committed. British soldiers in Derry on Bloody Sunday obeyed orders to shoot unarmed civilians and US soldiers in the Middle East; obeyed orders that led to prisoners being tortured and civilians being unjustifiably killed.

No. 145.

The Kerryman **4 April 2018**

Ireland Over-Hasty in Joining the Rush to Expel Russian Diplomats

The decision by the Irish Government to expel a Russian diplomat from Ireland, over alleged Russian Government involvement in the serious injuries inflicted on Sergei Skripal and his daughter Yulia in Salisbury, is at best premature and may be wholly unjustified. Other EU-neutral countries, including Austria and Malta, have not expelled Russian diplomats. Ireland as a sovereign state should not be dictated to by the EU, US, or UK. This attack was indeed a crime, but it is important not to exaggerate its seriousness. So far, no one has died and no credible evidence has been produced as to who perpetrated this crime. The fact that the nearby Porton Down Chemical Warfare Research Centre was so quickly able to claim to have identified the chemical involved indicates the likelihood that they already had some of this material. There are significant dangers in the current tensions with Russia that are being manipulated by the UK for domestic reasons, and by other NATO states for militaristic reasons. Well over two million people have died across the Middle East as a result of wars waged by the US, UK, and NATO. We now know that the invasion of Iraq was precipitated by false information about WMDs. The Russian Government had little to gain and much to lose by perpetrating this crime. In 1914, Archduke Ferdinand of Austria and his wife were assassinated in Sarajevo. This crime was orchestrated to precipitate World War I, costing over 18 million deaths. Let us not make similar mistakes that could precipitate World War III.

Comment: This short letter was written in response to the controversial rape trial in Belfast involving rugby players.

No. 146.
Irish Independent, Irish Daily Mail 2 April 2018
Where Are Our Rugby Heroes Gone?

Where have all our rugby heroes, past and present, disappeared to over the past several weeks? Rugby is supposed to be a character-building sport. It takes character to speak out against abuse. The silence has been deafening.

No. 147.
Irish Examiner 12 April 2018
False Flag War Crimes in Syria?

US President Trump stated: 'there will be a big price to pay after dozens killed in poison gas attack' (*Irish Examiner* April 8). He described Syrian President Assad as an animal, pre-judging the outcome of any investigation of this alleged chemical weapons attack. Reports that dozens have been killed in this latest alleged chemical attack have not been confirmed by reliable observers on the ground. There has been very little Western condemnation on the likelihood that Israel carried out a missile attack on a Syrian Government air base near Homs that reportedly killed fourteen people. Clearly all lives should matter, and if Israel did carry out this attack, it was in clear breach of international laws. Sources in Damascus indicate that this latest alleged chemical attack may have been a false flag attack orchestrated by one of the rebel groups to provoke US/NATO retaliatory attacks. On 8 February 2018, US Secretary of Defense General James Mattis stated in an interview with Newsweek that the US has 'no evidence' that the Syrian Government used the banned nerve agent Sarin against its own people. The Newsweek report states: 'Mattis offered no temporal qualifications, which means that both the 2017 event in Khan Sheikhoun and the 2013 tragedy in Ghouta are unsolved cases in the eyes of the Defense Department and Defense Intelligence Agency.' The people of Syria have been subjected to a series of disastrous and very complex multiple conflicts, involving civil war, and proxy wars being waged by regional and world powers at the enormous expense of the Syrian people. In addition, there is a risk of this conflict spreading regionally and even globally if the UN continues to be prevented from doing its primary job of creating international peace.

No. 148.
Irish Examiner 20 April 2018
Army Ranger Wing Served with NATO in Afghanistan

On the 17th of April, in answer to a parliamentary question by Clare Daly TD to the Taoiseach and Minister for Defence, the following information was provided: 'The Army Ranger Wing (ARW) are the Special Operations Forces of the Defence Forces. Personnel from the ARW served in the International Security Assistance Force (ISAF), Afghanistan from October 2006 to March 2007 and from September 2014 to March 2015.' And 'Specific details of the numbers of the ARW deployed overseas are not released into the public domain for security and operational reasons.' This was the first time that the Irish public, or indeed members of Dáil Éireann, were ever made aware that members of the Army Ranger Wing had served with the NATO ISAF force in Afghanistan. It is not clear from the written reply whether the total number of Irish Defence Forces personnel in Afghanistan during these periods exceeded twelve personnel, and if so, Dáil Éireann should have been asked to approve their presence in

Afghanistan. More seriously, the following questions must also be asked and answered. What were the ARW personnel doing in Afghanistan? Were they serving with US Special Forces, or British SAS troops? Were they involved in counter-insurgency or intelligence-gathering operations? Were any Afghan people killed during any of these operations? Why were the Irish people and members of Dáil Éireann not informed that members of Ireland's special forces had been serving with NATO in Afghanistan for a total of twelve months?

No. 149.
Irish Independent 2 May 2018
Irish Health Service Mismanagement

In the light, or darkness, of the most recent scandal to engulf our health services, we should spare a thought for and give support to our very many excellent health professionals who are continuing to do a great job under difficult circumstances. Our successive governments, Department of Health, HSE, and health administrators seem to have learned nothing from past disasters, including the manner in which Bridget McCole was treated, the hepatitis scandal, hospital waiting lists, A&E overcrowding, etc., yet our health professionals, especially our under-resourced nurses, have to continue to cope on a daily basis, and the vast majority of them do so in an excellent manner. A few years ago, I had to attend A&E with a hand injury, and more recently I attended with a family member who was seriously ill. On both occasions, I was very impressed with the level of care we received, in spite of overcrowding and staff working under pressure. If doctors or nurses make mistakes, they are usually held accountable, but we are continually failing to hold our government ministers, department of health, and HSE officials accountable for their very serious mismanagement of our health services. People who seek and achieve high office should not be immune from or protected from prosecution or accountability for their serious mistakes.

No. 150.
Irish Examiner 24 May 2018
Militarisation of a 'Peaceful' Europe

European Council president Donald Tusk's recent statement to EU leaders at their Sofia summit ('Capricious' Donald Tusk condemns Trump administration, *The Guardian* May 16) is deeply worrying for those who oppose the development of the EU into an aggressive superpower pursuing European interests and so-called 'European values' at the expense of our fellow human beings in regions exploited by past and present European colonial and economic abuses. Tusk stated that: 'Europe must be united economically, politically, and also militarily, like never before. To put it simply: either we are together, or we will not be at all.' Europe united economically, politically, and militarily, means a European super-state, not even in the interests of all EU citizens, or of all EU states, but in the interests of elite neoliberal groups within an elite group of EU states led by Germany and France. In one respect, Mr Tusk is right when he says: 'either we are together, or we will not be at all'. A militarised EU super-state representing part of Europe, excluding Russia and others, is not in the interests of all European peoples or in the interests of humanity as a whole. The peoples of Europe are being divided once again, instead of promoting peace and cooperation. Tusk's vision of being together in a militarised EU must be opposed, otherwise European Union, or unity, 'will not be at all' and will be replaced by a dangerous undemocratic threat to humanity.

No. 151.
Irish Independent 1 June 2018, *Irish Examiner* 4 June 2018
Incorrect Registration of Births

Yet another scandal has surfaced belatedly in Ireland, euphemistically being called 'incorrect registration of births'. An Taoiseach Leo Varadkar referred to this as 'another dark chapter of Irish history' in the Dáil on 30 May 2018. No, Taoiseach, this is not history; this is an ongoing serious crisis for thousands of people, including birth parents and adoptive parents, but most especially for those whose births were 'incorrectly registered'.

What happened is these cases were not simply 'incorrect registration' or simple mistakes. At the very least, falsifying official records may involve serious criminal offences unless, of course, the laws at the time were designed to avoid criminalising those elite persons in Irish society who were perpetrating or benefiting from these 'incorrect registration of births'. These elites include many medical professionals, male and female religious persons, as well as the fathers of many of the children involved. Mr Varadkar also stated that the issue 'must be dealt with sensitivity'. We must question whether the need for such sensitivity may be to protect the interests of these elites at the expense of the victims in this scandal, mainly the children whose births were knowingly incorrectly registered, and their vulnerable mothers. As with the cervical cancer scandal, it is vital that this latest scandal be resolved quickly before its victims conveniently die. What is needed now is not delaying enquiries or sensitivity, but some restorative justice where possible, fairness, and most of all truth instead of all the lies that were told.

No. 152.
Irish Independent, Irish Daily Mail 25 June 2018.
'Clinton Blackens TCD Name'

As a graduate and former employee of Trinity College, I am surprised and disappointed that Trinity College awarded an honorary doctorate to Hillary Clinton. Mrs Clinton was former US Secretary of State during the overthrow of the Libyan Government in 2011, which was largely assisted by US and NATO bombing campaigns. On 20 October 2011, the day that Gaddafi was brutally murdered, she was interviewed by CBS News. She laughed as she said, 'we came, we saw and he died'. She blames many people including Vladimir Putin, Barack Obama, James Comey, and Bernie Saunders for her defeat in the US presidential election, but the reality is that at a time when she represented the opportunity to be the first female US President, she should have been by far the preferred candidate, especially given the unsuitability of her main opponent, now President Donald Trump, it is clear that the majority of US citizens simply neither liked nor trusted Hillary Clinton. Why did Trinity College award an honorary doctorate to such a failed politician? Perhaps the answer is contained in TCD's website with regard to honorary doctorates, which states: 'Nominations are sought for individuals of […] exceptional achievement whose acceptance of an honorary degree would add lustre to this university.' This seems to suggest that the purpose of such awards is the self-serving one of adding lustre to the university. Awards like this one to Hillary Rodham Clinton are more likely to tarnish the long-standing reputation of TCD than add lustre to it.

Comment: The following letter was signed by Clare Daly TD, Mick Wallace TD, Maureen O'Sullivan TD and Catherine Connolly TD, Leinster House, Dublin, and Dr Edward Horgan, Castletroy, Limerick.

No. 153.
The Irish Times 29 June 2018
Helping the Vulnerable in Syria

The article by Annie Sparrow 'Ireland can help UN to stop Assad manipulating humanitarian aid' (Opinion, June 26) seems to be part of a well-orchestrated effort to prevent international humanitarian aid from reaching vulnerable Syrian people, traumatised by civil war, terrorist militias, and foreign military intervention. While the initial protests against Assad in 2011 did have justification, the involvement of ISIS and al-Qaeda terrorists forced many Syrians to abandon their opposition to the Assad government. US support for the overthrow of the Assad government led to military intervention by Russia and Iran, who feared that their countries might be the next US target for overthrow. The Syrian Government has regained control of most of Syria, but all the Syrian people are now in urgent need of humanitarian aid. A similar crisis occurred in Iraq during the US-driven sanctions in the 1990s, leading to the deaths of almost half a million Iraqi children. When then-US Secretary of State Madeleine

Albright was asked if these children's deaths were worth it, she replied, 'yes they were'.

A medical doctor such as Annie Sparrow should not be advocating withholding of humanitarian aid from very vulnerable people. She describes the Syrian situation as 'arguably the world's worst humanitarian crisis', but she focuses only on those opposed to the Syrian Government, ignoring all those killed and traumatised by opposition forces. A far more serious humanitarian crisis has been ongoing in Yemen, where the US is actively supporting the Saudi bombardment. The UNRWA UN organisation providing vital support to the people of Gaza is now facing a similar crisis because the US withdrew its contribution to UNRWA's funding. Dr Sparrow seems not to have written any articles in support of the humanitarian needs of the suffering peoples of Yemen and Gaza, indicating her article is primarily political. Ireland and other independent countries must reject US efforts to deny humanitarian aid to the most vulnerable members of humanity. Too many children have died already.

No. 154.
The Irish Times, Irish Independent, Irish Examiner, Irish Daily Mail
Wed 4 July 2018

UN Security Council Bid: Campaign Intensifies

Ireland's involvement with United Nations peacekeeping should make it very suitable for membership in the UN Security Council. (UN Security Council bid: Campaign intensifies, *Irish Examiner*, July 3). However, a surprising aspect of our government's campaign has been its failure to mention the word neutrality. Ireland's neutrality was a key factor in our participation in UN peacekeeping for many decades and this enhanced our reputation within the international community. It would appear from the UNSC campaign optics so far that our government is embarrassed by the issue of Irish neutrality. It well might be embarrassed, given that while Bono was entertaining 150 UN ambassadors in New York, a US Air Force Hercules C130 was being refuelled at Shannon Airport, probably on its way to contribute to wars in the Middle East. Pragmatically, if we are to have a reasonable chance of success when up against NATO members Norway and Canada, we must find ways of differentiating our application from theirs, and surely Irish neutrality should be a winning point with the large majority of the non-NATO members of the United Nations. The Canadian Air Force dropped 250 bombs on Libya in 2011 and the Norwegian Air Force dropped more than twice that, and both provided military support for US efforts to overthrow the Syrian Government. Ireland's application for a UN Security Council seat should be based on being a genuine neutral altruistic country, and the most appropriate way to commemorate the eighty-eight peacekeeping heroes who gave their lives for international peace will be to restore genuine Irish neutrality.

No. 155.
Irish Daily Mail 11 July 2018
Belgian Apologies to the Congo?

On 30 June 2018, the Mayor of Brussels renamed a square after Patrice Lumumba and carefully worded apologies were issued. Such apologies and token acts are cheap and are often attempts to avoid proper accountability. It is impossible to bring the millions of dead Congolese back to life, but it is possible to calculate the resources that Belgium exploited from the Congolese people and to estimate what level of exemplary reparations Belgium should be forced to pay. Belgium is not the only country that has failed to adequately compensate the victims of crimes against humanity. There is not enough space on this letters page to list the crimes of all the countries who committed crimes against humanity. It includes all the European colonial states, and many more, including the US, Japan, Soviet Union, and Turkey. After each atrocity, hollow cries of Never Again ring out, but in reality, the cry should have been Ever and Ever Again. Crimes against humanity continue to occur because most of the countries that committed such crimes are never properly held to account and are seen to have benefitted substantially from such crimes. The peoples of many

African countries, especially the Congo, are still being exploited by European and other first-world countries. Crimes against humanity are now occurring in Yemen, Palestine, and Myanmar without effective response from the international community, including the UN. The lessons that should have been learned from Cambodia and Rwanda are already forgotten. If the UN is prevented from acting in such cases, by one or more of its permanent members, then it may need to be replaced.

Comment: I was prompted to write the following short letter partly by a recent personal development. At seventy-three years of age, I was diagnosed with what will hopefully turnout to be a not-too-serious case of skin cancer in my face. What I optimistically term a small c rather than The Big C! Not surprising given my childhood living and working on a farm in the days when sun cream and sun hats were not the norm, combined with my many periods of service in hot climates as a military peacekeeper, and on democratisation and humanitarian work.

No. 156.
Irish Independent 19 July 2018
Never Too Old to Make a Difference

Anthony Woods (*Irish Independent*, Letters, July 17) writes that 'getting older need not be frightening'. The same applies to the inevitability of dying. Dying is only a problem if one has not lived a life worth living.

So, if one is fortunate enough to be getting old, knowing that far too many do not get the privilege of getting old, then getting old gives more urgency to the task of living a life worth living.

And so, life goes on, for some of the lucky ones, including this writer.

No. 157.
The Irish Times 27 July 2018.
Security, Defence, and Neutrality

The MacGill Summer School began with a row over gender balance and compounded this by an unbalanced team of speakers on Ireland's defence and neutrality ('Irish MEP says calm debate needed on security and defence', July 24). The vast majority of Irish people support Irish neutrality, so it is difficult to justify such a one-sided debate including Mairead McGuinness, Ben Tonra, and Joe Mulholland, while advocates of neutrality were excluded. Ms McGuinness said that 'Irish spending on defence was the lowest in the EU.' Irish defence spending should be the lowest in the EU, given that our geography as an offshore island and our neutrality are our best defences. She went on to say that 'Ireland must engage in a national debate… which does not descend into accusations of sending "our sons and daughters to war" '.

Advocates of abandoning neutrality want to avoid mentioning such unmentionables, on the centenary of the ending of the First World War when almost 50,000 of Ireland's sons were needlessly killed. The defence of the Irish people should include priorities such as health services and homelessness. Ben Tonra raised the spectre of global threats to Ireland 'such as terrorism, a resurgent Russia, and the rise of authoritarian regimes'. Terrorism threats are best dealt with by good policing and restoring genuine neutrality. A 'resurgent Russia' is mainly an invention to justify the militarisation of Europe, and authoritarian regimes are a serious issue within the European Union and NATO, rather than being a threat to Ireland. The statement by the French ambassador to Ireland Stéphane Crouzat that 'his country does not see Ireland as neutral' represents unacceptable interference in important Irish internal affairs.

No. 158.
Irish Examiner 6 August 2018
Mainstream Media Not to Be Trusted.

Timmy Dooley TD, Fianna Fáil proposed that the government provide €30M to support 'high-quality print and online journalism' (*Irish Examiner* July 31). Where this fund would come from is not clear. Traditional news media are under threat from alternative media, which they accuse of propagating fake news. But fake news can also be propagated by mainstream media as well as by manipulation of public opinion by governments, business interests, and elite groups nationally and globally. The proper role of independent media should be to hold governments and others in authority to account, but this proposal may indicate that politicians are worried about their inability to control alternative media sources. State funding for media could further compromise their integrity.

Deputy Dooley said that 'We have a proliferation of news content not properly researched or verified on digital platforms, which leads to fake news.' Yes, but how much of this disinformation is being spread by the governments using compliant media sources? One of the reasons for the explosion of alternative and social media is that many citizens no longer trust the traditional media. Let's not forget the examples of the Nice and Lisbon treaties referenda. In both cases, the Irish Government, political parties, media outlets, and business interests all combined to browbeat the citizens to approve both treaties. When the citizens voted democratically to reject both treaties, the Irish Government, backed by traditional media, undemocratically inflicted a rerun of both referenda on the Irish people. Deputy Dooley proposes 'the appointment of a minister with responsibility for media'. The Germans used to have a chap called Goebbels who was very good at that sort of thing during World War II when misinformation was used to devastating effect in Nazi Germany, and we already have a minister for communications.

At European and global levels, citizens are also getting very biased or untrue reports on important matters. Truth, integrity, and honesty should be hallmarks of all independent media, otherwise they just become propaganda.

No. 159.
Irish Examiner 13 August 2018
The Agony of Yemen Getting Worse.

The appalling situation in Yemen is getting worse. According to the United Nations, 10,000 people – two-thirds of them civilians, including thousands of children – have been killed and 55,000 injured. On the 9th of August, a bus carrying children to a summer school was hit by a Saudi air strike in the town of Dahyan in northern Yemen. At least forty-seven civilians, including twenty-nine children all under fifteen years of age, were killed. Col Turki al-Malki, spokesman for the US-backed Saudi-dominated coalition, said the attack was 'a legitimate military action, conducted in conformity with international humanitarian law'. On the 2nd of August, several explosions hit al-Thawra Hospital in the rebel Houthi-held city of Hodeidah, killing at least twenty-six people. The Saudi-led coalition claimed that bombing was carried out by Houthi rebels themselves, but independent analysts said the bombing was caused by 120 mm mortar shells, made by German company Rheinmetall Denel Munition, who supply munitions to Saudi Arabia and the United Arab Emirates. As well as the USA, three European Union countries, France, Germany, and the UK, supply large amounts of armaments and munitions to Saudi Arabia. Three of these countries – the US, UK, and France – are permanent members of the UN Security Council. Ireland is also supporting these bombings in Yemen. On the 10th of July, a National Air Cargo plane on contract to the US military was refuelled at Shannon Airport en route from an airbase in the US, and it went on to make deliveries to air bases in Kuwait, Afghanistan, and Djibouti, before returning through Shannon on July 12th. Djibouti is just across the Red Sea from Yemen.

No. 160.
The Irish Times **13 August 2018**
Ireland's Record on Torture Prevention

Sir, – The article by Deirdre Malone, 'Ireland has not ratified a protocol to prevent torture in places of detention' (Opinion, August 8), highlights the Irish Government's failure to comply with its duties to prevent torture. While the Operational Protocol to the Convention against Torture (OPCAT) deals primarily with people detained in state prisons, the elephant in the room with regard to Ireland is that the Irish Government was complicit in the US Extraordinary Rendition program whereby hundreds of prisoners were tortured. EU Parliament TDIP committee report found that CIA aircraft associated with the torture were refuelled at Shannon Airport. None of these aircraft was ever searched or investigated. This means the Irish Government is in breach of Article 4 UN Convention Against Torture (UNCAT): 'Each State Party shall ensure that all acts of torture are offences under its criminal law. The same shall apply to an attempt to commit torture and to an act by any person which constitutes complicity or participation in torture.' Prisoners being transported on aircraft under severe conditions that may amount to torture means that such an aircraft should fall under the provisions of the OPCAT as a place of detention, and therefore be subject to inspection. This may be the reason why the Irish Government is failing to ratify this important protocol. Torture is one of the most heinous of crimes, and while it may not be occurring within Irish prisons, the Irish Government is failing in its duties to ensure that Irish territory and Shannon Airport are not being used to facilitate or be complicit in torture. This may call into question Ireland's application for membership of the UN Security Council.

No. 161.
Irish Examiner **18 August 2018**
Immunity for US Soldiers in Ireland?

According to reports in the *US Navy Times* in March 2017 and August 2018, a US Navy officer was arrested by Gardai in March 2017, over an alleged rape of a female US Navy sailor in Dublin and accused of violating Section 4 of Ireland's Criminal Justice Act 1984, but instead of being charged with any offence in Ireland, the suspect was released back to US Navy custody. Both the accused and the alleged victim were crew members of the USS *Donald Cook*, a US Destroyer most probably armed with Tomahawk cruise missiles that was on a visit to Cobh harbour, in breach of international laws on neutrality. On 13 August 2018, the Chief Intelligence Specialist officer involved was charged before a US Navy court-martial at Norfolk naval base in the US with several sexual offences including rape. Article 29.5.1 of Bunreacht na hÉireann states that: 'Every international agreement to which the State becomes a party shall be laid before Dáil Éireann'. Yet it now transpires that either an official or an unofficial international Status of Force Agreement (SOFA) has been made with the USA without Dáil Éireann approval, whereby serious crimes committed by US military personnel in Ireland will not be prosecuted in Ireland. The questions that now need urgent answers include: Were the Attorney General and/or the Director of Public Prosecutions consulted or involved in these matters? Under what Irish law or legal process did An Gárda Síochána fail to prosecute this suspect and release him into the custody of a foreign power? What Irish Government ministers approved these matters and why?

No. 162.
Belfast Telegraph **24 Aug 2018**, *Irish Examiner* **25 Aug 2018**
'IRA Song' Inappropriate for Hurlers' Celebration

The winning of the All-Ireland hurling final by the Limerick team was a joyous occasion for all their friends and supporters and for the team themselves. For some, however, it is likely that the occasion was spoiled by repeated singing of a song associated with IRA violence, Sean South of Garryowen. It has been widely reported that the song was sung in the Croke Park dressing room, on the train journey to Limerick, at the Gaelic Grounds in Limerick, and elsewhere. No thought seems to have been given to the feelings of those very many people in all parts of Ireland who have been victims of such violence. In Limerick especially, where Detective Garda Jerry McCabe was murdered by the IRA in 1996, the singing of this song was inappropriate. Lest we forget, in addition to the very many people killed in Northern Ireland during the troubles, several people were also killed in the Republic of Ireland, including Pte Patrick Kelly and Garda Gary Sheehan during the Don Tidey kidnapping in 1983, and a Protestant member of the Oireachtas, Senator Billy Fox shot dead in Co Monahan 1974. Sport in Ireland should be a uniting factor and not a divisive one. The examples of our 32 country women's hockey team, and our Irish rugby teams, are very good examples of this. A huge step forward has been achieved by the Good Friday peace process, but arguably not enough has been done to promote genuine reconciliation. There are many other more appropriate songs that could have been sung to celebrate this victory. There is an isle, and there is an island of Ireland where we all need to learn to live in peace and show respect for each other's traditions.

No. 163.
Irish Examiner 27 August 2018
Facilitating the Killing of Children in the Middle East.

We must all welcome the statement by An Taoiseach Leo Varadkar to Pope Francis that there must be zero tolerance towards those who abuse children and facilitate that abuse. Crimes against children are the most heinous of crimes and sexual abuse of children is particularly serious, but by far the most serious crime against children is the killing of children. Tens of thousands of children have been killed in unjustified wars in the Middle East. Pope Francis has spoken out several times about violence in the Middle East and on 7 July 2018, he referred to the 'murderous indifference' of the great powers towards the violent wars in the Middle East and that children who endure war are its ultimate innocent victims. What is happening in the Middle East is not just 'indifference' by the great powers towards wars but active participation in these wars by the great and not-so-great powers. Successive Irish governments since 2001 have played a shameful role in facilitating these Middle Eastern wars by allowing US military use of Shannon Airport. It's now time for An Taoiseach Leo Varadkar to live up to his fine words, spoken to Pope Francis, that zero tolerance must be applied to those who facilitate the abuse of children. Facilitating the killing of innocent children is occurring almost daily at Shannon Airport. Our Irish Government must stop facilitating the killing of children right now.

No. 164.
Irish Examiner 11 September 2018, *The Irish Times* 17 September 2018

Peaceful Ways to End War Crimes

Brendan Butler (Sept. 8) is critical of the lack of international protest 'as Syria, Russia and Iran are allowed to act with impunity … in their assault against Idlib'. In reality, there has been very widespread international condemnation of Russia, Syria, and Iran for their military actions in Syria, some of it justified. From an international law point of view, Russia and Iran are not in direct breach of the UN charter by providing military support to UN member Syria, but in some cases, breaches of international and humanitarian laws have been committed by these countries when civilians were recklessly killed in air strikes, and human rights abuses were committed by Syrian Government forces. But it must be pointed out that the United States and its allies including NATO have been in very clear breach of the UN Charter by carrying out military attacks and supporting the attempted overthrow of the Syrian Government without UN approval. Tens of thousands of foreign and Syrian fighters associated with ISIS and al-Qaeda have been relocated to Idlib province. They have little prospect of returning to their own countries and many of these fighters are both perpetrators and victims. It's likely that the countries that helped train and finance them always intended to abandon them. In modern wars, innocent civilians, conscripted soldiers, and manipulated fanatics are slaughtered while the major war criminals and state terrorists go free. Similar massacres happened when US-supported forces captured and destroyed

Mosul in Iraq and Raqqa in Syria. Thousands of civilians were killed with very limited outcry in Western media. If humanity is to prevail and survive, we must find peaceful ways of preventing such atrocities and promoting reconciliation when such war crimes have been committed.

No. 165.
Irish Examiner, Irish Independent 14 September 2018
Nuclear Watchdogs are Failing to Bark

A report in *Penarth Daily News* on September 11 has revealed that up to 300,000 tons of nuclear-contaminated mud is being removed from the existing closed Hinkley Point nuclear power stations and is being dumped at the mouth of the Bristol Channel, just a mile offshore from the town of Penarth in Wales. A new nuclear power station is being built at Hinkley Point in Somerset at an estimated cost of over £20 billion sterling. It is being built by French company EDF jointly owned by the French Government and Chinese nuclear energy company CNG. This will be the most expensive power station in the world, and British energy users are likely to be paying for it for generations to come. The hidden costs of nuclear power are the decommissioning costs and the impossible-to-calculate costs of disposing of nuclear waste. Ireland should be worried about these Hinkley Point developments, but official silence is deafening. The majority of Britain's existing and closed nuclear plants, including the Sellafield reprocessing plant, are located on its west coast posing a serious threat to Ireland. The dumping of this contaminated waste mud could further pollute the Irish Sea, and pollution from the new Hinkley Point nuclear power station will add to the nuclear risks to Ireland. It seems that our watchdogs are failing to bark.

No. 166.
Irish Examiner **17 September 2018**
Genuine Reform of Garda Force Needed

Protesters who posted details of Gardai on social media that had nothing to do with inappropriate Garda behaviour or who unjustifiably abused Gardai during the occupation incident in Dublin, have done a disservice to civil liberties, and their actions have played into the hands of those seeking to justify unjustified Garda behaviour. Gardai on public duty should always be identifiable by wearing their Garda numbers and Gardai should be proud to be identified as Gardai. However, we do have serious problems with inappropriate Garda behaviour. A culture of Garda impunity has been encouraged by lack of accountability and inappropriate Garda training. The abuses by the so-called Garda heavy gang in the 1970s was neither the first nor the last example. Very serious, unjustified behaviour by Gardai occurred during the Shell to Sea protests in Co Mayo, yet in many cases only the victims of such abuses were brought before the courts. The Donegal Garda scandal involved wrongful convictions, yet the Morris Tribunal led to very little real accountability. In Co Clare, justifiable peaceful protests against US military use of Shannon Airport have resulted in some abuses by Gardai, but the main problems there have resulted from inactions by Gardai. Since 2001, Gardai at Shannon have consistently failed in their duties to investigate and prevent complicity in war crimes including torture. The fact that the victims of these war crimes are foreigners in faraway places, or Gardai obeying inappropriate orders, in no way justifies such Garda inactions. Genuine reform of An Garda Siochana is urgently needed.

No. 167.
Irish Examiner **24 Sept 2018**
Up to 1,000 Die on Day of Peace

Friday 21 September was International Day of Peace, so was all quiet on the conflict and war fronts? Well not quite, quiet. In Yemen at least fifteen people a day are being killed, not counting those dying from hunger and diseases. In Afghanistan, up to fifty-five people a day are dying in a war that has lasted seventeen years. In South Sudan, the world's newest state, up to 150 people a day have been dying in a civil war. About six million people have died in the Democratic Republic of Congo conflict, in spite of the presence of over 20,000 UN peacekeepers. As many as 1,000 people a day, including on International Day of Peace, are dying due to ongoing conflicts in many countries. The United Nations is not being allowed to carry out its primary responsibility to maintain international peace, partly because at least four of its Security Council permanent members are involved in several of these conflicts, three of them in clear breach of the UN Charter. With about 576 Irish soldiers serving on overseas missions, Ireland would appear to be doing its bit to promote international peace. However, over 500 of these soldiers are serving in Lebanon and in the Israeli-occupied Syrian Golan Heights in questionable peacekeeping missions while there are other conflicts with far greater humanitarian needs. Our Irish Government should be doing far more towards promoting international peace using our unique position as a neutral altruistic state, yet our support for unjustified US wars is helping to kill thousands of innocent people.

No. 168.
Irish Examiner 10 October 2018
Accountability for Economic Crash

On the 10th anniversary of the economic crash, we need to examine who will have paid the greatest price and why. Article 43 Bunreacht na hEIREANN guarantees the right to private property with some limitation in 'the exigencies of the common good.' This limitation has been seriously abused by recent governments. Our politicians and a foreign Troika decided without the approval of Irish citizens that the properties of the citizens would be unjustifiably expropriated to bail out bankrupt banks, not in the interests of the common good, but in the interests of reckless elite individuals, groups, and banks. The banks should have been allowed to go bankrupt and then their remnants taken over and nationalised by the state in 'the exigencies of the common good.' The victims of this abuse are not just this generation of Irish citizens, some of whom were responsible for the crash, but the younger and future generations. The Irish financial crisis was not solved by the bailout, it was postponed by the devious trick of long-term loans, and by selling off property belonging to present and future Irish citizens, without their permission. Yet politicians who made these decisions have repeatedly awarded themselves unjustified remuneration, while at the same time penalising ordinary citizens with austerity measures. The housing and health service crises are part of the price paid by many, and our homes and health are our property. Now we are again experiencing another boom, forgetting that it is our grandchildren that will pay for the crash ten years ago and the crash to come. We urgently need accountability and justice.

No. 169.
Irish Independent 25 October 2018
Zappone Commands the Moral High Ground, Unlike So Many

It was surprising to hear Minister Katherine Zappone say that she was doing what she was doing with regard to the Tuam babies scandal, because it was right. This seems almost unprecedented for a politician in Ireland. Minister Zappone did likewise with regard to problems with Scouting Ireland; she did what was clearly right. We owe her a sincere thanks for doing the right thing, in such matters, rather than opting for a 'pragmatic' or typical 'cute hoor' type of option, that many of our Irish politicians opt for. In our recent budget, it was clear that climate change needed to be seriously addressed yet the cabinet opted for doing virtually nothing significant due to lobbying by vested interests. The greatest environmental scandal in Ireland over the past century has been the peat industry, burning the land from beneath our feet and releasing huge amounts of damaging CO_2 and destroying very valuable carbon storage capacity and our precious environmental wealth. Even now this will be allowed to continue up until 2030. Bridget McCole was treated appallingly by the state for 'pragmatic' reasons and she was just one of many such persons treated with such contempt. Since 2001, our foreign policy ministers and officials have been behaving 'pragmatically' with regard to Irish neutrality and complicity in war crimes in the Middle East. If we had the likes of Katherine Zappone as Minister for Foreign Affairs, then our foreign policy might also be directed to doing what is right because it is right.

Thank you, Katherine Zappone, for doing what is right.

No. 170.
Irish Examiner 13 November 2018
La Francophonie and Cultural Colonialism

In 1939, the Irish Government declared that Ireland would be a neutral state, and in 1949 Ireland became a republic and left the British Commonwealth. These decisions have been supported by the majority of the Irish people. In 1973, we joined the European Union as an organisation of states with supposedly equal status but the EU has been evolving into a super-state with its own army and a two-tier system dominated by Germany and France. However, Fianna Fáil and Fine Gael have been trying to get Ireland ever closer to NATO and an EU Army by joining Partnership for Peace, EU PESCO, and questionable NATO and EU military missions. Now our government is taking us into La Francophonie even though French is spoken by very few Irish people. Brexit is cited as one of the reasons for this bizarre move. La Francophonie is not all it seems to be. In Africa especially, Francophonie has become a form of cultural colonialism used to enhance French neo-colonial interests, frequently enforced by French military interventions.

During the Rwandan genocide in 1994, the French Government provided active military and political support to the genocidal Rwandan Government, before, during, and after the genocide, in an attempt to prevent Rwanda from abandoning La Francophonie and becoming an Anglophone state. Books by credible authors such as Adam LeBor: *A people betrayed,* Linda Melvern - *The Role of the West in Rwanda's*

Genocide, Andrew Wallis: *Silent Accomplice: the Untold Story of France's Role in Rwanda Genocide*, and General Romeo Dallaire: *Shake Hands with the Devil*, document the role of France in the Rwandan Genocide.

Ireland's decision to join La Francophonie is a vain attempt to gain French support within a post-Brexit EU and is a serious mistake and should be reversed, or at least approved by Dáil Éireann.

No. 171.
Irish Examiner November 20, 2018
Media Ignoring Majority Interests

An international peace conference against US/NATO Bases took place in Dublin over the weekend of 16–18 November. It was one of the most significant civil society conferences to be held in Ireland in recent years, yet it was ignored by most of the mainstream Irish media. Good-quality independent and balanced reporting should be the hallmark of all media sources in a democracy, yet several elements in Irish media and our public broadcasting service behave more as if they were a government information service and represent only the interests of the elite sections of our society at the expense of the majority interests of the Irish people. Most of the speakers and over 300 attendees at this conference came from other countries from as far afield as Japan, Australia, and Argentina, and represented an important cross section of international civil society, yet their presence in Ireland was largely ignored by our mainstream media. Little wonder then that people are turning to alternative media sources, especially social media, for their news and information, in spite of the limitations and risks of misinformation on some alternative media. Irish and global society needs reliable, independent, balanced, and truthful media sources, in this time of increasing crises, yet the quality and integrity of our media is deteriorating when we need it most.

No. 172.
Article published in Proceedings of the First International Conference on US/NATO military bases, November 18 2018.
The Role of Individuals in Promoting International Peace and Justice

This paper will emphasise what we as individuals must do to promote peace, including getting rid of foreign military bases, especially US and NATO bases. There is a Just War Theory that suggests that wars can be just and justified. In modern times, with modern weapons of mass destruction, no war can be justified because there is always a peaceful or non-violent alternative, and wars only occur when these alternatives fail to be applied. Some will argue that capital punishment is justified in certain circumstances. Historical experience has shown that a high percentage of those sentenced to death were innocent, and those statistics should mean that capital punishment should be outlawed in all countries, as it is in all European Union countries. However, several EU countries are committing acts of capital punishment by killing thousands of people in air attacks in the unjustified so-called war on terror. The United States has been forced to partly abandon its practice of torturing prisoners of war due to international condemnation, but it has replaced much of its torture program with drone and special forces assassinations, which involve even more serious human rights abuses and gross breaches of international laws. US military bases in the Middle East are used to carry out these illegal targeted assassinations.

Human rights abuses occur primarily because of the deliberate actions of the abusers, and killing people is the ultimate and most serious human rights abuse. But human rights abuses, including mass killings, also occur because of the inactions of those who stand idly by and choose to do nothing. In the past, there was a presumption that good would overcome evil in the longer term, yet others argue that wars, short-term self-interest, greed, and man's innate brutal tendencies, will often overcome our better instincts. World Wars I and II tend to support the power of evil over good, but only if we forget that in the modern media, good news is no news and we are subjected to a barrage of daily bad news. Regardless of such arguments, humanity is now in a new level of crisis. With the advent of weapons of mass destruction, especially nuclear weapons, combined with the ongoing and increasing environmental damage to our living and survival environment, arguments about good and evil are almost irrelevant. The survival of humanity is at stake. If we fail to overcome the destructive forces that are destroying our societies and our living environment then we, as individuals and humanity, are heading towards extinction. Positively promoting peace, protecting life, and opposing war – these are no longer just nice and good ideas, they are essential tools of survival.

In 1914, in spite of a very active peace movement, Europe and the world carelessly and recklessly drifted into the hugely destructive World War I, which arguably did not really end in 1918 – the conflict just paused for two decades and resumed in 1939. A flawed peace agreement is just a temporary ceasefire, without comprehensive reconciliation and atonement by all sides. Humanity is now in my view at a very similar tipping point like 1913, only this time there may be no coming back to peace and normality. World War I was promoted as the 'war to end all wars', and this was very clearly just fake news. However, World War III, if it occurs, may indeed be the war to end all wars, because there may be no one or nothing left at the end of World War III to fight World War IV. Just as World War I was unnecessary and avoidable, and if World War I had been avoided, then World War II could also have been avoided, likewise World War III is avoidable, and the tools for avoiding World War III include actively promoting peace, combined with human ingenuity.

Human ingenuity has given us weapons of mass destruction, destructive neoliberal capitalism, slavery, colonialism, neocolonialism, and racism, all designed to enable the powerful elites in our societies and our countries to achieve a hugely undue share of the world's resources at the expense of the vast majority of humanity. The propaganda we are exposed to in the Western media is far more effective than the propaganda used by Reich Minister of Propaganda, Joseph Goebbels. It extolls the false virtues of warmongers such as John McCain and denigrates peace activists as troublesome utopian unrealistic individuals. We, as peace activists, must use our ingenuity and actively engage in peace propaganda, but unlike Joseph Goebbels and Donald Trump, our peace propaganda must be based on truth, justice, and ingenuity.

Our Western politicians cynically speak of American exceptionalism and values, and European civilisation and values. Yes, the very short American history has been exceptional in all the wrong ways since Amerigo Vespucci brought European invaders, genocide, slavery, and racism to the continent we now call America. European values and so-called civilisation included slavery, genocide, colonialism, and even today, destructive neocolonialism and resource wars.

Human agency – what humans do and don't do – is a matter of what human individuals do or fail to do, as distinct from what large organisations such as governments, states, international organisations such as the UN, or religious groups do. It is individuals within these organisations who take action or fail to take action. It was not the Nazi regime that perpetrated the Holocaust and World War II. The Nazi regime coordinated it but it was tens of thousands or millions of individuals in Germany and in many other European countries that perpetrated these actions, or allowed these actions to happen by failing to take appropriate actions to prevent or stop the Holocaust or World War II. Likewise, if World War III happens, it will be individuals like you and I who either cause it to happen, or who fail by our inactions to prevent it from happening. Far too many are still obeying orders that should never be obeyed. In the past, the Crusades were perpetrated on the peoples of the Middle East by religious and political leaders who abused the powers that they had assumed for themselves, to have their orders obeyed without question. We must use our conscience and intelligence to evaluate the ethics and correctness of all such orders. An example of how this should be applied can be seen in the oath taken by the soldiers of various armies. In most countries, soldiers take an oath to obey all orders from their superiors, on the presumption that their superiors are always correct. The oath taken by Irish soldiers stipulates that they must obey all LAWFUL orders from their superiors. This means that it is unlawful for an Irish soldier to obey an unlawful order, and this is one of the reasons for their very good reputation as United Nations peacekeepers. Oaths of obedience are also taken by many religious orders and, in both cases, this has led to very serious abuses of human rights, including war crimes and abuses of children by clergy.

In 1973–74 I served as a UN peacekeeper in the Middle East in the Sinai Desert at the end of the Yom Kippur War. Like many other peacekeeping soldiers, I was almost killed on a few occasions and eighty-eight Irish soldiers have been killed on UN peacekeeping duties. While such deaths are regrettable, they are justified in the cause of promoting peace, as distinct from waging war. Ireland and the Irish Defence Forces have successfully used Positive Neutrality to promote international peace, and other countries that are now supposedly making peace by making war should follow Ireland's example. Just as the crimes committed in the name of Christianity in the past were an abuse of religion rather than caused by religion, likewise the horrific crimes committed by ISIS and al-Qaeda have been a gross abuse of the Islamic religion. The abuses being committed by Israel against the Palestinian people are also an abuse of the Jewish religion. 'You shall not kill' is also a commandment of the Jewish religion. The same applies to the abuses being committed by members of the majority Buddhist community in Myanmar against the minority Muslim Rohingya community. In all such cases, it is individuals who are committing these crimes, and these crimes are being facilitated by the inactions of many more individuals. The words Yom Kippur stand for A Day of Atonement in the Jewish religion. All religions and all countries should consider introducing days of atonement and genuine acts of atonement, reparation, and reconciliation.

Humanity is now facing a coming together or confluence of crises that could destroy humanity and our living environment on this very vulnerable Planet Earth.

The existing or impending crises in possible order of priority include:

1. The real risk of nuclear war

2. Climate change and catastrophic damage to our environment

3. Unjustified conventional wars causing millions of deaths, infrastructural and environmental damage

4. The resulting refugee and migrant crisis

5. The economic chaos being caused by destructive neoliberal global economic systems

6. Political upheaval across the world.

1. The real risk of nuclear war:

World War I and World War II were dreadful and avoidable catastrophes. However, it was not until the US dropped atomic bombs on Hiroshima and Nagasaki that humanity achieved the capacity to utterly destroy itself and all of its living environment. That risk has not lessened with the end of the Cold War, and it has increased significantly in the past few years with irresponsible leadership in many Western countries. It is not just Donald Trump and Kim Jong-un that we need to worry about. Our neighbours, Britain and France, also have stockpiles of nuclear weapons and probable policies of first use of these nuclear bombs, and the manner in which Russia is being unjustifiably encircled and threatened economically and militarily is a recipe for nuclear disaster.

2. Climate change and catastrophic damage to our environment:

While nuclear war is a possibility, climate change and disastrous damage to our living environment is not only likely it has already occurred and the damage is increasing exponentially. Human ingenuity is capable of reversing most of this damage provided we do not allow it to reach a point of no return, which we are approaching. Small improvements like getting rid of plastic packaging and recycling some materials are no longer adequate. We now need urgent major environmental projects, including banning nuclear power and weapons, ending the use of fossil fuels, restoring our forests in large areas of the planet, cleaning up and protecting our seas and the marine life, and protecting our agricultural lands from soil erosion and from damage by pesticides and herbicides. We have the technology and the resources and the ingenuity, but we need to use them now before it is too late.

3. Unjustified conventional wars causing millions of deaths and infrastructural and environmental damage:

The global Military Industrial Complex (MIC), has grown to be more powerful than even the Government of the United States, and instead of taking its orders and instructions from the various governments, the MIC is dictating foreign and war policies for the benefit of arms industries and the benefit of those who benefit from wars. Neutral countries such as Switzerland, Ireland, Sweden, Finland, and Austria are being threatened if they do not go along with the wishes of the warmongers. NATO's so-called Partnership for Peace, which now includes all these neutral countries, is simply an attempt to drag these countries into the NATO alliance and make us complicit in their war crimes. It is a Partnership for War, not a Partnership for Peace. In each of these countries there are individuals and groups who have vested interests in wars, under the false guise of Humanitarian Intervention, as the people of the former Yugoslavia know to their cost.

The overthrow of the Libyan Government in 2011 is one of the more dreadful examples. The NATO attack on Libya in 2011 launched over 14,000 air attacks on Libya. Nineteen states were involved in this so-called humanitarian operation misusing an unjustified UN Security Council Resolution. These countries included EU states Belgium, Denmark,

France, Italy, Spain, the UK, Bulgaria, Greece, Netherlands, Romania, in all of which capital punishment is outlawed, as well as Canada, Norway, Qatar, the US, Jordan, and the United Arab Emirates. Denmark dropped 107 so-called precision bombs on Libya. Neutral Sweden, not to be denied the opportunity to miss out on demonstrating and selling their fighter jets and weapons, joined in and provided eight fighter jets in support of the NATO mission. Peace-loving Norway dropped nearly 600 bombs on Libya, all of course in the supposed interests of bringing peace, freedom, human rights, and democracy to Libya. We have seen in the meantime how well these spurious objectives have been achieved.

It was not just the fighter pilots who dropped these bombs that were responsible for these war crimes. It was the individual citizens of these countries who failed to prevent their governments from unjustifiably attacking the people of countries such as Libya, Afghanistan, Iraq, Syria, and Yemen. Of course, peaceful neutral Ireland would never participate in such dreadful behaviour, would it? During all these wars since 1999, including the NATO war against Yugoslavia, the neutral Irish Government allowed the US military to use Shannon Airport as a refuelling stop for thousands of US military aircraft, in gross breach of international law on neutrality. Three million armed US troops have travelled through Shannon Airport, and tens of thousands of aircraft associated with the US military have been refuelled at Shannon.

4. The resulting refugee and migrant crisis:

The victims of these wars and economic abuses are fleeing across the Mediterranean, and we are now refusing to pick them up and are letting them drown in large numbers. Those few we do rescue we are now sending back to dreadful concentration camps in Libya, where gross human rights abuses, including slavery and sexual abuse, are rampant, and to other countries that we have already destroyed. We should begin by changing the missions or orders our countries give to our naval services that were initially being used to genuinely rescue these drowning migrants. Now their role has been changed to sinking the smugglers' boats, and transporting those few that we do pick up out of the sea back to Libya. Our European Governments have taken a positive decision to stop rescuing migrants from the Mediterranean and this is not just unethical, it is in clear breach of international law of the sea; it is a crime against humanity. Genuine humanitarian rescue ships are being denied access to ports in the European Union to deliver the migrants they have rescued. This is truly shameful. If the word Ethics means anything, it must mean that we cannot allow thousands of innocent people fleeing from wars, human rights abuses, and gross poverty to drown before our eyes in the Mediterranean. Of course, it is easy to avert our eyes and pretend we don't see them drowning. We can behave like the three monkeys, seeing no evil, hearing no evil, and speaking no evil.

5. The economic chaos being caused by destructive neoliberal global economic systems:

This economic chaos may not seem very real here in prosperous Europe. However, if we step out of the privileged bubbles that we live in and walk through the back streets of Cairo, Jakarta, and Kinshasa, and other even poorer countries, as I have, we realise or should realise that our privileged bubbles are at the expense of these poorer societies. Kinshasa and the Congo are good or dreadful examples. The Congo is probably the richest country in the world from a resources point of view, but its people are among the poorest and the most exploited. It is we Europeans who have exploited and are still exploiting such countries and their peoples. Davos in Switzerland is not just a nice ski resort. It is also where the elite of the world meet each year at the World Economic Forum to plot and ensure that their group remains the elite at the expense of everyone else.

6. Political upheaval across the world:

Political upheaval across the world has resulted in right-wing, left-wing, and religious fundamentalist groups destroying our existing political and social systems. Our political and social systems are not perfect, they never will be, and we must always be working to update and improve our governance systems. However, over the past few years, far from improving our social and governance systems, there has been very significant deterioration and damage to our governance systems. The rule of law at international level has been abandoned. The UN Charter has been virtually torn up. It is no longer dictators such as Saddam Hussein, Muammar Gaddafi, or Idi Amin who are the biggest threat to humanity, but some of the democratically elected leaders in Western countries. These are our democratic countries, and our leaders, and it is our responsibility to hold our leaders to account.

We individuals are almost brainwashed by governments and other large organisations into believing that we individuals are almost powerless to do anything to prevent these organisations, or the individuals who control and benefit from these organisations, from doing what they want to do, regardless of the destruction they are causing. The so-called military industrial complex includes NATO, which is by far its most powerful and most damaging part. A European Union Army officially does not yet exist, but the recent Permanent Structured Cooperation (PESCO) developments are clearly intended to create a real and powerful additional European army. The last thing humanity needs is another large army, to further destroy our environment.

It is vital that we as individuals understand that we are not powerless and that we can and must take action to prevent our world, our civilisation, and our very vulnerable living environment from being destroyed. We can also achieve results at times by inactions – such as refusing to cooperate with the destructive plans of destructive organisations, refusing to serve in unjustified wars, refusing to be the equivalent of the stationmasters who helped by obeying orders to transport millions of people to the Holocaust death camps.

We are here today in a nice relaxed, cordial atmosphere, yet the Barbarians are at the gates. And the Barbarians are not the usual hordes coming from the East wielding swords. Genghis Khan and the Soviet Union no longer exist. Today's Barbarians are coming from the West, coming from within our own democratic countries and wielding so-called smart bombs fired from unmanned drones. We must take urgent action now.

The International Conference Against US/NATO Military Bases in Dublin was supported by a wide range of peace and anti-war organisations. However, the success of this important conference and the prospects for building on this success rests primarily with all the dedicated individuals who organised and participated and networked to make this conference such a huge success.

There are very many reasons why we should oppose military bases, promote peace, and campaign against wars. However, one of the most basic reasons for opposing modern wars is that with modern military weapons and modern methods of making war, especially by the United States and its allies including NATO, tens of thousands of children are recklessly killed in these wars. I am involved in a project called Naming the Children that is attempting to name and commemorate in appropriate ways as many of the children as possible who have been killed or who have died as a result of US-led wars in the Middle East since the first Gulf War in 1991 (www.namingthechildren.com). Our estimate is that up to one million children have died as a result of these wars. Children, by definition, are totally innocent victims of such wars and their deaths are inexcusable, and amount to crimes against humanity.

For many in our privileged Western societies, these dead children are just Collateral Damage, resulting from a so-called War on Terror in faraway places. Far too many consider it none of their business.

I will finish by listing just a small sample of the names of some of these dead children from some of the countries we have so far included in our list. I will begin with those children killed by acts of terror in Western countries, and then include some from the very many more killed by acts of terror, including state and NATO terrorism, across the Middle East and parts of Africa.

In the attack on New York that was wrongfully used to justify the war on terror, one Irish child, Juliana Clifford McCourt, was killed when the plane she was on was crashed into the Twin Towers in New York in an unjustified act of terror. Seven other children were killed in that attack.

— Ireland, New York, 9 Sept 2011, Juliana Clifford McCourt age 4
— France, Nice, 14 July 2016, Léana Sahraoui, age 2
— Germany, Munich, 22 July 2016, Sabina Sulaj, age 14
— Spain, Barcelona, 17th August 2017, Julian Cadman, age 7
— Britain, Manchester, 22nd May 2017, Saffie Rose Roussos, age 8
— Afghanistan, Afghanistan air strike: UN confirms 30 child deaths in April attack 2018
— Yemen, Asma Fahad Ali al Ameri, age 3 months, January 2016
— Syria, Maher al-Tarni, Aleppo, 26 April 2017
— Palestine, 3 August, 2014, Maria Mohammed Abu Jazar, age 2, Rafah, and her twin brother Firas Mohammed Abu Jazar, age 2 Rafah, 3 August, 2014
— Israel, 6 March 2008, Segev Peniel Avihail Hashahar, Jerusalem, age 15. 2,149 Palestinian children and 134 Israeli children have been killed since September 29, 2000
— Pakistan: Maezol Khan F Drone, age 8
— Iraq: As many as 576,000 Iraqi children may have died since the end of the Persian Gulf War because of economic sanctions imposed by the UN Security Council.

US Secretary of State, Madeleine Albright, once asked General Colin Powell, 'What is the point of having such a great army, if we don't use it.' When questioned about the Iraqi sanctions and whether it was worth the deaths of over half a million Iraqi children she replied: 'Yes, it was worth it.'

Let us pause and say a silent prayer for all those children who have died because of these unjustified wars. May they rest in peace, because they certainly were not allowed to live in peace.

The lives of all children are equally precious and we must avoid treating their deaths as just collateral damage. Joseph Stalin is credited with saying that 'one man's death is a tragedy – one million deaths is just a statistic'. He went on to create many such 'statistics'. A Palestinian child is as precious as an Israeli child, or a Syrian child or a Yemeni child or an Irish child.

The just war theory tells us we must wage war with *Jus ad Bellum* and *Jus in Bello*.

With modern powerful conventional weapons and weapons of mass destruction, there is no justification or justice towards making war, and there is no justification or justice in how war is made.

Let us make peace instead.

*Edward Horgan, International Secretary, Irish Peace and Neutrality Alliance

No. 173.
Irish Examiner 23 November 2018.
Ireland Does Little to Help with the Famine in Yemen

In 1847, the Choctaw Indians donated $170 toward famine relief in Ireland. Also, in 1847 Ottoman Sultan Abdülmecid I personally offered £10,000 in aid to Ireland, but British diplomats advised him that it would be offensive to offer more than Queen Victoria, who had only donated £2,000. It was suggested that he should donate £1,000. Genuine humanitarian efforts recognise no ethnic or religious divides. Why then is Ireland doing so little to address the suffering of the Yemeni people who are undergoing a similar famine caused by foreign aggressors? Eighty-five thousand children under five years of age have starved to death in Yemen, yet Ireland and the international community have stood idly by and continue to support oil-rich Saudi Arabia and United Arab Emirates (UAE) who are perpetrating violence and famine on the Yemeni people.

In February this year, the UN Security Council renewed sanctions against Yemen, exacerbating the famine, which is further exacerbated by a blockade enforced by Saudi Arabia and UAR, yet no sanctions have been imposed on the main perpetrators of Saudi Arabia and UAE. The Houthi rebels in Yemen are defending their people against internal corruption and external aggression, yet because they are Shia Muslims, they are being attacked by their more powerful Sunni Muslim neighbours.

The answer as to why the Irish Government is doing so little to help starving Yemeni people is probably that we do a lot of trade with Saudi Arabia and UAE and none with Yemen. Ireland is also complicit in these famine deaths by allowing US military to resupply Saudi munitions through Shannon Airport.

No. 174.
Irish Daily Mail **6 Dec 2018**, *Irish Examiner* **7 Dec 2018**
Why Do Laws Stop People Voting? Votes for Irish Citizens Living Abroad

About half of all countries allow their citizens who live outside their country to vote in national elections, albeit with some restrictions. Most Irish citizens except government employees working abroad are denied this privilege. Proposals to amend the constitution to allow them to vote but only in presidential elections are so inadequate that it would arguably be a waste of public money to bring in such an almost meaningless change, given that our presidency has a mainly ceremonial role. It is essential that all Irish citizens living outside of Ireland should be entitled to vote at least in all Dáil Éireann and European Union elections, otherwise their Irish citizenship is meaningless. My understanding of Bunreacht na hÉireann is that Article 16 does not prohibit Irish citizens living outside the state from voting in Irish elections. It states as follows:

Article 16.1.2.

i. All citizens, and

ii. such other persons in the state as may be determined by law,

without distinction of sex who have reached the age of eighteen years who are not disqualified by law and comply with the provisions of the law relating to elections to Dáil Éireann, shall have the right to vote at an election for members of Dáil Éireann.

It is my view that the qualification or limitation 'in the state' in subparagraph ii above applies only to 'such other persons', for example, British citizens living in the state, and does not apply to 'all citizens' mentioned in subparagraph i above. Therefore, all Irish citizens regardless of where they live, should be entitled to vote in Dáil Éireann elections, unless they are prohibited by law from doing so. If they are prohibited from voting by laws passed by An Oireachtas, then it should only be necessary for An Oireachtas to change the laws to allow all Irish citizens to vote in Dáil elections making a constitutional referendum unnecessary.

We must also ask why our existing laws or regulations prohibit most Irish citizens living outside the state from voting in Irish elections. It may be that Irish politicians have feared retribution or accountability from those hundreds of thousands of Irish citizens who have been forced to emigrate due to failed economic policies of successive Irish Governments.

No. 175.
Irish Examiner 13 Dec 2018
Should Scouting Ireland be Disbanded?

Revelations about child sexual abuse in the Irish scouting movement are truly shocking. 317 alleged victims have come forward and 212 alleged perpetrators identified, and these figures may rise substantially. This is yet another dreadful scandal. It should call into question the continued existence of Scouting Ireland and the broader scouting movement. We should begin by examining the roots of the scouting movement and its original raison d'être. It was founded by Robert Baden Powell, a British colonial army officer who became a British media hero because of his alleged heroic defence of the town of Mafeking during the Boer War. However, his military competence was questioned by his superiors, and he was subsequently removed from active service command. We must question also the wisdom of regimenting young children with all the trappings of military units, including uniforms, flags, insignia, ranks, and blind obedience, when we should be encouraging children to think for themselves and develop their own particular skills, rather than have someone else's skills and ethos imposed on them. There has been no adequate accountability for most of the previous scandals in Ireland, and the taxpayers have been repeatedly forced to pay compensation. Many of the perpetrators escaped punishment because far too many were complicit in cover-ups so many perpetrators had died of old age before their crimes were exposed. The Irish Government and the board of Scouting Ireland should be actively considering disbanding Scouting Ireland both as an exemplary action to prevent further similar abuses and because it has proved to be not fit for purpose.

No. 176.
Irish Independent 26 December 2018
Crises Facing Our World Are the Fault of Humankind, Not God or Religion

Since religion in Ireland and elsewhere has become discredited due to real abuses, it's important not to throw out the morality baby with the religious bathwater. Political systems and democracy are also deteriorating. It is not religion or democracy that causes the problems, but the abuses of religion and democracy. To avoid chaos, humanity needs a well-structured system of morality, even if we were all atheists. Democracy is deteriorating across the world, not just in areas like Turkey, the Middle East, and Africa, but in Western countries including the US, UK, Ireland, and the European Union. Self and national interests have replaced altruism and international cooperation which are vital for the survival of human society. Humanity now faces multiple crises including environmental damage, the risk of nuclear war, ongoing conflicts, and political turmoil that are likely to lead to catastrophic chaos because these crises are not being resolved and are intensifying. Humanitarianism at international level has been corrupted by rendering the United Nations powerless and by the degradation of international laws. Humanitarian intervention has come to mean overthrowing governments and destroying countries in order to more easily steal their resources. It is not God or religions that are causing these problems, it is irresponsible humans. If we destroy this beautiful planet, we do not have the capacity to move to another planet, and even if we had, we would not deserve such a second chance.

No. 177.
The Irish Times **9 January 2019,** *Irish Examiner* **10 January 2019**
Revoking Irish Citizenship

Sir, – Dr Umar Al-Qadri has said 'naturalised Irish citizens who travel abroad to take part in conflict should have their citizenship revoked' (News, January 8). This suggestion is understandable, but it puts the onus on the Irish State to remove their citizenship. It also singles out one particular group who chooses to take a particular side in these conflicts while ignoring many others, including Irish citizens who go abroad to fight in these same conflicts but choose to fight on the other side. We in Ireland should be especially conscious of the blurred distinction between terrorists and freedom fighters. Do we treat a person with a name like Seán Ó Murchú fighting with the Kurdish separatist group in Syria differently from a person with a Muslim name fighting for ISIS? Do we ignore Irish citizens who leave Ireland and join British, French, or US armies? Why is it considered acceptable for some Irish citizens to kill other humans in wars that are very often unjustified, but not okay for other Irish citizens to do likewise? The solution may well be to make a radical change in the Constitution, whereby after a specified date, any Irish citizen who joins any foreign army or armed militia group would automatically lose their

Irish citizenship. If this were enacted, then the revoking of their Irish citizenship would be implemented by the person themselves on their joining a foreign army or militia. It would also have the beneficial results of preventing neutral Irish citizens from unjustified killing of our fellow humans. This prohibition should also apply to Irish citizens joining any NATO or European Union army. The only exceptions should be genuine United Nations peacekeeping. – Yours, etc,

No. 178.
Irish Daily Mail 11 January 2019
Irish Army Ranger Wing is Likely to be Sent to Mali

An Taoiseach Leo Varadkar, while on a visit to Mali, has indicated that the Irish Army Ranger Wing is likely to be sent to Mali in Africa as part of an EU military mission. It has been suggested that our government is seeking the support of Mali for Ireland's bid to join the UN Security Council, and is likely also to be seeking French Government support. Irish Defence Forces involvement in foreign military missions should be confined to genuine UN peacekeeping missions and should be strictly in the humanitarian interests of the people suffering from serious conflicts and not in Irish national interests or in the broader European interests. What has been happening in Mali and other former French colonies in Africa are not straightforward anti-terrorist situations but a complex series of civil wars that ISIS and others, including France, have taken advantage of. By supporting compliant undemocratic regimes, France has ensured that virtually all its former colonies are held in neo-colonial circumstances for the exploitation of these valuable resources in 'French national interests'. Also, the Irish Army Ranger Wing is an elite special forces unit and is not trained or organised for peacekeeping. Their proposed deployment to Mali may be an attempt to justify their continued existence because An Garda Siochana has consistently failed to allow the Ranger Wing to have any real role in internal security or anti-terrorist type operations in Ireland. This issue should be resolved in Ireland and not in Mali and the Irish Defence Forces should not be used to promote European neo-colonial interests.

No. 179.

Irish Examiner 29 January, *The Irish Times* 30 January 2019

Intervention by US Has Left Nations in Chaos

The UN Charter prohibits wars of aggression, and overthrowing sovereign governments yet since 2001, the US and NATO have waged illegal wars of aggression, and overthrown the governments of Afghanistan, Iraq, and Libya, assisted the overthrow of governments in Egypt and Ukraine, and tried to overthrow the government of Syria. Far from bringing freedom and democracy to these countries, US intervention left all of them in chaos. We are now witnessing the attempted overthrow of the elected government of Venezuela, which has the world's largest oil reserves, led by the USA and supported by EU members Germany, France, Spain, and Britain, who have announced that they will recognise Juan Guaido as 'Interim President' if elections are not held within eight days, which is administratively impossible. When Nicolas Maduro was elected president in May 2018, the main opposition Democratic Unity coalition, boycotted the election, thus virtually guaranteeing that Maduro would be the democratically elected president. In any state, the position of 'interim president' can only exist if the incumbent either dies or is removed, neither of which has occurred in Venezuela. Even the CIA World Factbook states that President Nicolas Maduro is both chief of state and head of government, clearly indicating that Venezuela has a presidential rather than a parliamentary type of government, and that the Executive Vice President is Delcy RODRIGUEZ Gomez who should be the obvious replacement if President Maduro is removed. Since Juan Guaido was not even a candidate in the 2018 elections, his claim to be the 'Interim President' is spurious. An Irish Government statement that 'Ireland has consistently supported the democratically elected National Assembly of which Mr Guaido is President', ignores the fact that the system of government in Venezuela is a French-type Presidential system. The Irish Government should not be interfering in the sovereign affairs of other countries in such a manner.

No. 180.
Irish Independent **2 February 2019**
It is Time to Suspend Work on Children's Hospital
The exorbitant cost overruns in the children's hospital must not be allowed to become the straw that broke our dysfunctional health service. We do need a functioning children's hospital but not one costing up to two billion euro. Many of our best nurses have been forced to emigrate, and those nurses now justifiably on strike are being threatened with penal sanctions, while our politicians have no difficulty awarding themselves outrageous salaries, expenses, and pension pots. This is just the latest in a litany of such scandals involving our public services, including the Gardai, public/private infrastructural projects and our natural resources including oil, gas, and fisheries. Topping it all was the disastrous economic crash due primarily to corrupt and reckless bankers, builders, and developers, which Irish taxpayers were forced to bail out by our incompetent politicians. We have unjustifiably mortgaged future generations without their permission and this latest scandal will only add to this. Work on the children's hospital should be suspended. The board members who were supposed to be managing this project should be dismissed. Some persons must have been set to gain substantially unjustified amounts from these overruns. Enough is enough. It is time to deal with this scandal in an exemplary manner. In the short term, additional resources should be given to the existing children's hospitals and a proper investigation carried out by a non-Irish investigation team. In the long-term interests of all the Irish people, especially children, this latest scandal must be used to initiate real reform of the Irish health system and those responsible must be held accountable.

No. 181.
Irish Examiner **6 Feb 2019**
Punish Corruption in the Here and Now
What if there is no heaven or hell to reward the just, and punish those who commit heinous crimes? An increasing percentage of educated people are now very sceptical about heaven and hell and the likelihood of an afterlife.

Globally, corrupt politicians, dictators, and corporate executives are usually allowed to live out their lives in relative luxury even after being exposed. Cambodian genocide perpetrator Pol Pot is just one such example. After being overthrown in 1978, he continued to be recognised by the UN as Cambodian leader and was supported by the USA, Britain, and others, and died of old age three decades later surrounded by his family. Perpetrators of disastrous wars in the Middle East are further examples. In Ireland, corrupt and incompetent politicians and high-level public servants are allowed to retire with lavish pensions, and some are given additional lucrative public service appointments. Some of our most incompetent former politicians are given platforms in our media as if they were competent or suitable experts. Too many shrug off this reality on the basis that hopefully they will encounter justice in the next life. It's time to insist on justice and accountability in this life here on Planet Earth and if further accountability and justice can also be achieved in the next life, then that's all the better. Let the powers-that-be on the other side sort out any issues of double-jeopardy! Imagine there's no heaven.

No. 182.
Irish Examiner 20 February 2019
Ireland Complicit in Deaths of Yemeni Kids

There is supposed to be a ceasefire in Yemen but each day children are still dying, by bombing, gunfire, disease, and starvation. According to UN sources, at least 85,000 children have died. Like the Syrian conflict, there are many internal and external factions involved but the main culprits include Saudi Arabia and the United Arab Emirates supported by armaments supplied by the US, UK, France, and Germany. They support the UN-recognised Yemeni government that is not supported by the vast majority of Yemeni people. While Iran is accused of supporting the Houthi rebels, any such support is small for geographical and logistical reasons. The UAE is reported to be using mercenaries to carry out assassinations of politicians and Yemeni tribal and religious leaders, while the US has been carrying out assassinations by special forces and drone attacks from a US base called Camp Lemonier in Djibouti. On the 4th and 5th of this month, an aircraft on contract to the US military was refuelled at Shannon Airport on its way to and from the US to Camp Lemonier in Djibouti. In response to written questions by Clare Daly TD, our Minister for Transport confirmed that: 'An exemption for the carriage of munitions of war under the Air Navigation (Carriage of Munitions of War, Weapons and Dangerous Goods) Orders, 1973 and 1989, was sought and granted for this flight'. Our Minister for Foreign Affairs gave the following Orwellian reply. 'Consistent with our stated policy, my department recommends against the carriage of munitions, with exceptions made for unloaded personal weapons or those intended for international crisis management and peace support operations. Regarding the civil aircraft detailed in this instance, my department was asked for and duly provided its observations in accordance with that policy.' The US-supported war in Yemen is causing an international crisis rather than managing one, and it most certainly is not a 'peace support operation'. Ireland is thereby complicit in the deaths of innocent Yemeni children.

No. 183.
The Irish Times 23 March 2019, *Irish Examiner* 28 March 2019
Irish Troops Need to Stay Out of the Golan Heights

Sir, – US President Donald Trump has reached a new low in disregarding international laws by calling for recognition of Israeli annexation of the Syrian Golan Heights. Irish soldiers have been serving on the Golan Heights for over four years. It was a serious mistake to send them there in the first instance, and their presence there has little to do with peacekeeping and serves mainly to protect Israeli illegal annexation and Israel's attempt to acquire Syrian oil resources on the Golan Heights. All Irish troops should be withdrawn from the Golan Heights immediately and the replacement contingent of Irish troops that are scheduled to arrive on the Golan Heights in the near future should remain in Ireland and possibly be sent instead to other conflict areas where genuine peacekeeping is urgently required, such as the Democratic Republic of Congo, or South Sudan. – Yours, etc,

Comment: My letter below published in the Irish Examiner on 5 April 2019 was in response to the Irish Examiner Editorial on 1 April 2019 which concluded that Irish neutrality looks ever more like an indulgence than a noble principle.

No. 184.
Irish Examiner 5 April, 2019
Reader's Blog: Neutrality Has Never Been More Important

Humanity needed an effective UN to create international peace, but it has failed to achieve this vital objective because it has not been allowed to by its five controlling veto-wielding powers, three of whom, the US, UK, and France are also NATO powers.

Perhaps your editorial (April 1) on NATO's 70th anniversary was intended as an April Fool joke, but one should not play such games when so many peoples' lives are at stake. You describe the UN, EU, and NATO as three great alliances. Humanity needed an effective UN to create international peace, but it has failed to achieve this vital objective because it has not been allowed to by its five controlling veto-wielding powers, three of whom, the US, UK, and France are also NATO powers. The EU began as a great project. It did play an important role in maintaining peace in Western Europe. However, since then, the EU is evolving into a militarised super-state, intent on using its military power to promote European interests and exploit the resources of weaker states. The three-legged stool you refer to has one strong military NATO leg, one flawed EU leg that seeks to become another military leg, and one broken UN leg. Putting these three organisations or legs together to form a security stool for humanity makes no sense. NATO could be said to have given some protection to Western Europe during the Cold War, if it were not for the reality that any such protection was compromised by its MAD (mutually assured destruction) nuclear weapons stockpiles and strategy. NATO's actions since the end of the Cold War, by waging wars of aggression contrary to the UN Charter in Serbia, Afghanistan, Iraq, Libya, and Syria, have stripped the UN of its capacity to maintain international peace. Irish neutrality is dismissed as looking 'ever more like an indulgence than a noble principle'. Eighty-eight Irish soldiers gave their lives, not fighting with NATO, but bravely endeavouring to maintain international peace. Their sacrifice was not 'an indulgence' or part of 'a dishonest evasion'. It was an essential part of positive Irish neutrality. Our altruistic foreign policy helped send many thousands of Irish volunteers overseas to provide genuine humanitarian assistance to our fellow humans who were most in need. You are correct when you say that 'times – and the threats we face – have changed'. The threats to Ireland and to humanity today include uncontrolled wars of aggression and resources by the US and NATO, environmental damage and climate change accelerated by militarism and destructive neoliberal capitalism, and the erosion of genuine democracy and human rights across the world. Irish positive neutrality was never more important for Ireland and for humanity.

No. 185.

The Irish Times 13 April 2019
Julian Assange Facing Conspiracy Charges

Sir, – British Foreign Secretary Jeremy Hunt said that 'Assange is no hero' and 'No one is above the law'. He is wrong on both counts. Julian Assange is a hero. He may not be a perfect person, and may even be flawed in several respects, but his contribution to human rights, transparency, and exposing the truth have been immense (Front page, April 12). It is worth citing the First Amendment of the US Constitution, passed in 1791. 'Congress shall make no law . . . abridging the freedom of speech, or of the press; . . .'. Assange, using freedom of speech and access to various press and media, has made a huge contribution to exposing the truth concerning very serious war crimes by US forces in Afghanistan and Iraq, and even on issues such as CIA use of Shannon Airport. His arrest in London on April 11 is more likely to damage the reputation of the US, UK, and Ecuadorean governments than to enhance the rule of law as Jeremy Hunt implies when he falsely claims that 'No one is above the law.' The wars of aggression waged by the US and its allies in the Middle East, and especially the conflict in Syria (in which four permanent members of the UN Security Council, the US, UK, France, and Russia, participated without UN Security Council approval in breach of the UN Charter) clearly show that these four countries and their political leaders are above the rule of international law; and in the cases of the US and UK in particular have been in gross breach of the rule of international laws. Assange is being punished for being a genuine whistleblower and for exposing these breaches of the rule of law. Humanity urgently needs more courageous whistleblowers like Assange and less cowardly politicians who enable war crimes. – Yours, etc,

No. 186.
Irish Examiner **27 May 2019**
We Are All Complicit in US Aggression

Some will argue that we should welcome the visit to Ireland by US President Trump in Ireland's national interests. However, his behaviour as president is doing huge damage to humanity. Given that the USA is primarily a nation of migrants that treated its indigenous population appallingly, his attitude and treatment of migrants, especially Muslim migrants, is unacceptable, as is his attitude towards women and towards the gay community. His greatest danger to humanity arises from two closely related areas: climate change denial and wanton destruction of our living environment on the one hand, and unjustified wars of aggression for reasons of theft of other countries' resources, on the other hand. Oil-rich Venezuela and Iran are the most recent targets. The US military has become the world's greatest destroyer of our environment, in addition to using up a huge proportion of scarce resources. He has approved the use of torture in contravention of international law, and he and the US Government have abused so many other aspects of international law, including the UN Charter, that makes the US an outlaw state, albeit the most powerful state in the world. US military use of Shannon Airport, approved by successive

Irish Governments, makes all Irish citizens complicit in US wars of aggression that have caused the deaths and catastrophic injuries to millions of people, especially children, in the Middle East. No amount of jobs at Shannon or Doonbeg can justify this complicity. We must protest against President Trump's visit and we must end US military use of Shannon Airport.

No. 187.
The Irish Times, Irish Daily Mail 18 June 2019
Irish Troops and a War in Mali

Sir, – Ruadhán Mac Cormaic raises important questions regarding where Irish soldiers should be sent on overseas missions ('Ireland has quietly joined a dangerous war', Opinion & Analysis, June 15).

We are a small neutral country with a small army. While this is appropriate to our security and economic priorities, our neutral status and our Defence Forces' performance on genuine UN peacekeeping missions have enabled Ireland to achieve exceptional results towards enhancing international peace, promoting sustainable development, and genuine humanitarianism. In recent decades, these achievements have been eroded by our government sending Irish soldiers on inappropriate overseas missions with NATO and the European Union, and even on some inappropriate UN missions such as UNDOF on the Syrian Golan Heights, protecting illegal Israeli annexation.

We need to focus our limited peacekeeping and humanitarian resources towards those humanitarian crises of greatest need.

A neutral country should not be intervening in the civil war in Mali.

But this is not just a civil war. France has been the worst of the former colonial powers in its failure to allow its colonies to develop genuine freedom and democracy and is engaged in neo-colonial exploitation.

The Irish Defence Forces should be confined to genuine peacekeeping, and only in very exceptional circumstances should they become involved in peace enforcement.

The primary purpose of the Army Ranger Wing is internal security within Ireland. They should not be used to support French national interests towards exploiting African people. If Irish soldiers are killed on such missions, their deaths will not have been justified. – Yours, etc,

No. 188.

Irish Examiner 20 July 2019

Our Defence Forces Need to be Treated with More Respect

In recent times, our Irish Defence Forces have been treated with serious neglect bordering on irresponsibility by the Irish Government. This happened previously after World War II, and as a result, when Irish soldiers were sent to the Congo in 1960, several soldiers died due to inadequate equipment and training. While some improvements were achieved, when the conflict in Northern Ireland erupted, the Defence Forces transport fleet was so unreliable that it took some units weeks to deploy to border areas. Now this is all happening again at a time when Brexit could increase security needs, and international terrorism could bring serious security threats due to US military use of Shannon Airport. While good equipment and training are necessary, good morale and conditions for our soldiers are far more important. While the Irish Defence Forces active numbers have been reduced to below 8,800, the Department of Defence has well over 300 civilians not only duplicating many of the responsibilities of serving army officers, but also exercising a stranglehold over most aspects of military management regardless of their lack of military knowledge.

Ireland does not have an army and should never need an army unless we plan to invade some other territory. What we should have is an adequate Defence Force capable of ensuring the sovereignty of Irish people and Irish territory. The present strength, equipment, and morale of the Irish Defence Forces falls so far short of this vital requirement that our government leaders could be accused of treasonous behaviour. Ireland does not need expensive squadrons of fighter aircraft and battle tanks to defend its sovereignty. We have never had the capacity to defend Ireland by conventional military means and never will have. The only way Ireland can be defended is by actively planning, training, and equipping our Defence Forces for guerrilla warfare, which is how we got our independence. Our neutrality and island geography are vital parts of this defence. This requires a well-resourced volunteer Permanent Defence Force, backed up by equally well-resourced Reserve Defence Forces and Civil Defence organisation. Good morale and working conditions are vital towards achieving this, and these three defence elements can also be tasked to do many other useful services including UN peacekeeping, as hopefully they will never be required to defend our sovereignty, which was achieved at a huge cost.

No. 189.

Irish Independent 24 July 2019
When Will State Take Some of the Blame for America's Wars?

One of the realities of war crimes trials is the unjustified impunity for some and justified imprisonment for others. Radovan Karadžić and Ratko Mladić were justifiably convicted for Bosnian war crimes.

The Dutch Supreme Court has ruled the Dutch state bears 10 per cent responsibility for the failure of its military peacekeepers to protect Srebrenica Muslims towards whom they had a duty of care (Irish Independent, July 20). Why have we not heard similar levels of responsibility being applied to the higher UN echelons and the five permanent members of the UN Security Council?

No US, British, French, Russian, or Chinese generals or politicians have ever been convicted of war crimes. The absolute power they gave unto themselves when they drafted the UN charter gives them immunity and impunity to abuse power absolutely.

Just as Bosnian Serb leaders bear the major share of responsibility for atrocities committed in the Bosnian War, and Dutch peacekeepers a minor share, the United States now bears a large share of responsibility for the carnage and infrastructural damage that has occurred due to unjustified wars in the Middle East.

However, we must not overlook the significant minor share of responsibility that rests with countries and their political leaders who actively assisted these US wars.

When will we see the Irish Supreme Court apportion a just percentage of responsibility and reparations due to the victims of wars in the Middle East that were facilitated by US military use of Shannon Airport?

No. 190.
Irish Independent 1 September 2019
Solving the Beef Farming Crisis

Sir - Coming from a farming background, I understand and empathise with the present plight of Irish beef farmers.

There seems to be no easy solution to the crisis they are facing.

Dairy farmers had similar problems in the past, so they opted into the cooperative movement and set up cooperative creameries and achieved ownership of the processing stage of their business.

Perhaps the long-term solution to the beef farmers' crisis is for beef farmers to set up cooperative meat processing plants and they should be supported in this by all the farming organisations.

The beef barons will always maximise their profit, so the beef farmers need to become their own beef barons and cut out the middlemen.

No. 191.
Irish Examiner 5 October 2019, *Limerick Leader* 12 October 2019.
The Celtic Interconnector with France Connects to Nuclear Energy

The Celtic Interconnector, involving a one-billion-euro electricity interconnector between Ireland and France, seems like a great idea, and is described by Minister Richard Bruton as a reliable source of green renewable energy. Likewise, the construction of a large natural gas storage and processing plant at Ballylongford on the Shannon Estuary is being hailed as beneficial to Ireland's long-term energy needs. However, we need to examine such projects more closely. About 75 per cent of French electrical energy comes from nuclear power stations. France gets most of the uranium for its nuclear power stations from its former colony Niger, which has never managed to achieve full independence from its former coloniser. The people of Ireland rejected nuclear power in the 1970s, so why have we not been consulted about this major decision to import energy from France that is mainly produced by nuclear power? The proposed gas plant on the Shannon Estuary will be supplied with gas from fracking gas wells in the United States, which will then be transported in ships across the Atlantic. Ireland has banned fracking gas exploration in Ireland for very valid environmental reasons, yet our government thinks it is OK to import fracking gas from the US disregarding the huge environmental damage being caused by fracking in the US.

Such short-term poorly considered national interests should not be pursued at the expense of long-term serious damage to our global environment.

No. 192.
Irish Daily Mail, Irish Examiner 16 October 2019
President is Right to Speak Truth to Power

President Michael D. Higgins was speaking truth to abuse of power when he criticised the Turkish military intervention in Syria: 'I am appalled by any possibility of coercion or forced returns of refugees and underline in the strongest terms that any attempt at demographic change is not acceptable.' Civilians have already been killed and there are reports of Kurdish prisoners being executed. This military action by Turkey is in clear breach of the UN Charter, but Turkey is not alone in breaching international laws.

While the US has been criticised for betraying the Kurdish people, of far more importance is the fact that the US and its allies, especially EU members Britain and France, have been waging wars of aggression not only in Syria, but also in Afghanistan, Iraq, and Libya, all in contravention of UN Charter Article 2.4 which states: 'All Members shall refrain in their international relations from the threat or use of force against the territorial integrity or political independence of any state …'. They are also in contravention of Nuremberg Principle VI 'The crimes hereinafter set out are punishable as crimes under international law: (a) Crimes against peace: (i) Planning, preparation, initiation or waging of a war of aggression…'. The US, Britain, and France, as permanent members of the UN Security Council, have a special responsibility to uphold international laws, yet they are abusing their powers of veto so as to enable them to ignore and abuse the rule of international law.

The people of the Middle East, and the people of Syria especially have suffered far too much. It's time to stop making war and make peace instead.

No. 193.
Irish Daily Mail 23 October 2019
Tough Laws Needed

Many of our politicians seem to think that abusing the voting system in Dáil Éireann is not an important issue. The Electoral Act 1992, lists a wide range of electoral offences, including impersonation for which Irish citizens may be prosecuted in relation to electing TDs to Dáil Éireann, and the Penalties under Section 157 may include 'on conviction on indictment to a fine not exceeding £2,500 or, at the discretion of the court, to imprisonment for a period not exceeding two years or to both such fine and such imprisonment'. While these are serious offences against democracy, one citizen from an electorate of several million has little capacity to alter the election results. In representative democracy, the citizens elect TDs to the very important task of making legislation on their behalf, which is the very foundation of the rule law. Each TD so elected may then represent up to 10,000 or more voters when voting in Dáil legislation votes. This important task is therefore arguably up to 10,000 times more important than a citizen voting in a polling station. Yet there seems to be no equivalent legislation or penalties for Dáil deputies impersonating or otherwise abusing the Dáil legislation voting system. Such legislation, backed up by appropriate penalties is urgently needed.

No. 194.

The Irish Times 29 October 2019
Rescuing Refugees in the Mediterranean

Sir, – On October 24, 2019, our European Parliament voted against improving search and rescue for refugees in the Mediterranean. A collection of far-right and mainstream conservative parties including four Fine Gael MEPs defeated the plan to pressure member states to step up their efforts and comply with their duties under the UN Convention on the Law of the Sea 1982, Article 98.

'Duty to render assistance: 1. Every State shall require the master of a ship flying its flag, in so far as he can do so without serious danger to the ship, the crew or the passengers: to render assistance to any person found at sea in danger of being lost; to proceed with all possible speed to the rescue of persons in distress, if informed of their need of assistance, in so far as such action may reasonably be expected of him;

'2. Every coastal State shall promote the establishment, operation and maintenance of an adequate and effective search and rescue service regarding safety on and over the sea and, where circumstances so require, by way of mutual regional arrangements cooperate with neighbouring States for this purpose.'

According to the UN International Organization for Migration, about 18,000 people have died in the Mediterranean since 2014. Many more will die because of this failure by the EU MEPs, and EU states, including Ireland, to comply with their humanitarian and international law obligations. – Yours, etc,

No. 195.
Irish Examiner 9 November 2019
Europe's Vision Includes War

German Foreign Minister Heiko Maas has written that 'Europe must fight to preserve the international order, and become the heart of an alliance for multilateralism'. History shows that visions for Europe envisioned by past European leaders were flawed and some were disastrous. Mr Maas excludes Russia from his vision for Europe. Yet it was Russia/USSR that defeated the WWII German fascist vision for Europe at enormous cost to the Russian people.

He acknowledges Gorbachev's role in the peaceful transition from the Cold War but fails to mention the betrayal of promises that NATO would not expand into Eastern Europe. It was the threat of further NATO expansion that precipitated the crises in Georgia and Ukraine. The Iron Curtain removed from Germany in 1989 has been transferred to Russia's borders.

Maas tells us 'we must do more to defuse the conflicts in the Donbass, Syria and Libya'. He ignores the role that EU states including Germany are still playing in these conflicts as well as in Afghanistan, Iraq, and Yemen, millions of whose people have been killed, injured, and forced to flee as refugees because far from defusing these conflicts, EU states and NATO helped to ignite them.

He says: 'We need a genuine European Defence union alongside NATO that is able to act independently where necessary.' That means we will have two large armies in Europe focused primarily on a non-existing threat from Russia, since an expansionist USSR no longer exists. The victims of NATO bombs in the Balkans, North Africa, and the Middle East know what NATO's ability 'to act independently' means. It means waging wars of aggression in breach of existing international laws including the UN charter, and protecting European interests means using force to gain access to an undue share of the world's limited resources.

The United Nations gets no mention in Maas's vision for Europe. The UN Charter would be an inconvenience for such a vision.

No. 196.
Irish Examiner 22 November 2019
Concerned at Fracking Extremists

David Nabhan's article (19 November) 'Calls to end fracking put our elderly population in jeopardy' beggars belief unless it is part of a concerted lobbying effort by the oil and gas industries. He raises the spectre of pensioners dying of hypothermia unless we import and drill for fracking gas. In an article in the Times of Israel he uses similar language 'Self-styled environmental activists, ... said "no" in 2014 to a hydraulic fracking pilot project in the Adullam region between Tel Aviv and Jerusalem. They frowned in 2015 at petitions by Afek Oil and Gas to extract vital petroleum and methane from the Golan Heights.' He fails to mention that Israeli extraction of oil and gas from the Syrian Golan Heights is a breach of international law. Large chunks of his *Irish Examiner* article are copied from his *Israeli Times* article. 'Every living thing requires fixed nitrates since the double-helices of the DNA in our chromosomes can't be constructed without nitrogenous bases' etc. He is also described as an expert on earthquakes and seismic forecasting. He criticises the UK Government decision that fracking will no longer be allowed at the Cuadrilla fracturing site at Preston, but fails to reveal that this decision was taken 'because of new scientific analysis' including multiple earth tremors caused by fracking.

He outrageously tries to link the Irish famine 'in the middle of the 1800s' in support of his pro-fracking arguments. 'Those calling for an end to everything – cars, meat, oil, aviation, coal, plastic, fracking – are naively appealing for no people as well.' He labels those opposed to fracking gas and burning of fossil fuels as 'eco-extremists' but the tone and content of his articles indicate it may be the fracking extremists we need to be far more concerned about.

No. 197.
The Irish Times 26 November 2019
By Our Silence And Inaction, We Are Complicit

The Irish Times is to be commended for publishing the leaked documents on the treatment of Uighur people detained in camps in Xinjiang in China ('More than a million people detained in camps in China', Colm Keena, November 25). It is vital that all such abuses be exposed. The Chinese Government may justify its actions as necessary for preventing terrorism.

Terrorism is best prevented by the proper application of the rule of law towards those accused of terrorism, combined with respect for the human rights of all those hundreds of thousands of Uighur people reported as being held in detention camps.

This unacceptable pattern of human rights abuses on the pretext of prevention of terrorism is not confined to China.

The United States and its allies have been using the so-called war on terrorism to wreak havoc and human rights abuses across the Middle East since 9/11, the scale of which far exceeds what is happening in Xinjiang, although this in no way justifies or mitigates the abuses by Chinese authorities.

A credible report by the Watson Institute, Brown University estimates that several million people have died as a result of these US-led wars, yet criticism of these abuses has been far too muted in our Western media and governments.

The United Nations, which should be taking action against these abuses, is prevented from doing so by its flawed charter. The UN Charter prevents the UN from interfering within states and allows its five UN Security Council permanent members to commit crimes against humanity with impunity by misuse of their powers of veto over the UN.

The Irish Government should not remain silent on all these abuses. By our silence and inaction, we are complicit.

No. 198.
Irish Examiner, Irish Daily Mail 21 January 2020
Parties of Law and Order?

Fianna Fáil and Fine Gael are portraying themselves as parties of law and order. Fianna Fáil are recommending a change in legislation so that the opinion of a Chief Superintendent should be accepted as evidence that a person is a member of a criminal gang. This has implications for civil liberties and for justice. Fine Gael are claiming that Sinn Féin are not suitable to be in government because they allege that Sinn Féin takes their orders from the IRA. Yet both Fianna Fáil and Fine Gael originated from backgrounds of violent conflict and their predecessors were the IRA. Sinn Féin have embraced the peace process in Northern Ireland and are supportive of international peace. The law and order claims of Fianna Fáil and Fine Gael do not appear to extend to respecting international laws due to their supporting US wars of aggression by continuing to allow the US military to use Shannon Airport. It can also be argued that they take orders from their neoliberal bosses in Washington and Brussels, sometimes to the detriment of Irish citizens from whom they should be taking orders.

Justice and the rule of law at national and international levels are more important now than they ever were, and should not be misused as political footballs.

No. 199.
Irish Examiner **2 March 2020**
Coronavirus Threat at Shannon Airport

Coronavirus is now in several Middle East countries including Iran, Syria, Iraq, Kuwait, several Balkan countries and in Italy, Germany, South Korea, Japan, and the US itself. The United States military has multiple bases in most of these countries and has imposed severe sanctions on some of them, such as Syria and Iran, as a result of which they are incapable of controlling the spread of the virus. Air travel is one of the ways this deadly virus is being spread, as demonstrated by confirmed cases having arrived at Dublin Airport. While the US has cancelled military exercises in South Korea, they have not cancelled larger NATO exercises in Europe, and there has been no let-up on US military use of Shannon Airport. At 6 p.m. on Friday 28 February, there were three aircraft transporting US troops to Kuwait being refuelled at Shannon Airport. These three aircraft returned to Shannon Airport for refuelling on Saturday 29 February, most likely transporting US soldiers returning from various countries in the Middle East. These soldiers enter the terminal building, mingle with other civilian passengers, and use the duty-free, restaurants, and toilets. This poses a severe and unnecessary danger of spreading the coronavirus into Ireland. The US military should never have been allowed to transit through Shannon Airport on their way to war zones. The risk of spreading coronavirus is yet another reason for ending US military use of Shannon.

No. 200.
Sunday Independent **8 March 2020**
International Women's Day?

Sir - Today, March 8, is the United Nations' designated International Women's Day.

We should ask whether this is just pointless tokenism, given how relatively little progress has been made towards genuine equality for women internationally and even in Ireland.

Internationally, we have seen the US and NATO wage wars of aggression across the Middle East and North Africa using bogus humanitarian excuses, including liberation and equality for women.

The US has just signed a peace deal with the Taliban, who are now likely to regain power in Afghanistan after almost twenty years of war, in which women and children have suffered catastrophically.

Have the women of Libya been liberated by the NATO overthrow of Gaddafi? Have the women of Iraq or Syria been liberated by the UN, or by the UN's most powerful members?

Or has the UN stood idly and powerlessly by as its most powerful member states wage wars in contravention of the UN Charter?

In Ireland, some equality has been achieved, but not nearly enough, especially in areas such as equality of earnings, the numbers of women in politics, and especially the almost total exclusion of women from the leadership of the Catholic Church. It's time to stop this tokenism and create real equality for all.

It's especially long past time to end unjustified wars where women and children are by far the most victimised.

No. 201.

Irish Independent 4 April 2020
Us Military Should Not Be Using Shannon Airport

Dr Paddy Mallon, UCD professor of microbial diseases and leading infectious disease expert, has called on the government to consider closing Irish borders to slow the spread of coronavirus. Dr Mallon stated: 'We should be looking seriously over the next week at protecting our borders and stopping new infections coming in because it will give us the ability to control the infections that we have.' Italian supporters for the Ireland/Italy rugby match and the Cheltenham festival were missed opportunities to prevent the importation and spread of the Coronavirus. Even though most

Irish citizens except essential services are now on virtual lockdown, and US President Trump announced severe restrictions on US military travel within the US and overseas, several aircraft carrying US soldiers are being allowed to land at Shannon Airport on a daily basis, with the approval of Irish Minister for Transport. The US Embassy has stated that US soldiers on these flights are now prohibited from entering the Shannon Airport terminal building 'except in certain circumstances', but these circumstances are not explained. Several of these aircraft have had long stopovers at Shannon in excess of twelve hours, for crew resting and other purposes. These crew members are most likely entering the terminal building and staying in local hotels. All such US military traffic through Shannon Airport should be prohibited immediately in the interest of public health.

No. 202.

Sunday Independent 12 April 2020, *Irish Examiner* 10 April 2020

Need to Question Draconian Decisions

While Ireland is justifiably on partial lockdown, it is important to question the effectiveness and effects of the draconian decisions being taken. Restricting people, except essential workers, to within two kilometres of their homes is justified, but this is not being applied to people entering Ireland through air and ferry ports. Several ferries are arriving at Dublin each day, and while this is necessary for cargo purposes, passengers arriving from the UK especially should be restricted due to the worsening COVID-19 situation there. Ryanair and Aer Lingus are still bringing in passengers from London, as well as from countries in Europe such as France and Poland. Any passengers arriving from these countries should be obliged to self-isolate and their travel around Ireland should also be curtailed as they pose a far more serious threat than the millions of Irish citizens now on lockdown. We should also question why there are daily flights between Dublin and Kerry airports, connecting with incoming flights from the UK.

The other issue that must be questioned is the cocooning of all people over seventy within their homes. This draconian measure amounts to virtual imprisonment without trial. A US scientific study in 2018 found that isolation was a major cause of premature deaths. Some over 70s are vulnerable because of their medical condition, but many are not. Those who are medically vulnerable should be advised to isolate within their homes but not compelled, as the risks associated with isolation for elderly people may be greater for them than the risks associated with coronavirus. Also, the over-70s as a group are likely to be a lesser risk of spreading the coronavirus than the younger members of the community, and they could and would still be restricted to two kilometres from their homes. We know to our cost that our politicians don't always get things right.

No. 203.

Irish News **Belfast 15 April 2020**

For the Future of Democracy, It Is Vital That Sinn Féin Are Part of the Next Government

Democracy is rapidly going out of fashion, when most needed, as humanity is facing a range of existential crises, including environmental destruction, coronavirus, and wars of aggression waged by senior UN members whose role should be preventing wars. Likewise, the European Union should be a vital force for peace, transnational cooperation, caring for refugees, promoting democracy, and solidarity. The EU is failing on all these counts. It allows several of its members to wage wars of aggression and others to degrade democracy within their states. Ireland risks going down a similar route, as it almost did when the virus of fascism spread across Europe. Yet, in 1932, Fine Gael agreed to facilitate the transfer of government to Fianna Fáil and rejected its fascist wing led by Eoin O'Duffy. Now, while everyone is focused on the coronavirus, we find ourselves with an interim government that was elected out of office on February 8, misusing the coronavirus crisis to prolong their period in power, supported by Fianna Fáil, both attempting to engineer sharing power for the next five years, ignoring the wishes of the people. This is a time for national government.

Those who say Sinn Féin, the party that gained the biggest percentage of votes in the election, are not suitable for government, are contradicting the democratic wishes of a significant proportion of the people. For the future of democracy in Ireland, it is vital that Sinn Féin be part of the next government. Those who question the competence of Sinn Féin in government should ask themselves, could Sinn Féin in government possibly be any worse than Fianna Fáil and Fine Gael have been, both parties that originated as violent revolutionaries.

No. 204.

Sunday Independent **19 April 2020**

Criticism in a Crisis Can Help Save Lives

There is a dangerous consensus gathering steam whereby any criticism of the government's response to the coronavirus emergency is deemed a failure to put on the green jersey.

Green jerseys and flag waving will not save lives. But critical evaluation of actions and procedures, and of government policies, will save lives.

The vast majority of our frontline healthcare workers are doing a tremendous and dangerous job but in several cases they have not been getting the vital support they need.

People in crowded nursing homes and other institutions are also the most vulnerable to the virus. In the first weeks of this emergency, decisions were made, or failed to be made, that have resulted in the deaths of far too many elderly and vulnerable people. That is fact.

Care of the elderly and vulnerable should not be outsourced on a privatised for-profit basis. We must learn from this – and I hope we will.

No. 205.
Irish Independent 24 April 2020
SF Deserves to Be Invited to Join National Government

The three parties being wooed by Fine Gael and Fianna Fáil to join a coalition government received a combined total of 14.4 per cent of the vote in the February election (Green Party 7.1 per cent, Labour Party 4.4 per cent, Social Democrats 2.9 per cent), yet it seems they are now being made attractive offers if they go into government.

The hidden purpose of this may well be to prevent the Sinn Féin, the party that got the highest percentage of the vote, from being part of the government.

In this time of very serious health, environmental, and economic crises, we need a genuine national government that includes the changes the electorate voted for.

The coronavirus crisis must not be used as an excuse to deny the electorate's wishes.

No. 206.
Irish Examiner 4 May 2020
Too Many Compromises

Negotiations to form a government were never more urgent than at present, not only because of the coronavirus pandemic but also because of even more serious long-term emergencies, including the climate/environmental crisis and international peace. Most of humanity will survive the coronavirus crisis, but a huge proportion of humanity will not survive the environmental crisis or the real risks of a nuclear war, unless we actively undo the damage already done. Ireland needs a vibrant Green/environmental party but the credibility of our existing Green Party was severely damaged by its involvement in the Fianna Fáil-led Government, including facilitating US military use of Shannon Airport. If it compromises too much on key environmental issues, it will have betrayed its raison d'etre. A 7 per cent reduction in carbon emissions is not too much, it is arguably too little.

Likewise, Ireland needs a Labour Party representing workers, now more than ever, but the credibility of the Labour Party was severely damaged by its compromises on foreign policy and austerity during its participation in the Fine Gael-led Government. Inequality in Ireland has reached an all-time high, highlighted by the statement by the Minster for Finance Paschal Donohoe that government ministers will not be taking a COVID-19 pay cut. In opposition, Labour always supported Irish neutrality and opposed US military use of Shannon Airport but when in government caved in on these issues. The treatment of our elderly and other most vulnerable people in nursing homes, direct provision, and other institutions by the present government has led to far too many avoidable deaths. Our health, our essential living environment, our foreign policy of neutrality, and promoting vital international peace must not be compromised and must be red-letter issues.

No. 207.
Irish Daily Mail 24 May 2020
Varadkar's €10M Military Transport Plane

The *Sunday Business Post* says 'Varadkar eyes purchase of €10M military transport plane' (Michael Brennan 17 May). The justification for a large military transport plane is as flawed as the case for a large multi-role naval ship. The €10M cost cited is the minimum purchase price of the Hercules C130, but like the children's hospital debacle, the eventual costs involved will be many multiples thereof. Why squander such a large amount of money when we have far more pressing needs to be financed? Due to servicing and maintenance downtime, two such aircraft would be needed to ensure 24/7/365 availability. This immediately doubles the cost to over €20M before other costs, such as spare parts, recruitment, and training of air crews etc. Cathal Berry TD, former army officer cites the prestige issue: 'it reflects very poorly on the country ... very embarrassing that we are literally hitch-hiking on German and Spanish aircraft to get our people out of Mali'. It reflects far more poorly on our country to have so many homeless, poor health services, and crippling national debt. By the time these two Hercules are purchased and operational, the temporary needs that exist at present will hopefully have passed, and anyway, it is far cheaper to hire commercial aircraft to do such very occasional tasks than to have large transport aircraft sitting idle in their Baldonnel hangars for most of every year. Our Defence Forces were never intended to be an invading army.

No. 208.
Irish Examiner 3 June 2020
Civilian Control of Defence is Democratic

A number of former officers of the Irish Defence Forces (including Dorcha Lee and Ray Cawley) have very justifiably criticised the present depleted condition of our Defence Forces and the manner in which recent governments have treated our serving soldiers, and I agree with their concerns. However, I urge caution on the suggestion in the report 'Ex-senior officer seeks commission to examine Defence Forces' (Irish Examiner, May 27) that a former army officer should be appointed as Irish defence minister. I have no doubt that former officer Cathal Berry was a very capable officer and will make a very capable politician. We need people with this level of intelligence and capability in our government and this is demonstrated by the incompetence of so many of our senior politicians over recent decades. Since the 1930s especially, there has been very clear civilian democratic control over our defence forces and this is essential in a democracy. In many other countries, the Eoin O'Duffys of this world have done serious damage to democracy, although I have no doubt that Cathal Berry TD is not in this category. Doctors don't necessarily make the best ministers of health, former police don't necessarily make the best ministers of justice (remember Sean Doherty?), and teachers don't necessarily make the best ministers of education, due to being too close to the vested interests of their professions.

I think that Cathal Berry should set his sights a little bit higher than minister for defence.

Edward Horgan (Comdt. retired)

No. 209.
The Irish Times, Irish Examiner, Irish Daily Mail **19 June 2020**
Ireland's Place on the UN Security Council

Our Irish diplomats are to be congratulated on the success of Ireland's campaign for membership in the UN Security Council. It would have been a travesty if two more NATO countries had been elected in addition to the three NATO countries of the US, UK, and France, who are permanent members of the Security Council. The primary role of the UN is to maintain international peace, yet those three permanent members have abused their powers of veto to usurp the role of the UN and wage wars of aggression with impunity since the end of the Cold War. These wars have caused the deaths of millions of people, including an estimated one million children, in Iraq, Serbia, Afghanistan, Libya, and Syria, and the US, UK, and France are supporting conflicts in Yemen, Palestine, and elsewhere. Successive Irish governments have been silent in failing to criticise these wars of aggression and have allowed the US to misuse Shannon Airport to wage these wars. The recently published programme for government makes reference to 'active military neutrality'. Active neutrality should not mean actively supporting wars.

On 29 May 2020, in Ireland's opening statement to the WFUNA, Ambassador Geraldine Byrne Nason said 'we are an independent neutral country beholden to no one'. Our independence and our neutrality have been recklessly compromised. We have become beholden to the successive US government administrations in a manner that threatens our historically friendly and kinship relationships with the people of the United States. Ireland's two-year membership of the UN Security Council should be used to restore Ireland's credibility as an independent neutral state and towards restoring the UN to its proper role of maintaining international peace and justice.

No. 210.
Belfast Telegraph **20 Oct 2020**
Ireland Has Blood on Its Hands for Letting US Military Use Shannon

The report in the Belfast Telegraph (News, October 12) that the New IRA leadership discussed a possible attack on Shannon Airport is deeply worrying. There will always be a minority in society who advocate violence as a solution to their often misperceived ideals, or in pursuit of their own self-centred interests. Peace activists in Northern Ireland, led by John Hume and others, were pushed to one side and sometimes vilified by those who went on to pursue their objectives by violent means at enormous cost to lives.

However, the unjustified use of violence is not confined to extremist individuals and paramilitary groups. The vast majority of unjustified deaths, injuries, and destruction are caused by wars perpetrated by member states of the United Nations, including several permanent members of the UN Security Council.

Those who work to promote international peace are also pushed aside by those who pursue national and self-interests at the expense of the vast majority of humanity. Ireland should be at the forefront of states promoting international peace and justice, and we were for many decades as a genuine neutral state. Since March 20, 2003, Ireland abandoned its status as a neutral state by allowing the US military to use Shannon Airport as a forward airbase to wage unjustified wars in the Middle East.

This decision by the Irish Government (backed up by a vote in Dáil Éireann) has made Ireland complicit in millions of deaths in the Middle East and was likely one of the reasons why the New IRA were considering acts of unjustified violence at Shannon Airport.

No. 211.
Irish Daily Mail 3 Dec 2020
'Rule of Law' in EU

Deep divisions within the EU have arisen over 'rule of law' issues in Hungary and Poland. Both countries are now holding up the passing of the EU 2021 budget because the EU has linked the rule of law issues to the budget. A report in the *Guardian* by Daniel Boffey on 1 Dec quotes EU President Von der Leyen: 'Hungary and Poland should take the EU to court rather than make millions suffer by blocking its €1.8tn (£1.6tn) budget and recovery fund.' The rule of law is a vital issue not only for the EU but for all of humanity. Hungary and Poland should be held accountable for breaches of EU rule of law standards. Several other EU member states have been involved in far more serious breaches of the rules of laws at international levels, yet the EU has been silent on these matters. One of the most important rules of law justifiably enforced by the EU is its ban on capital punishment. EU member states who are also members of NATO have engaged in gross breaches of international laws and conventions and in very clear breaches of the UN Charter. These EU/NATO member states have participated in the overthrow of the governments of Afghanistan, Iraq, and Libya, and the attempted overthrow of the government of Syria. Ireland has also been complicit in these wars and in breaches of the UN Convention Against Torture. These breaches of international laws have cost the lives of millions of innocent people. The European Union claims to be a project for peace, democracy, and justice and should begin to live up to these ideals.

No. 212.
Irish Independent 9 Dec 2020
175 Years On, We Still Have a Lot to Learn from the Famine

Tomorrow, December 10, is Human Rights Day. The Story of the Irish Famine on RTÉ should persuade those who live in today's well-resourced

Ireland that such contrived or assisted atrocities should never be allowed to happen in these sophisticated times.

Yet deprivation is happening locally, nationally, and internationally. Homeless people are dying on our streets, and some of our most vulnerable are dying because they are denied adequate access to our two-tier healthcare system.

There should be a priority of human rights, with the right to life, and the right not to be killed or die prematurely, being at the top of the human rights priority list.

The Irish Famine experience and the resulting forced migration should mean that we Irish, including our government, should be at the forefront in campaigning on behalf of others who are today suffering very similar famine and forced migration. However, the opposite is the case.

Ireland's intake of refugees and asylum seekers is one of the lowest in Europe. Our government has been too silent on the war and famine in Yemen, perhaps to avoid offending the perpetrators of such atrocities.

We continue to support sanctions on Syria and Iran that are causing suffering and death and we helped facilitate the overthrow of the Afghan and Iraqi Governments. Our support for the Palestinian people is inadequate, lest we offend Israel.

Worst of all is our government's decision, along with the EU, to stop rescuing drowning refugees from 'coffin ships' in the Mediterranean and sending those they do find back to face gross abuses of their human rights.

If justice, the rule of law, and human rights were given the correct priority at all levels, then every day would be a human rights day.

No. 213.
Sunday Times January 10 2021 (Letter as Published)
Abuses Of Human Rights Off the Scale

David Quinn ('Turning a blind eye has secured us UN success', Comment, last week) rounds up the usual suspects, Russia, China, and Saudi Arabia, in relation to Ireland's failure to criticise human rights abuses. This is only partly true. Ireland did expel a Russian diplomat in March 2018 over the death of Sergei Skripal, but has indeed been silent on human rights abuses in China and Saudi Arabia. Quinn justifiably criticises the UN for human rights abuses by some of its peacekeepers. One of the reasons why these abuses by UN peacekeepers go unpunished is that they have effective immunity from prosecution in the countries where they operate. This also applies to US forces in their foreign bases, yet Quinn fails to mention the far greater scale of human rights abuses they have committed.

(Letter as submitted)

Dear Editor

David Quinn ('Turning a blind eye has secured us UN success', January 3) makes some valid points. He tells us that Ireland should be 'even-handed in who it chastised, or even-handed in its silence'. He rounds up the usual suspects, Russia, China, and Saudi Arabia, on Ireland's failure to criticise human rights abuses. This is only partly true. Ireland did expel a Russian diplomat in March 2018 over the death of Sergei Skripal, but has indeed been silent on human rights abuses in China and Saudi Arabia. He justifiably criticises the UN for human rights abuses by some of its peacekeepers. One of the reasons why these abuses by UN peacekeepers go unpunished is that they have effective immunity from prosecution in the countries they operate in. This sort of immunity also applies to US forces in all US foreign bases, yet Quinn fails to mention the far greater scale of human rights abuses committed by US soldiers compared to those of UN peacekeepers. 'Contrast this with Ireland's continual lecturing of Israel and condemnation of various Israeli Government policies and actions' writes Quinn. Is he suggesting that Ireland should remain silent on Israel's very serious human rights abuses against the Palestinian people? David Quinn should be more even-handed in who he chastises, or even-handed in his silence.

No. 214.
Irish Examiner 12 Jan 2021
Apologies Are No Substitute for Justice

Fianna Fáil leader and Taoiseach, Micheál Martin, will apologise on behalf of the State to the survivors of the mother and baby homes. He will do so when the Dáil resumes after the Christmas break.

This scandal did not occur over a short period or in secrecy: It occurred throughout our State's existence. It is still going on, to some extent, as demonstrated by the premature leaking of the commission of investigation report and the sealing of records.

Was the leaking a tactic to take some of the focus off the perpetrators of abuse in the homes, and off those who were complicit?

Fianna Fáil, and, for a shorter time, Fine Gael, were in power throughout the lifetimes of the mother and baby homes. They had a duty of care, which they failed to honour.

We have heard far too many, far too belated apologies for this and for other scandals, so much so that such cynical apologies should, perhaps, be ended.

The focus should be on achieving real justice, for this and for other scandals. We must also focus on accountability for those who are culpable, in spite of the unforgivable delays.

The mothers and babies who were treated so cruelly need justice and not crocodile tears.

No. 215.
Irish Examiner **15 January, 2021**
What of Culpability of the Fathers?

I listened carefully to the apology issued by An Taoiseach Micheál Martin for the mothers and baby homes scandal. I listened in vain for any mention of the culpability of Irish political parties and Irish politicians in this scandal. Yes, he did mention the role and culpability of 'the State', but as leader of the Fianna Fáil party, he never once mentioned the failures by Fianna Fáil, which was the governing party for vast majority of that period.

Fine Gael was the governing party leader on all the occasions when Fianna Fáil was not in power. It's easy to blame the State and society and to avoid all accountability by specific individuals. Likewise, it is easy to blame the Catholic Church, when it was individual priests, nuns, and bishops who perpetrated these crimes by their actions or culpable failures.

Why was there no mention of the culpability of the fathers of all those children born in these institutions?

No. 216.
Irish Independent, Irish Examiner **January 19, 2021**
An Effort to Right the Wrongs or a Bid to Limit the Damage?

In his interview on RTÉ Radio's This Week programme (Sunday, January 17), Archbishop Eamon Martin suggested that religious congregations might be scapegoated for their role in the mother and baby homes and said: 'They were commissioned by the State and local authorities, county councils, and expected to intervene when the rest of society had basically banished these mothers.'

He seemed to be trying to apportion a significant part of the blame onto 'the rest of society' in a similar way that Fianna Fáil politicians did during the economic crash.

By using the phrase 'they found themselves in the front line' he even seemed to suggest that these religious congregations were performing a similar role to our present health workers during the COVID-19 pandemic.

His statement that: 'If it's just, proportionate, and if it's in account of the findings of the Commission, I do feel the Church needs to do reparation for this' also seems designed to limit any such reparation payments, especially as the Commission's findings with regard to accountability have been widely criticised.

His interview sounded more like a carefully crafted damage limitation exercise than a genuine effort to right the dreadful wrongs perpetrated on so many women and children.

No. 217.
Irish Examiner 25 January, 2021
Time to Ground Shannon Stopover

Irish people scattered around the world welcome the transition in the USA to Irish American President Joe Biden. However, Ireland is not the 51st state of the USA, or another one of its occupied territories. We are an independent sovereign country.

We represent just 0.07 per cent of the population of Planet Earth. We can never be a military power, and if we align ourselves with foreign military powers, all our soldiers will ever be is cannon fodder or mercenaries, 'War dogs hungry and grey, Gnawing a naked bone, Fighters in every clime, For every cause but our own.' These are the words of Emily Lawless in her poem *Clare Coast* 1710.

That same Clare Coast at Shannon Airport has seen Irish sovereignty, independence, and neutrality compromised severely since 2001 by the wholly unnecessary transit of over 1m armed US soldiers on their way to and from US wars in the Middle East. If President Joe Biden wishes to show his love and respect for the country of his forebearers, he will direct the US military to cease using Shannon Airport. Irish American ties and friendship are as deep as the Atlantic that separates us. Now is the time to repair and restore that friendship and kinship.

No. 218.
Irish Examiner 25 February 2021
Shannon and US Military's COVID Risk

Over the past few weeks three aircraft transporting at least 300 US soldiers and aircraft crew members to and from the Middle East, were allowed to spend overnights at Shannon Airport and most of these 300 US personnel were allowed to enter Ireland and were accommodated in several different hotels in Counties Limerick and Clare, without complying with proper COVID-19 regulations. Included were a US Navy aircraft on January 25 with forty-eight soldiers and five crew, an Omni Air aircraft on contract to the US military on January 28 with 226 soldiers plus crew, and a US Air Force aircraft on February 8 with an estimated three crew members and four passengers.

On February 22, the Department of Health statistics revealed that Limerick had the highest percentage of COVID-19 cases in the country. While there are multiple sources for these cases and they might not be associated with the US military, it is irresponsible for the Irish Government and the authorities at Shannon Airport to continue to allow the US military to be transiting through Shannon Airport, especially during this most dangerous period of the pandemic.

No. 219.
Irish Daily Mail 29 March, 2021
COVID-19 Exemptions for US Military at Shannon Airport?

A report in the Medical Independent (David Lynch, 25 January) reveals that US military are not required to have a pre-departure 'not detected' PCR test when travelling through Shannon Airport. Many of these soldiers enter the airport terminal building and interact with airport personnel. Since early January, over 400 US military personnel were accommodated overnight in hotels in Limerick and Clare without complying with Irish Government COVID-19 regulations, thereby increasing the risks of spreading COVID-19. US military should not be transiting through Shannon Airport at all, as this makes Ireland complicit in US serious breaches of international laws. The report by David Lynch also states that Minister for Foreign Affairs Simon Coveney told the Dáil in November that the use of Shannon Airport by the US military was 'a long-standing practice, which has been in place for over fifty years'. Most of the US soldiers transiting through Shannon Airport fifty years ago were engaged in peacetime garrison duties in Germany, but even this was also in breach of international laws on neutrality, especially while the US was engaged in illegal wars such as the Vietnam War, causing the deaths of over three million people in Indochina. If a group of bank robbers were successfully robbing banks fifty years ago, that does not give them a right to continue robbing banks up to the present times. This equally applies to facilitating war crimes and other breaches of international laws. On St Patrick's Day, President Biden refused to share US surplus vaccines with Ireland. Ireland should now refuse to continue sharing the use of Shannon Airport for US military illegal wars.

No. 220.

Irish Daily Mail 2 April 2021, My response to John Carey's letter
US Abused the Law

John Carey (*Irish Daily Mail*, 31 March), questions my statement (Letters, March 29) that 'US involvement in Indochina was illegal' and cites Article 51 of the UN Charter that the 'US acted within international law when it assisted South Vietnam against communist aggression'. Both Vietnam/Indochina wars, first involving French attempts to prevent the decolonisation of Vietnam, Cambodia, and Laos from 1946 to 1954, and then involving the US from 1955 to 1975 resulted in the most serious breaches of the UN Charter, the Geneva Conventions on War, and other international human rights conventions, between the founding of the UN and up to present times. These two permanent members of the UN Security Council abused their UN veto powers to prevent accountability for their actions. These totally unjustified wars led to the deaths of over four million people, and involved use of torture, massive use of chemical weapons (Agent Orange) and carpet bombing and were a contributing factor to the subsequent Cambodian genocide. The UN itself was in breach of its own UN Charter by continuing to recognise the genocidal Khmer Rouge regime of Pol Pot after he was overthrown in 1979 right up to 1991. These wars did irreparable damage to the rule of international law and to the role of the UN in maintaining international peace.

No. 221.
Irish Examiner April 6, *Irish Daily Mail*, April 7 2021
Ireland Needs to Help in Myanmar

The international community was very much aware that the Cambodian genocide and the Rwandan genocide were occurring but took no action to prevent or stop these genocides. War crimes are happening in many countries, some of which are being committed by permanent members of the UN Security Council.

Three conflicts are occurring in Myanmar: ('Myanmar death toll mounts', Irish Examiner, April 3) virtual genocide in north Myanmar against the Rohingya people, mass murder by the military dictatorship in central Myanmar, and air bombing attacks in southeast Myanmar in Karen state. Myanmar is in violent chaos but the international community, including the UN, are standing idly by as happened also with Cambodia and Rwanda. Ireland was elected to the UN Security Council as a neutral independent state with an impressive record for helping to create international peace. Now is the time for Ireland to live up to the serious responsibilities that go with our membership of the UN Security Council. The government, through the Department of Foreign Affairs, should now be playing a leading and independent role towards creating peace and restoring democracy in Myanmar and elsewhere. Otherwise, our two-year membership of the UN Security Council will just be a cynical self-serving status symbol.

No. 222.
Irish Daily Mail 22 April 2021, *Irish Examiner* 23 April 2021
Why We Must Speak Up to Prevent More Genocides

Genocide is the most serious crime against humanity. The Holocaust caused the deaths of six million people, most of whom were Jewish. The UN was founded to prevent such crimes against humanity and the Genocide Convention was passed in 1948 to ensure the words NEVER AGAIN actually meant what they said. Genocides occurred prior to the Holocaust, committed against indigenous people in the Americas. by Germany in Southwest Africa and by the Ottoman Turkish Government during WWI. Genocides have continued to occur in breach of the Genocide Convention, especially in Cambodia, East Timor, Bosnia, and Rwanda. Genocides will continue to occur unless positive actions are taken to prevent or stop genocide, and its perpetrators must be exposed and held to account. Genocides continue to occur because past genocides are perceived to have been successful. The Armenian genocide began in 1915 during WWI, causing the deaths of over one and a half million Armenian, Greek, and Assyrian people. Subsequent governments of Turkey have denied that what occurred was genocide, thereby avoiding accountability or reparations. Recent conflicts across the Middle East from Libya to Myanmar have the potential to lead to acts of genocide. Now is the time to act to prevent further acts of genocide. The Armenian genocide has been recognised by the parliaments of thirty countries including sixteen EU countries, the US Congress, and the EU Parliament. Ireland has so far failed to do so. We the undersigned call on members of the Oireachtas, including the Dáil and Seanad, to pass a motion formally recognising the Armenian genocide as an initial step towards helping to prevent further acts of genocide.

Signed by the following:

Mairead Maguire, Cofounder of The Peace People,
Roger Cole, Peace and Neutrality Alliance,
Barry Sweeney, World Beyond War, Ireland Chapter,
John Lannon, Shannonwatch,
Davy McCauley, Derry Anti-War Coalition,
Edward Horgan, Veterans For Peace Ireland,
Niall Farrell, Galway Alliance Against War,
Joe Murray, AFRI, Action From Ireland,
Martin Leavy, Ireland Yearly Meeting Quaker Peace Committee,
Rob Fairmichael INNATE.

No. 223.
The Irish News **22 June 2021**
Ireland's Neutrality Should Not Be Undermined

There is a determined campaign afoot to undermine and abandon Irish neutrality. The British-based *Sunday Times* seems to be leading the Charge of the NATO Brigade into some valley of death (June 13, 'Neutrality has no place in an increasingly hostile world'). The article claims that the ransomware attack on the HSE was a security wake-up call for Ireland, but this is a criminal matter best dealt with by Irish and international police rather than for military action. It claims without justification that Russia has shown 'a lack of respect for our sovereignty' and goes on to falsely claim that Russian 'military aircraft have entered Irish airspace on more than one occasion in the past year' with their transponders switched off. There is no evidence that the Russian Air Force has ever violated Irish airspace, which extends only out to twelve miles around our coast. The Russian Air Force is fully entitled to fly through international air space beyond those twelve coastal miles. The only serious breaches of Irish neutrality in recent decades have been by three million US troops transiting through Shannon Airport to Middle East wars. Not only have US military aircraft violated Irish sovereign airspace, but more than 10,000 of these have landed and refuelled at Shannon Airport since 2001.

Even more worrying is the virtual decommissioning of the Irish Army Air Corps, while at the same time, there has reportedly been a secret agreement to allow the British Air Force operational access to Irish sovereign air space. This is tantamount to a reversal of the 1938 handover of the three Irish ports that enabled Ireland to remain neutral during the Second World War. Irish freedom and sovereignty cost a lot of valuable lives and should not be thrown away for spurious reasons.

No. 224.
Irish Examiner 28 June 2021
Weapons Transport at Shannon Airport

Richard O'Donohue TD has raised concerns with Foreign Affairs Minister Simon Coveney TD over the risks associated with the transport of US arms through Shannon Airport (*Irish Examiner* June 25). Mr Coveney stated that US military flights 'are routinely required to meet strict conditions, including that the aircraft is unarmed, carries no arms, ammunition or explosives', etc. It is US military practice that US soldiers travelling to war zones carry their personal weapons, and many of these military flights have been transporting soldiers. Therefore, it is inconceivable that weapons have not been transported through Shannon on US military aircraft.

Mr Coveney stated: 'In order for a civilian aircraft carrying US military personnel who are carrying arms on their person to travel through Shannon Airport, there needs to be an exemption for that. This is different from using Shannon Airport as a stopover to carry munitions or arms to a theatre of war. That does not happen.' Over three million US soldiers have travelled through Shannon Airport since 2001. Therefore, over three million US weapons were transported through Shannon Airport.

If it is not acceptable for US military planes to carry weapons through Shannon, why is it acceptable for civilian planes on contract to US military to do so?

Civilian aircraft have also been transporting US war materials through Shannon Airport. One example confirmed by documents released by the department shows that between June and September 2018, fifty-seven new Bearcat Armoured vehicles were transported from the USA through Shannon Airport to Erbil in Iraq.

Hundreds of thousands of people have been killed due to US-led wars in the Middle East. Ireland's role in these wars must be ended.

No. 225.
Irish Daily Mail 2 July 2021
Death of Donald Rumsfeld

The death of Donald Rumsfeld should prompt us to pause for reflection. While most of us are reluctant to speak ill of the dead, we should not hesitate to speak what we believe to be the truth about individuals who have caused unjustified suffering to others. Many such individuals avoid accountability for their actions during their lifetimes, so perhaps some accountability may be due after they have passed from this life. While Donald Rumsfeld was not the worst of individuals, he was a malevolent force in international politics and had significant responsibility for hundreds of thousands of deaths in US-led wars in the Middle East, especially in Iraq. We are all capable of making genuine human mistakes but knowingly doing something wrong that causes death and suffering is not a genuine mistake, it is an act of evil. Since he was a very capable and intelligent man, it is inconceivable that he did not know that his actions in Iraq and elsewhere were wrong. He died in relative luxury and good care surrounded by his family, as did others who committed far more heinous crimes such as Pol Pot and Idi Amin. Far too many of their victims died in traumatic and horrific circumstances. All war criminals and human rights abusers should be held to account for their actions while they are still alive.

No. 226.
Irish Daily Mail 21 July 2021
Very Little Justice for Victims of Abuse

I will begin with a word of thanks to Teresa Lavina for the documentary *Untold Secrets*, to Catherine Corless for her exposure of the Tuam babies scandal, to the late Anne Silke for her courage and strength of character, and to Caelainn Hogan and the *Irish Examiner* for publishing the article 'Anne Silke: Fostered to a Fianna Fáil TD, beaten, and abused' (26 July 2021).

Anne Silke's story is just one story of the many thousands of stories of abused children in Ireland that will forever be a shameful stain on the history of the Republic of Ireland during the 20th century.

These crimes against our most vulnerable citizens were not committed by foreign occupiers, but by so-called Christians, including priests, nuns, and Irish politicians and officials all of whom had a serious duty of care.

The exposure of the serious abuses inflicted on Anne Silke by a senior Fianna Fáil politician, Mark Killilea Jr, senator, TD, and MEP, begs some questions.

How many more politicians and other Irish officials were involved in such abuses?

In whose interests was it decided to seal the records of the Commission of Investigation into Mother and Baby Homes for thirty years?

In response to questions from the *Irish Examiner*, Donagh Killilea, son of the late Mark Killilea Jr, described the allegations made by Anne Silke as both 'unverified' and 'inaccurate' but said 'we have nothing to hide', adding that 'everyone involved in this has passed away'.

Justice delayed in such cases is justice denied and so far, very little justice has been achieved for these children.

No. 227.
Irish Daily Mail **19 August 2021**
Diplomacy Trumps Force

The Afghan people have suffered greatly over the past forty years due to foreign interference and military aggression by the Soviet Union, foreign jihadists, internal warlords, and religious fundamentalists, and especially over the past twenty years by the US- and NATO-led unjustified war. Ireland's role in facilitating this war makes us complicit in the suffering of the Afghan people.

Given this history, I find it amazing that Independent TD and former Army Ranger, Dr Cathal Berry (Speaking on RTÉ radio's Today show) has called on Ireland to deploy special forces to Kabul airport to coordinate the extraction of Irish citizens. It is especially inappropriate that as a member of Dáil Éireann, Dr Berry TD has recommended that 'up to twelve members of the Army Ranger Wing could be sent without requiring the resolution of the Dáil'. This undermines the authority of Dáil Éireann. Ireland and the Irish Defence Forces were not part of the solution in Afghanistan, they were part of the problem due to their participation as part of the NATO occupation force. This makes it likely that members of the Army Ranger Wing would be seen as hostile to the new Taliban Government and its military activists. Dr Berry stated that the job of the Army Ranger Wing is 'to protect Irish citizens, at home and abroad'. Yes, the job of the Irish Defence Forces is to protect Irish citizens at home, but the only function of the Irish Defence Forces abroad should be as genuine peacekeepers to protect the citizens of those countries to which they are assigned by the United Nations. Diplomatic negotiation and not military force is by far the best way to help extract the Irish citizens from Afghanistan.

No. 228.
Irish Independent 25 September 2021
Links Between Climate Change and Our Security

Taoiseach Micheál Martin gave a well-crafted speech to the UN Security Council on Thursday. He carefully avoided the large elephants in the Security Council room, and these were not just Chinese, Indian, and Russian elephants. An Taoiseach said: 'The impact of climate change is global and our collective security is at risk.'

NATO and its allies are the largest collective security organisation on Earth. An Taoiseach and the UN Security Council have got the wrong end of the climate change stick.

NATO and its associated militarism are among the greatest polluters on the planet, even in peacetime. However, the US, NATO, and their allies have been waging aggressive resource wars across the wider Middle East since the end of the Cold War, causing massive destruction and hugely contributing to climate change and causing millions of unjustified deaths.

He went on to say: 'Around Lake Chad, the combination of conflict and the impact of climate change has led to violence between communities.' While climate change may be one of the causes of conflict there, another elephant in the room and a major cause of conflicts in Africa has been and still is French neo-colonial abuses, including the arguable misuse of UN and EU peacekeeping forces, who are intervening in civil wars or anti-colonial wars rather than genuine peacekeeping. Closer to home, the US military use of Shannon Airport has substantially contributed to the chaos and climate change in the Middle East.

No. 229.
The Irish Times **28 November 2021**
Human Cost of US, EU, UN Sanctions

Sir, – Sanctions imposed by the United States, the United Nations, and the European Union have been causing the deaths of millions of people in the most impoverished countries of the world.

Various humanitarian agencies within the UN have been highlighting the hundreds of thousands of children who have died as a result of such sanctions for many years. Just one example was the sanctions on Iraq during the 1990s imposed by the UN Security Council and implemented by the US and its European allies. A very credible UNICEF report in 1999 estimated that these sanctions caused the deaths of up to 1.5 million Iraqi people, including over 500,000 children.

At present, the US is imposing sanctions on up to thirty countries, or on individuals or organisations within these countries, while the EU (which includes Ireland) is likewise imposing sanctions on up to thirty-two countries and the UN (which also includes Ireland) imposes sanctions on at least fifteen countries.

The peoples of some of the most impoverished countries in the world are victims of these sanctions, imposed by, or enforced by all three of the US, UN, and the EU, especially the impoverished peoples of Yemen, Libya, Syria, Iraq, and Afghanistan, all of which have been left in ruins by wars of aggression by the US and its NATO and Middle Eastern allies.

Children, especially, are dying in huge numbers due to these sanctions. Ireland is sitting silently on the UN Security Council that is helping to impose these murderous sanctions. By our silence we are complicit.

– Yours, etc,

No. 230.
Irish News 9 November 2021, *Irish Examiner* 6 November, *Irish Daily Mail* 3 November

Further Steps Needed Towards Taking Violence Out of Irish Politics

The decision by Sinn Féin to recognise the Special Criminal Courts marks a significant step forward for Sinn Féin but further steps are needed on the journey towards taking violence out of Irish politics. Such steps must also be taken by other parties, especially Fianna Fáil and Fine Gael, whose very foundations were laid with violence.

As we approach the centenary of the civil war, it is important to point out that more Irish people died in that civil war than died in the war for independence. The number of people who died due to the more recent Troubles in Northern Ireland was almost as many as died in the war for independence and the 1920s civil war combined.

If the argument by Fianna Fáil and Fine Gael is that Sinn Féin are unsuitable to be in government because of their violent past, then that same criterion should have been applied to themselves.

We should not whitewash or censor those parts of history that we would like to forget, lest we go on repeating past mistakes.

There is a valid case to be made for a truth commission into the killings during the Troubles in Northern Ireland, as documented in *Lost Lives*, edited by David McKittrick et al. There should also be more honest discussion on all the unjustified killings that occurred during the war for independence and the civil war. Many wars are caused by intelligent people making stupid decisions. The First World War was one such dreadful example.

John Redmond was an intelligent man who opposed the war for independence, but he actively supported the First World War where up to 50,000 Irish men lost their lives, including his brother Major Willie Redmond.

As the centenary of the civil war approaches, now is a good time for Fianna Fáil, Fine Gael, and Sinn Féin to admit and apologise for all the unjustified deaths and injuries caused by their past and more recent associates.

No. 231.
Sunday Times (edited) 5 December 2021, *Irish News* 1 December 2021
Inappropriate Assertion

Statements made by the Chief of Staff of the Defence Forces, Major General Sean Clancy, (Ireland 'a target for hostile states' *Sunday Times*, November 21) should cause concerns for the Irish Government and the Irish people. Without naming Russia directly, he nonetheless has targeted Russia as a hostile state, using questionable reports of 'foreign military vessels and aircraft having entered Irish-controlled waters and airspace with their transponders switched off'.

Clancy goes on to say that hostile states 'represent not just a risk to critical infrastructure but to every aspect of Irish society as they use hybrid warfare to undermine democracy'. Russia and NATO have been engaging in dangerous confrontations, usually hundreds of miles off the Irish coast but there has been no credible evidence that Russia is a 'hostile state' towards Ireland.

Such an inappropriate assertion is a serious diplomatic insult to a friendly state. Those who threaten Irish sovereignty and Irish neutrality are not the Russians, who have never been a threat to Ireland. During the Second World War, it was Germany and Britain that posed a serious threat to our sovereignty.

A few Russian bombers flying many miles off the Irish coast must not be compared with an estimated 15,000 aircraft associated with the US military landing and refuelling at Shannon Airport over the past twenty years. The most serious threats to democracy internationally in recent decades come, not from Russia, but from the US and its NATO allies.

No. 232.
Irish News 6 January 2022, *Irish Daily Mail* 29 December 2021
Why Are Irish Soldiers in Mali?

The *Financial Times* article (December 22) seeks to answer the question: 'How France lost Mali: failure to quell jihadi threat opens door to Russia.' Ireland should be asking the question of why Irish soldiers are stationed in Mali in the midst of one of the most dangerous and confusing conflicts. The UN MINUSMA peacekeeping mission may well be contributing to this confusion. This UN mission has soldiers from sixty-five different countries including Ireland's Army Ranger Wing. MINUSMA has lost more than 200 peacekeepers killed since 2013. France has attempted to maintain an economic and political stranglehold over all its former colonies and in recent years has persuaded the EU, including Ireland, to support its neo-colonial enterprises in the Sahel region of Africa. In addition to the UN mission, the EU also has a training mission called EUTM including twenty more Irish soldiers propping up what has become a military junta. Far from creating peace and preventing terrorism, the EU and UN are interfering in a civil war in Mali.

Further confusion is caused by the presence in Mali of French-led Operation Barkhane with soldiers from five Sahel region former French colonies, Burkina Faso, Chad, Mali, Mauritania, and Niger. ISIS and other terrorists are taking advantage of the chaos in Mali, using the Libyan chaos, largely created by NATO, as their staging post and source of weapons.

Irish soldiers should never have been deployed to Mali when there are more urgent peacekeeping needs, such as in the Congo DRC, one of the potentially richest countries in the world, but where tens of thousands of children are starving at present.

No. 233.

Irish News 25 January 2022, *Irish Examiner* 16 January 2022

Accountability for Torture

The conviction in a German court of Syrian former colonel Anwar Raslan, who was found guilty of crimes against humanity and torture, is to be welcomed by all who oppose such dreadful crimes. No such sentence will ever compensate the victims of such crimes, but may achieve some accountability.

Far too many state leaders and officials who commit such crimes are never brought to justice. Ireland should examine Germany's 'universal jurisdiction laws' which would allow for the prosecution of such crimes in Ireland. Media coverage of this trial has focused on Raslan's crimes committed during the Syrian civil war that began in 2011. However, Raslan left Syria in 2012 and was also involved in torture prior to 2011, as confirmed by one of the witnesses. Raslan may well have been responsible for torture at this prison in 2002/2003 when the US was sending prisoners to Syria for interrogation and torture.

The Washington Post in December 2002 described the rendition of captured al-Qaeda suspects from US custody to Syria, Uzbekistan, Pakistan, Egypt, Jordan, Saudi Arabia, and Morocco, where they were tortured. Most of these countries are still allies of the US and are ruled by dictatorships of various types.

Ireland's complicity in such crimes also needs to be properly investigated, and accountability is also needed for torture committed by British forces in Northern Ireland.

No. 234.
Irish Independent **25 January 2022**
What About All the Western Military Operations Near Us?

Foreign Affairs Minister Simon Coveney is to raise concerns and express the government's unhappiness with the Russian ambassador over planned Russian naval exercises 240km off the southwest coast of Ireland.

This Russian military exercise is fully in accordance with international laws.

No such concerns were raised when Britain and its NATO allies staged several naval exercises off the north coast of Ireland in recent years, coming as close as 32km from Malin Head on April 29, 2021.

Damien McCallig, chief engineer on the RV *Celtic Explorer*, took photos of a possibly nuclear-armed submarine and told the *Irish Examiner*: 'The sub passed us this morning at 6 a.m. Twenty miles northwest of Malin Head.'

In October 2020, a total of eleven NATO nations took part in exercise Joint Warrior, bringing twenty-eight warships, two submarines, and eighty-one aircraft off the coasts of Scotland, some of which came within 80km of the Inishowen Peninsula.

The departments of Foreign Affairs and Transport have approved the refuelling of an estimated 15,000 US military-associated aircraft at Shannon Airport over the past twenty years, transporting over three million armed US soldiers and an unknown quantity of munitions to and from illegal wars in the Middle East that have cost the lives of millions of people.

Is this the behaviour of a genuine neutral country towards promoting international peace and justice in accordance with Article 29 of Bunreacht na hÉireann?

No. 235.

9 February 2022. Article on Veterans Global Peace Network (VGPN) International Neutrality Project was printed in the Czech newspaper *Halo Noviny*. It was also published in the March edition of Polish monthly newspaper *Mysl Polska* 'Polish Thought'.

International Neutrality Project

Initiated by the Veterans Global Peace Network (VGPN www.vgpn.org)

Since the end of the Cold War, wars of aggression for the purpose of grabbing valuable resources have been waged by the USA and its NATO and other allies in gross violation of international laws and the UN Charter. All wars of aggression have been illegal under international laws including the Kellogg-Briand-Pact, August 27, 1928, which was a multilateral agreement attempting to eliminate war as an instrument of national policy.

The UN Charter opted for a more pragmatic system of 'collective security', a bit like the Three Musketeers – one for all and all for one. The three musketeers became the five permanent members of the UN Security Council, sometimes known as the five policemen, who were tasked with maintaining or enforcing international peace. The US was the most powerful country in the world at the end of WWII. It had used atomic weapons unnecessarily mainly against Japanese civilians to demonstrate its power to the rest of the world. By any standards, this was a serious war crime. The USSR detonated its first atomic bomb in 1949, demonstrating the reality of a bipolar international power system.

In this 21st century the use, threat to use, or even possession of nuclear weapons should be considered a form of global terrorism. In 1950 the US took advantage of the USSR's temporary absence from the UN Security Council (UNSC) to push through UNSC Resolution 82, which had the effect of the UN declaring war on North Korea, and that war was fought under the UN flag. This precipitated the Cold War, as well as corrupting the role of the UN and especially the role of the UN Security Council, from which it has never recovered. The rule and abuse of force had superseded the rule of international law.

This situation could and should have been resolved peacefully after the end of the Cold War in 1989, but the leaders of the US perceived the US to be once again the unipolar most powerful country in the world and moved to take full advantage of this. Instead of retiring the now redundant NATO, as the Warsaw Pact had been retired, US-led NATO ignored promises made to Russian leader Gorbachev not to expand NATO into the former Warsaw Pact countries.

The problem now is that the US, backed by the UK and France, have a majority of the five permanent members of the UN Security Council (UNSC) who hold the power of veto over all UNSC decisions. Because China and Russia can also veto any UNSC decisions, this means that the UNSC is almost permanently deadlocked when important international peace decisions are needed. This also allows these five UNSC permanent members (the P5) to act with impunity and in breach of the UN Charter that they are supposed to uphold, because a deadlocked UNSC can take no punitive actions against them. Since the end of the Cold War, the main perpetrators of such abuses of international laws have been the three NATO P5 members, the US, UK, and France, in cahoots with other NATO members and other NATO allies.

This has led to a series of disastrous illegal wars, including the war against Serbia in 1999, Afghanistan 2001 to 2021, Iraq 2003 to 2011 (?), Libya in 2011. They have taken the rule of international law into their own hands, and become the greatest threat to international peace. Instead of providing genuine security for Western Europe that it was established to do, NATO has become an international protection racket. The Nuremberg Principles outlawed wars of aggression, and the Geneva Conventions on War sought to regulate how wars are fought, as if wars were just a sort of game. In the words of Carl von Clausewitz, 'War is the continuation of politics by other means.' Such views on war must be rejected, and the huge amounts of resources spent on war and preparations for wars must be transferred towards genuinely creating and maintaining peace.

In theory, only the UN Security Council can authorise military actions against member states of the United Nations and then only for the purposes of maintaining genuine international peace. The get-out excuses that many countries are using include claiming that their wars of aggression are necessary for the self-defence of their countries or to protect their national interests, or bogus humanitarian interventions.

Armies of aggression should not exist in these dangerous times for humanity where abusive militarism is doing untold damage to humanity itself and to humanity's living environment. Genuine defence forces are necessary to prevent the warlords, international criminals, dictators, and terrorists, including state-level terrorists such as NATO, from committing huge human rights abuses and destruction of our Planet Earth. In the past, Warsaw Pact forces engaged in unjustified aggressive actions in Eastern Europe, and European imperial and colonial powers committed multiple crimes against humanity in their former colonies. The Charter of the United Nations was meant to be the foundation for a much-improved system of international jurisprudence that would put an end to these crimes against humanity. The replacement of the rule of law by the rule of brute force by the US and NATO, will almost inevitably be copied by those countries who feel that their sovereignty and security are being threatened by NATO's ambitions to become a global enforcer.

The international law concept of neutrality was introduced in the 1800s to protect smaller states from such aggression, and The Hague Convention V on Neutrality 1907 became and still remains the definitive piece of international law on neutrality. In the meantime, the Hague Convention on Neutrality has been recognised as Customary International Law, which means that all states are bound to comply with its provisions even if they have not signed or ratified this convention.

It has also been argued by international law experts such as L. Oppenheim and H. Lauterbach that any state that is not a belligerent in any particular war, is considered to be a neutral in that particular war, and is therefore bound to apply the principles and practices of neutrality during the course of that war. While neutral states are forbidden from participating in military alliances, there is no prohibition on participation in economic or political alliances. However, the unjustified use of economic sanctions as a form of hostile collective punishment should be considered as aggression because of the devastating effects such sanctions can have on civilians, especially children. International laws on neutrality apply only to military matters and participation in wars, except for genuine self-defence.

There are many variations in the practices and applications of neutrality in Europe and elsewhere. These variations cover a spectrum from heavily armed neutrality to unarmed neutrality. Some countries such as Costa Rica have no army at all. The CIA factbook lists thirty-six countries or territories as having no military forces, but only a small number of these would qualify as fully independent states. Countries such as Costa Rica rely on the rule of international law to protect their country from attack, in a similar way that citizens of various countries rely on the rule of national laws to protect themselves. Just as police forces are necessary to protect citizens within states, an international policing system is needed to protect smaller countries against larger aggressive countries. Genuine defence forces are needed for this purpose.

With the invention and spread of nuclear weapons and other weapons of mass destruction, no country, including the US, Russia, and China, can any longer be assured that they can protect their countries and their citizens from being overwhelmed. This has led to what is a truly mad theory of international security called Mutually Assured Destruction, appropriately abbreviated to MAD. This theory is based on the arguably mistaken belief that no national leader would be stupid or mad enough to start a nuclear war, yet the USA did start a nuclear war against Japan on the 6th of August 1945.

Switzerland is considered to be the most neutral country in the world, so much so that it did not even join the United Nations until as recently as 2 September 2002. Some other countries such as Austria and Finland have neutrality enshrined in their constitutions, but in both cases, neutrality was imposed on them after the end of World War II, so both may now be moving towards ending their neutral status. Sweden, Ireland, Cyprus, and Malta are neutral as a matter of government policy and in such cases, this can be changed by a government decision. Constitutional neutrality is the better option because it is a decision made by the people of that country rather than by its politicians, and any decisions to abandon neutrality and go to war can only be made by a referendum, with the exception of genuine self-defence.

The Irish Government acted in serious breach of international laws on neutrality by allowing the US military to use Shannon Airport as a forward air base to wage its wars of aggression in the Middle East. Cyprus's neutrality is compromised by the fact that Britain still occupies two large so-called Sovereign Bases in Cyprus that Britain has used extensively to wage its wars of aggression in the Middle East. Costa Rica is an exception as one of the few genuinely neutral states in Latin America and a very successful neutral one at that. Costa Rica 'squanders' a lot of its financial resources on health care, education, and looking after its most vulnerable citizens, and is able to do this because it has no army and is not engaged in wars with anyone.

After the end of the Cold War, the US and NATO promised Russia that NATO would not be expanded into the eastern European countries and other countries on the borders with Russia. This would have meant that all the countries on Russia's borders would be considered neutral countries, including existing neutral Finland, but also the Baltic States, Belarus, Ukraine, Romania, Bulgaria, Georgia, etc. This agreement was quickly broken by the US and NATO and moves to include Ukraine and Georgia as members of NATO forced the Russian Government to defend what it considered to be its national strategic interests by taking back the Crimea and taking the provinces of North Ossetia and Abkhazia under Russian control.

There is still a very strong case to be made for neutrality of all states close to the borders with Russia, and this is urgently needed to prevent escalation of the conflict in Ukraine. History demonstrates that once aggressive states develop more powerful weapons that these weapons will be used. The US leaders who used atomic weapons in 1945 were not MAD, they were just BAD. Wars of aggression are already illegal, but ways must be found to prevent such illegality.

In the interests of humanity, as well as in the interest of all living creatures on Planet Earth, there is now a strong case to be made to extend the concept of neutrality to as many countries as possible. A recently established peace network called Veterans Global Peace Network www.VGPN.org is launching a campaign to encourage as many countries as possible to enshrine military neutrality in their constitutions and we hope that many other national and international peace groups will join us in this campaign.

The neutrality we would like to promote would not be negative neutrality where states ignore conflicts and suffering in other countries. In the interconnected vulnerable world that we now live in, war in any part of the world is a danger to us all. We wish to promote positive active neutrality. By this, we mean that neutral countries are fully entitled to defend themselves but are not entitled to wage war on other states. However, this must be genuine self-defence and does not justify spurious pre-emptive strikes on other states or bogus 'humanitarian interventions'. It would also oblige neutral states to actively promote and assist with maintaining international peace and justice. Peace without justice is just a temporary ceasefire as was demonstrated by the First and Second World Wars.

Such a campaign for international positive neutrality will begin by encouraging the existing neutral states to maintain and strengthen their neutrality, and then campaign for other states in Europe and elsewhere to become neutral states. VGPN will actively cooperate with other national and international peace groups to achieve these objectives.

There are some important variations on the concept of neutrality, and these include that of negative or isolationist neutrality. An insult that is sometimes thrown at neutral countries is a quote from the poet Dante: 'The hottest places in Hell are reserved for those who, in a time of great moral crisis, maintain their neutrality.' We should challenge this by responding that the hottest places in hell should be reserved for those who wage wars of aggression.

Ireland is an example of a country that has practised positive or active neutrality, especially since it joined the United Nations in 1955, but also during the interwar period when it actively supported the League of Nations. Although Ireland has a very small defence force of about 8,000 soldiers, it has been very active in contributing to UN peacekeeping operations since 1958 and has lost eighty-eight soldiers who have died on these UN missions, which is a high casualty rate for such a small Defence Force.

In Ireland's case, positive active neutrality has also meant actively promoting the decolonising process and assisting newly independent states and developing countries with practical aid in areas such as education, health services, and economic development. Unfortunately, especially since Ireland joined the European Union, and especially in recent decades, Ireland has tended to be dragged into the practices of the EU larger states and former colonial powers in exploiting the developing countries rather than genuinely assisting them. Ireland has also seriously damaged its neutrality reputation by allowing the US military to use Shannon Airport in the west of Ireland to wage its wars of aggression in the Middle East. The US and NATO members of the EU have been using diplomatic and economic pressure to try to get the neutral countries in Europe to abandon their neutrality and are being successful in these efforts. It is important to point out that capital punishment has been outlawed in all EU member states and this is a very good development. However, the most powerful NATO members who are also members of the EU have been unlawfully killing people in the Middle East for the past two decades.

Geography can also play an important role in successful neutrality and Ireland's peripheral island location on the extreme western edge of Europe makes it easier to maintain its neutrality, combined with the reality that unlike the Middle East, Ireland has very little oil or gas resources. This contrasts with countries such as Belgium and the Netherlands that have had their neutrality violated on several occasions. However, international laws must be enhanced and applied to ensure that the neutrality of all neutral countries is respected and supported. Geographical factors also mean that different countries may have to adopt a form of neutrality that suits their geographical and other security factors.

The Hague Convention (V) respecting the Rights and Duties of Neutral Powers and Persons in Case of War on Land, signed on 18 October 1907, can be accessed at this link:

https://ihl-databases.icrc.org/applic/ihl/ihl.nsf/ART/200-220001?OpenDocument

While it has many limitations, the Hague Convention on Neutrality is regarded as the foundation stone for international laws on neutrality. Genuine self-defence is allowed under international laws on neutrality, but this aspect has been very much abused by aggressive countries. Active neutrality is a viable alternative to wars of aggression. Since the end of the Cold War, NATO has become the greatest threat to international peace. This international neutrality project must be part of a wider campaign to make NATO and other aggressive military alliances redundant.

Reformation or Transformation of the United Nations is also another priority, but that is another day's work.

Peace organisations and individuals in all regions of the world are invited to participate in this campaign either in cooperation with Veterans Global Peace Network or separately and should feel free to adopt or adapt the suggestions in this document.

No. 236.
Irish Examiner **11 February 2022**
Simon Coveney Chops and Changes the Rules

Defence Minister Simon Coveney has justifiably ordered an independent investigation by a senior counsel into a party held by soldiers in an outdoor area at Defence Force Headquarters.

Foreign Affairs and Trade Minister Simon Coveney initially failed to order an independent investigation into an indoor celebration held by Department of Foreign Affairs officials at their headquarters.

Are different rules being applied by a different Simon Coveney?

No. 237.
Irish Independent **12 February 2022**
We Must Not Become a Stopover on Way to War

On Wednesday, at least three B52 US Air Force bombers were deployed from Minot air base in Dakota to RAF Fairford in England (UK Defence Journal, February 10).

A US Air Force statement read: 'The mission focused on enhancing readiness and interoperability for the controllers responsible for co-ordinating airstrikes to support ground forces.'

As the people of Vietnam discovered, the speciality of these monstrous Stratofortress aircraft is carpet bombing from 40,000 feet.

Will Ireland be facilitating the transit of these weapons of mass destruction through Irish sovereign airspace or Irish-controlled airspace in the event of a war in Ukraine?

Germany has recently been refusing to allow weapons deliveries to Ukraine to pass through German airspace.

These are not just harmless war games; they are deadly serious preparations for war.

In the interests of international peace and justice, Ireland should immediately cease allowing foreign military aircraft to land in Ireland or transit through Irish sovereign airspace, with the exception of diplomatic flights.

Comment: Some of my letters appear in unusual places. This is a report by the Syrian Arab New Agency about an article that appeared in a Czech Republic paper 'Halo Novini'.

No. 238.
Halo Novini, **Prague and SANA, Syria, 12 February 2022**
US Sanctions on Syria and Cuba Are Described as Aggression by Irish Peace Activist

Irish activist Edward Horgan, a university professor and former officer in the Irish forces, stressed that the unilateral coercive measures imposed by the United States of America and the West on Syria, Cuba, and some other countries should be considered a described aggression, pointing out that its repercussions are devastating and affect civilians, including children and women.

Horgan, who worked in several United Nations military missions in the world, pointed out during an article published in the Czech newspaper *Halo Novini* today that the United States, along with its allies and NATO, has carried out many aggressive wars since the end of World War II, which represented a clear violation of the law. He stressed that all these aggressive wars were illegitimate and tragic in accordance with international law, including the occupation of Afghanistan and Iraq and the aggression against Libya and Serbia.

Horgan stressed that since the end of the Cold War, NATO has become the biggest threat to international peace, pointing out that the United States and the NATO alliance countries that are also in the European Union use diplomatic and economic pressure to force neutral countries in Europe to abandon their neutrality.

No. 239.
***Irish Independent* 16 February 2022, *Irish Examiner* 19 February 2022**

We Should Facilitate Peace, Not US Troop Movements

On Monday, five Omni Air aircraft on contract to the US military were refuelled at Shannon Airport while transporting up to 1,000 armed US soldiers from the United States to an airport called Rzeszow-Jasionka in southeast Poland, which is just 90km from the western borders of Ukraine. These five aircraft were refuelled again at Shannon Airport on their return journeys to the US.

This is happening with the approval of Minister for Transport Eamon Ryan and arguably in contravention of the Department of Foreign Affairs' insistence that US military aircraft are not allowed to transport weapons or to be involved in military operations while landing in or overflying Irish territory.

As a neutral state, Ireland should be using its membership of the UN Security Council to promote peace in Eastern Europe and elsewhere and should not be facilitating preparations for war by belligerent states.

No. 240.
***Irish Examiner* Opinion Article 14 March 2022 by Edward Horgan:**

Ireland Must Use Active Neutrality to Promote Peace in Ukraine

War is being over-simplified as a clash between good and evil. Neutrality for Ukraine would have and should have prevented this conflict
https://www.irishexaminer.com/opinion/commentanalysis/arid-40827671.html

The tragic conflict in Ukraine is being used by those with a vested interest in the militarisation of Europe and in aggressive resource wars to challenge the neutrality not only of Ireland but also of the other European neutral states, especially, Sweden, Finland, and Austria.

The war in Ukraine has complex local and international causes but is being over-simplified in the Western media as a clash between good and evil.

Simplistic solutions to deal with this conflict include pouring in weapons and munitions, adding fuel to the fires of war, and attempting to make peace by making war.

Neutrality for Ukraine would have and should have prevented this conflict. Those who are calling for the abandoning of Irish neutrality and joining NATO are at best mistaken, including those calling for the expulsion of the Russian ambassador.

We should recall the words of George Orwell, who wrote in his novel 1984: 'War Is Peace. Freedom Is Slavery. Ignorance Is Strength.'

New proxy war

These words now seem appropriate to the broader conflict between Russia and US-dominated NATO, which has turned the Ukrainian conflict into a new proxy war.

They are also very relevant to Irish neutrality as well as for Ukraine and other countries.

The lies that were told to justify wars in Serbia, Iraq, Afghanistan, Libya, and elsewhere, under the guise of humanitarian interventions are now being erased – war is peace and lies become the truth.

These regime-change wars were serious breaches of international laws made possible by the abuses of the powers of veto by the US and its NATO allies Britain and France.

Putin and the Russian Government were concerned that the expansion of NATO up to its borders indicated that Russia was being targeted for regime change.

Russia felt justified in launching its own war of aggression, which is also in breach of international law. None of these illegal wars are justified but they do demonstrate that Ireland should have nothing to do with such destructive military alliances and should focus its efforts on promoting international peace by reinforcing its neutrality rather than abandoning it.

The Irish people are genuinely concerned about the suffering and killing of Ukrainian people. In this 21st century, it is not just conflicts in Europe that should concern us, but all military conflicts that are doing huge damage to humanity as a whole, and to our vulnerable living environment.

The greatest threat facing humanity now is climate change, yet this is being ignored and progress to deal the environmental damage is being reversed.

The key issue for us as a nation should be how we can protect and defend the best interests of the Irish people, including our huge diaspora scattered around the planet, while at the same time promoting international peace and justice by peaceful means.

We should have learned from the First World War – which cost the lives of up to 50,000 Irish soldiers – that Ireland will never have the capacity to be anything other than cannon fodder as part of a military alliance.

Since 1958, Ireland has played a huge role in promoting international peace and has achieved this through the courageous peacekeeping by our Defence Forces combined with our positive neutrality foreign policy.

Proposals to increase defence spending, and purchase fighter jets and naval warships ignore the reality that the territory of Ireland, or of any small country, can never be defended from invasion by conventional military means.

The best and only practical way to defend the Irish people is by reinforcing our neutrality.

As a deterrent against the very unlikely event of an invasion, Irish defence policy and practice should be radically changed from one of conventional military defence to one of being prepared for guerrilla warfare in the event of any such invasion. This is how we achieved our independence and how we managed to avoid entanglement in the Second World War, and how the people of Vietnam and Afghanistan defeated French, US, and USSR military powers.

If foreign powers encroach on our air or sea spaces, do we shoot them down or sink them with our newly purchased jets if they refuse to leave? If a civilian aircraft full of passengers hijacked by terrorists is flying through our airspace, do we shoot it down killing all on board? Allowing the British RAF to do so over Irish territory is also a reckless policy.

Irish neutrality has a long and respected history dating back to Wolfe Tone in the 1790s. The Irish Neutrality League was active in 1914 to keep Ireland out of the First World War, using the slogan: 'We serve neither king nor kaiser, but Ireland.'

Our neutrality became more firmly enshrined during the Second World War, when Ireland successfully remained neutral in spite of threats of occupation from the Allies and Axis belligerents.

After we joined the United Nations, our neutrality took on a more positive role with our Defence Forces playing an active role in UN peacekeeping from 1958 to the present time.

Some eighty-eight Irish soldiers have died while serving overseas. Abandoning neutrality means abandoning this proud peacekeeping tradition as we join the breakers of international law.

This positive neutrality enhanced the reputation of Ireland internationally so much so that we have been elected to the UN Security Council on five occasions.

Successive Irish governments have sought to compromise or end Irish neutrality by allowing US military forces to use Shannon Airport while waging wars of aggression in the Middle East.

The Irish people have remained committed to maintaining positive neutrality – a recent poll by Amárach Research in February showed 76 per cent of the Irish people in favour of neutrality.

There are important moral, legal, humanitarian, and existential reasons why Ireland should maintain a policy and practice of positive neutrality.

The moral reasons are based on the old-fashioned 5th Commandment 'Thou shall not kill'.

Unjustified wars in the Middle East from Libya to Afghanistan since 1991 have caused the deaths of up to five million people, including over one million children.

Now Russia is also waging an unjustified war in Ukraine because of the failures by all concerned to find peaceful solutions to this conflict.

The legal reasons are based on the importance of the rule of law at national, regional, and international levels, as opposed to the rule of abusive force.

At national legal level, An Garda Síochána is obliged to investigate and prevent serious crimes, including crimes of torture and war crimes committed elsewhere which people in Ireland may have facilitated or been complicit in.

At regional level, the European Union has outlawed capital punishment. However, twenty-one EU member states are also members of NATO, and NATO has been involved in illegal wars resulting in the deaths of millions of people. This is capital punishment by means of war.

At international law levels, Adam Lupel of the International Peace Institute writes that: 'Small states are by definition vulnerable in a world where international law is compromised and only might makes right.' Small states like Ireland need to uphold the rule of international law rather than join the lawbreakers.

Humanitarian reasons for Irish neutrality should be a priority for the Irish people, given our history of occupation by a foreign power that committed crimes against humanity against our people, forcing millions of Irish people to seek refuge in other countries.

Irish facilitation of Middle East wars of aggression contributed to the refugee crisis, and our government is failing to promote peace in the Ukrainian conflict.

The existential reasons for neutrality are highlighted by the risks of nuclear accident or nuclear war due to the present conflict in Ukraine and the possession of and threats to use nuclear weapons by at least nine countries.

Promoting peace by peaceful means using our positive active neutrality is the only sensible and practical policy for Ireland in the future.

Dr Edward Horgan BA, M.Phil., PhD, Commandant (retired), served on several occasions with the Defence Forces as a UN military peacekeeper in the Middle East, worked with the EU, OSCE, UN, and Carter Centre on election monitoring missions in post-conflict situations in the Balkans, Eastern Europe, Asia, and Africa. In 2008, he completed a doctoral thesis on international peace and reform of the United Nations.

No. 241.
Irish Examiner and in British-based *Morning Star* 19 March 2022
President's Statement Not Reported in Media

When the president of any country makes a statement on important matters, that country's mainstream media usually reports on such statements. On the 15th of March 2022, President Michael D. Higgins published such a statement concerning his letter to the presidents of a group of fifteen non-executive European Heads of State on the conflict in Ukraine.

Most of the Irish mainstream media has ignored this presidential statement.

President Higgins describes the Russian invasion of Ukraine as involving: "clear breaches of International Law, Humanitarian Law and the basic Charter of the United Nations".

This statement and letter contain the following points:

· The President notes the specific possibilities contained in the perspective which can be brought by the group of those nations who are neutral countries within the twenty-seven member countries that form the European Union.

· The neutral member's perspective, ... has real possibilities in creating the atmosphere for a meaningful ceasefire and a further move to meaningful talks for Ukraine and its people.

· The demand for peace must return to our lives and streets, and we must give time to confront the outrage that is contained in the suggestion that the sole version of a shared life on our vulnerable planet must rely on armaments rather than a shared peace.

· The inevitability of war must be rejected if we are to retain hope.

President Higgins should be complimented on this important initiative and on the wisdom of his words.

No. 242.
Irish Independent 5 April 2022, *Irish Daily Mail* 11 April 2022
Putin Knows He Won't Face Justice for His War Crimes

Reports of war crimes, including the crime of making a war of aggression committed by Russian forces in Ukraine, are shocking and are probably accurate. Nothing justifies such war crimes. The reality is that most modern wars involve serious war crimes against civilians. Most claims by belligerent states and non-state aggressors that civilian casualties are just 'collateral damage' due to 'military necessity' are false. Widespread shelling of civilian apartment buildings by Russian forces in Ukraine are war crimes. The International Criminal Court (ICC) should prosecute all suspected war crimes, but in most cases, it is powerless to do so. Three permanent members of the UN Security Council, China, USA, and Russia have not signed up to and have not ratified the ICC and can use their veto to prevent their leaders or citizens from being prosecuted by the ICC. Only 123 of the 193 UN member states have ratified the ICC.

Many war crimes occur because those committing war crimes know that they are unlikely to be brought to justice because the rule of international law, including the UN and the ICC, are grossly inadequate. In recent decades, the UN has failed to achieve its primary role of creating and maintaining international peace. Wars and war crimes occur because of the failures to prevent them, and the failures to bring the perpetrators to justice.

The rule of international law needs to be substantially improved and then enforced if global justice is to be achieved.

No. 243.
Irish Daily Mail 13 April 2022
Push for Peace

'Weapons, weapons, weapons' was the demand by Ukrainian Foreign Affairs Minister Dmytro Kuleba to NATO foreign ministers. Billions of dollars worth of weapons are being poured into Ukraine to make war, and it seems as if not a single dollar is being spent on making peace. Shares in the world's largest arms manufacturer Lockheed Martin are rising daily, but so are the cost of living and inflation all over Europe. The damage being done by the war in Ukraine and other wars to the global environment is huge. Tens of thousands of people including hundreds of children have been killed in the Ukraine conflict since 2014, not just in Western Ukraine but also in the Russian-speaking Donbas region. Humanity seems to be rushing blindly into World War III. Perhaps we are already in WWIII if we take the illegal and unjustified wars in Iraq, Afghanistan, Libya, Syria, and Yemen into account. These wars, including the US/NATO and Russian proxy war in Ukraine, are not just isolated local wars, they are resource wars by the elite countries of the world, including Ireland, in our bid to maintain control of our planet's depleting resources. While the Ukrainian refugee crisis is getting the response it deserves from EU countries, the response to the refugee crises resulting from wars in the Middle East and Africa has been shamefully inadequate. Instead of using our traditional positive neutrality to promote international peace, our Irish Government has been supporting these US- and NATO-instigated resource wars. The warmongers are everywhere but where are the peacemakers?

No. 244.
The Irish Times 22 April 2022
The European Peace Project?

Sir, – Justin Kilcullen has vast humanitarian experience working worldwide with Trócaire. I was surprised therefore to read (Letters, April 19) his negative comments on Irish neutrality and his description of the European Union as 'a haven of peace and democracy'.

Yes, the EU did a lot to promote peace within Europe, and by providing an alternative vision for governance compared with communist-controlled Soviet Union. Since the end of the Cold War, however, the EU has largely failed to promote peace within Europe, and especially within the wider world. This is partly due to the reality that several of the EU's most powerful states, especially France, have never fully abandoned their colonial exploitation.

Added to this is the failure of the international community, including the EU, US, and NATO, to promote peaceful cooperation with our neighbour Russia within the broader Eurasian sphere. The counterproductive continuing existence of NATO and the reality of NATO expansion has been a major cause of the unjustified Russian war against Ukraine. The EU's role as a peace project has been fatally compromised by the fact that twenty-one EU member states are also members of NATO.

Irish neutrality, supported by the vast majority of Irish citizens, is something to be proud of because it has enabled us to achieve far more towards international peace and justice than we could ever achieve as an insignificant belligerent state.

The 'trials of war' are not confined to the 'heart of Europe' and the people of Ireland are correct in wanting to bring peace and justice not only to

Europe but especially to our sisters and brothers in Africa and the Middle East. – Yours, etc,

No. 245.
Irish Daily Mail **12 May 2022**
Neutrality Gone AWOL?

April 27th, *The Defence Post* military journal reported that: 'Australia will deliver six M777 155mm lightweight towed howitzers and ammunition to Ukraine as part of a 26.7 million Australian dollar ($19 million) package to bolster the country's defenses against the Russian invasion.'

On 4 May, a large Ukrainian Antonov 124 transport aircraft, registration number UR-82072 took off from Amberley Royal Australian Air Force base near Brisbane Australia. It made refuelling stops in Japan, Anchorage in Alaska, and Edmonton and Goose Bay in Canada. It arrived at Shannon Airport on Saturday 7 May about 17.40 p.m., stayed overnight at Shannon and took off on Sunday 8 May at about 12.11 p.m. and flew to Rzeszow airport in southeast Poland, which is the main delivery airport for sending weapons and munitions into Ukraine.

If this aircraft was transporting weapons and munitions, which is very likely, it would have needed the approval of the Minister for Transport, Green Party leader Eamon Ryan TD and probably also the approval of Minister for Foreign Affairs and Defence Simon Coveney TD. Over two-thirds of the Irish people support Irish neutrality. If democracy means government of the people, by the people and for the people, then our government should not be acting against the wishes of the Irish people and in serious breach of international laws on neutrality.

No. 246.
The Irish Times, Irish Daily Mail 27 May 2022.
French Ambassador is Not Helping Matters

The carefully and diplomatically worded comments on Irish neutrality by French ambassador to Ireland Vincent Guérend (Neutrality will not stop Russia harming Ireland, *Irish Times* and *Irish Examiner*, May 24) need to be challenged. He stated that 'Neutrality is not respected by Russia and China in the way Ireland would like to think it is.' While nothing justifies Russian war crimes in Ukraine, there is no basis for accusing China of breaching the neutrality of any foreign country in recent decades. France itself arguably committed very serious breaches of Libyan neutrality in 2011 when it led the efforts to overthrow the Libyan Government by abusing the terms of the UN no-fly-zone resolution, leaving Libya in chaos ever since. Rwanda was arguably a neutral state when France intervened in Rwanda's internal affairs by militarily supporting the genocidal Rwandan Government in 1974 with catastrophic consequences for the people of Rwanda. NATO and the European Union NATO members, twenty-three of whom will also be members of NATO when Finland and Sweden abandon their neutrality, appear to be engaged in a campaign towards eliminating the concept of neutrality in Europe. On such sensitive matters, ambassadors should remain silent to avoid being seen to interfere in the democratic processes of their host countries.

No. 247.
Letter as was sent to *Sunday Times* 5 June 2022.
Choosing Which Refugees Not to Welcome Is Racist

David Quinn (May 29th) says that choosing who to welcome to Ireland is not racist. International laws and conventions put obligations on all states to rescue people in distress and give refuge to refugees fleeing from wars and persecution, regardless of their colour or religion. No one that I know of has criticised the taking in of Ukrainian refugees. What they have done is to criticise how we and the European Union failed in our duties towards refugees from Africa and the Middle East. Libya, for example, is a similar distance from Ireland as Ukraine, yet we and the EU have stopped rescuing migrants from Libya in the Mediterranean and are sending many of them back to dreadful conditions in Libya in breach of the UN Convention on Refugees. Quinn writes that everyone 'accepts that our greatest obligation is to our family' and then prioritises others, including our nearest neighbours and those of 'a common culture and heritage'. Our Christian beliefs emphasise that our neighbours are all humankind, not our families or those who look like us and share our beliefs. Quinn uses a very flawed argument based on the atrocity in Uvalde in Texas saying that we are more interested in this event than in a similar event in Mexico, because 'America, with its language and culture, is far more familiar to us'. Uvalde is just fifty miles from the Mexican border, and if Quinn had bothered to read the list of children and their teachers who were killed, he should have realised that virtually all of their names were of Mexican or Latin American origins.

Letter as Published, *Sunday Times*, 5 June 2022
We are all humankind

David Quinn writes that everyone 'accepts that our greatest obligation is to our family' and then prioritises others, including our nearest neighbours and those of 'a common culture and heritage'. Our Christian beliefs emphasise that our neighbours are all humankind, not our families or those who look like us and share our beliefs.

Edward Horgan, Castletroy Co Limerick

No. 248.
Irish News 23 June 2022, *Irish Independent*, *Irish Daily Mail* 21 June 2022
International Law Has Been Flouted by the Irish State For Years

Taoiseach Micheál Martin, Tánaiste Leo Varadkar, and Foreign Affairs Minister Simon Coveney have all justifiably criticised the UK Government for its proposal to enact UK legislation that will be in breach of international law with regard to the Northern Ireland Protocol and the Good Friday Agreement.

It is good to see such respect for international laws by our senior government leaders on such matters. Yet far more serious breaches of international laws and Irish legislation have been occurring due to the US military use of Shannon Airport since 2001.

In April 2003, Judge Nicholas Kearns in the High Court ruled that the Irish Government was in breach of customary international laws on neutrality, including the Hague Convention (V) on neutrality. The UN Convention Against Torture (UNCAT) has been brought into Irish legislation by the Criminal Justice (UNCAT) Act 2000. Article 4.1 of UNCAT states: 'Each State Party shall ensure that all acts of torture are offences under its criminal law. The same shall apply to an attempt to commit torture and to an act by any person which constitutes complicity or participation in torture.'

US military and CIA use of Shannon Airport has arguably made the Irish State complicit in war crimes and acts of torture.

No. 249.
Irish Examiner 1 July 2022, *Irish Independent, Irish Daily Mail* 28 June 2022.

Human Rights Abuse in Sahara

Last Saturday, at least thirty-seven African migrants died while attempting to cross a six-metre-high fence from Morocco into the Spanish enclave Melilla. Moroccan and Spanish security personnel were accused of brutality and using unjustified force by Amnesty International and other human rights observers.

The Melilla enclave is just one of the many flashpoints on the borders between the European Union and Africa that have their roots in colonial abuses by former European powers.

This recent tragedy results partly from a Spanish-Moroccan agreement in which the Spanish Government has recognised Moroccan annexation over the sovereignty of Western Sahara in exchange for buying a guarantee from Morocco to prevent asylum seekers from entering Spanish and EU-controlled territory.

In 1976, the UN reaffirmed the right to self-determination of the Sahrawi people, but Morocco continues to occupy most of Western Sahara and its illegal occupation or annexation is now supported by several EU states and the United States.

US military forces recently participated in major multi-state military exercises in southern Morocco and Moroccan-occupied Western Sahara. The UN has had a peace mission in Western Sahara called Minurso for over thirty years, to which Ireland has been contributing a small number of unarmed observers.

Ireland's contribution to Minurso ended in July last year, arguably at a time when genuine neutral observers were most needed by the people of Western Sahara who have been experiencing serious human rights abuses.

No. 250.
Irish Independent 23 July 2022.
Western Nations Failing to Uphold Marine Obligations

International organisations like the UN, EU, and Red Cross are mandated with promoting and defending essential values such as democracy, freedom, human rights, equality, international peace, and justice.

A recently published book by Irish journalist Sally Hayden, *My Fourth Time, We Drowned*, exposes the failure of these organisations to uphold such vital ideals and obligations.

Questionable Western economic interests are being pursued at the expense of gross human rights violations and abuses of international laws and humanitarian obligations. Tens of thousands of refugees and economic migrants have died while attempting to flee conflicts and dire poverty in the Middle East and Africa. Several of these conflicts have been precipitated by US/NATO wars of aggression and the overthrow of governments.

Initially, Ireland and other EU states provided their naval services to rescue thousands of migrants from the Mediterranean. This humanitarian rescue response was abandoned and replaced by more aggressive EU pushback policies backed up by EU border control mechanisms and financial deals with the Turkish government.

What has been happening in Libya, the Mediterranean, and in the wider Middle East and North Africa is comparable with what happened in Cambodia and Rwanda, as exposed by brave journalists like Fergal Keane.

Western nations and international organisations said: 'Never again.' Once again, they never really meant it.

No. 251.
The Irish Times, 25 July 2022.
EU policies and migration response
Aggressive EU Pushback Policies

Sir, – International organisations like the UN, EU, and Red Cross are mandated to promote and defend essential values such as democracy, freedom, human rights, equality, international peace and justice. A recently published book by Irish journalist Sally Hayden called *My Fourth Time, We Drowned* exposes the failure of these organisations to uphold such vital ideals and obligations. Questionable Western economic interests are being pursued at the expense of gross human rights violations and abuses of international laws and humanitarian obligations. Tens of thousands of refugees and economic migrants have died while attempting to flee from conflicts and dire poverty in the Middle East and Africa. Several of these conflicts have been precipitated by US/NATO wars of aggression and the overthrow of governments. Initially, Ireland and other EU states provided their naval services to rescue thousands of drowning migrants from the Mediterranean. This humanitarian rescue response was abandoned and replaced by more aggressive EU pushback policies backed up by Frontex EU border control mechanisms and financial deals with the Turkish Government. EU naval forces are now preventing rescue operations in the Mediterranean and funding the Libyan coastguard to prevent migrants from escaping to Europe and forcing them back to dreadful concentration camps in Libya where murder, rape, human trafficking, and slavery are being perpetrated.

What has been happening in Libya, the Mediterranean, and in the wider Middle East and North Africa, is comparable with what happened in Cambodia and Rwanda, as was exposed by a few brave journalists like Fergal Keane. Western nations and international organisations said never again, and once again they never really meant it. Will the truths exposed by Sally Hayden also be ignored again?

No. 252.
Irish News 3 August 2022, edited version *The Irish Times* 2 August 2022.
Unreasonable Criticism

Sabina Coyne Higgins has been a lifelong advocate for peace and justice and so has her husband, President Michael D. Higgins. She has been subjected to unreasonable criticism and abuse simply because she called for a negotiated ceasefire in the Ukrainian conflict. She has never suggested that the Russian invasion of Ukraine was justified. Bunreacht na hÉireann Article 29 states that: 'Ireland affirms its devotion to the ideal of peace and friendly cooperation among nations founded on international justice and morality' and that 'Ireland affirms its adherence to the principle of the pacific settlement of international disputes by international arbitration or judicial determination.' Those who criticise her are in effect calling for a continuation of the war in Ukraine which has already caused the deaths of tens of thousands of people, including many children. For every day this war continues, hundreds more people will be killed. It is so easy for politicians in Ireland and elsewhere to oppose a negotiated ceasefire but we must ask 'qui bono' – who benefits as the killing continues?

Since the first Gulf War in 1991, up to one million children have died due to unjustified war-related reasons across the wider Middle East. Now innocent Ukrainian children are being added daily to this dreadful statistic. The real risk of a nuclear war is also being ignored.

The Irish Government should be using its membership of the UN Security Council to work for peace in Ukraine as they are mandated to do under Article 29 of our Constitution.

No. 253.
Irish News 15 August 2022
Sinn Féin Not Only Ones Who Seek to Justify Political Violence

Sinn Féin vice president Michelle O'Neill was asked in an interview for the BBC Red Lines podcast: 'Do you still feel that it was right at that time, for members of your family and others, to engage in violent resistance to British rule here?' She replied: 'I think at the time there was no alternative …'

In human interactions, there are always peaceful alternatives to political violence. Violence begets further violence. The statement by DUP leader Jeffrey Donaldson that: 'There is no justification for how the IRA targeted Northern Ireland citizens who were from all faiths and backgrounds and entirely innocent' is a valid one, but it also applies to unjustified violence by loyalists and by British security forces. Sinn Féin are not the only ones who seek to justify political violence. William T. Cosgrave, leader of the Free State government during the civil war, is quoted as saying: 'I am not going to hesitate and if the country is to live and if we have to exterminate 10,000 republicans, the three millions of our people are bigger than the

10,000.' Fine Gael and Fianna Fáil should use the centenary of the civil war to apologise for crimes committed by their predecessors during the War for Independence and the civil war. If Sinn Féin is to lead this country into the future and into a genuine unity of all the people living on this island, it too needs to acknowledge the mistakes and the crimes committed by IRA volunteers otherwise the cycle of political violence will continue. Internationally, far more needs to be spent on conflict prevention and far less on arms production and militarisation.

No. 254.
Irish Independent 30 August 2022
If EU Sends Troops to Ukraine, Then Ireland Should Refuse

The European Union is considering a large-scale training mission for the Ukrainian military.

Ireland is also considering providing Irish soldiers for this mission. EU foreign policy chief Josep Borrell stated: 'The conflict in Ukraine is a large-scale war and therefore, any mission has to be equal to the conflict.'

The increasing militarisation of Europe, and indeed of the whole world, should be deeply worrying to all of humanity.

As a neutral country, Ireland should be using our membership of the UN Security Council to promote peace and should not be taking sides in this disastrous war.

While the Russian invasion of Ukraine was the immediate cause of this war, unjustified NATO expansion was the principal background cause. Now that the vast majority of EU member states are also full members of NATO, this is eroding the EU's claim to be a genuine force for peace.

Ireland's ever-closer integration with NATO and the increasing militarisation of the EU are diminishing Irish traditional positive neutrality, something that is supported by the vast majority of the Irish people.

If the EU becomes a war project rather than a peace project, Ireland's membership of the EU may be called into question.

No. 255.
Irish Daily Mail 19 September 2022, *Irish News* 28 September 2022
Don't Rush to Judgement

In an article in *The Journal* on 16 Sept. Irish Minister for Foreign Affairs, Mr Simon Coveney TD, states that: 'Ireland "needs to hold Russia to account" after the discovery of mass graves in Ukrainian city (Izium)'. All war crimes need to be investigated and all war criminals held to account. Mr Coveney said that: 'Countries like Ireland need to insist on international law applying and on Russia being held to account.' I fully agree that Ireland needs to insist 'on international law applying', but it is vital to add that international laws don't just apply to Russia but apply and should be enforced on all states and on all individuals who commit very serious breaches of international laws, including the UN Charter, and on those who are complicit in such breaches of international laws. We should know from our own Irish history that war crimes are often committed by all sides in wars, as was demonstrated during our civil war in the 1920s and in the more recent Troubles in Northern Ireland. It is also unwise to rush to judgement on very recent violent conflicts. War crimes need very careful scientific and judicial investigation and should not be used for propaganda purposes.

In addition to the war crimes being committed in the conflict in Ukraine, the international community seems to be applying convenient amnesia to the reality that war crimes were committed by the US and NATO forces and their other allies, and by their opponents, in Afghanistan, Iraq, Libya, Serbia, Yemen, and Palestine. The Irish Government should condemn all war crimes and their perpetrators but should do so in a rational, judicial, and balanced manner and should be doing a lot more to promote international peace and justice.

No. 256.
Irish News **4 October 2022**
Silence of the Sheep

An Taoiseach Mr Micheál Martin has labelled Russia as a rogue state in a very partisan manner. Successive Irish governments have actively facilitated serious breaches of international laws, including the UN Convention Against Torture, and breaches of the UN Charter, and international laws on neutrality, by allowing the US military to transit through Shannon Airport. Is this not one rogue state name-calling another state as a rogue state? Because of our government's complicity in US and NATO war crimes in the Middle East, our leaders have been silent and have failed in their duties to promote international peace while serving on the UN Security Council. This is the silence of the sheep.

No. 257.
Irish News **10 October 2022**
Gas Pipeline Retaliation

The article 'NATO believes Baltic Sea gas leaks were sabotage' (September 29) quotes NATO sources as saying they would retaliate against the perpetrators of the attacks on gas pipelines off Denmark and Sweden. Given that it is most unlikely that Russia would attack its own gas export pipelines, and that there are increasing indications that these gas pipeline attacks may have been carried out by the US, are NATO members going to retaliate against one of their own member states? This and related issues, including the deteriorating dreadful war in Ukraine, have very serious implications not only for the Republic of Ireland but also for Northern Ireland and mainland UK. If the US did attack the Nord Stream pipeline, it may provoke Russian retaliatory attacks on vital undersea communications links and energy supply links through Irish and UK territorial and economic zone sea areas.

No. 258.
Irish Independent **15 October 2022**
Apologising for Past Violence and Renouncing It into the Future Will Unite Us – Not IRA Chants

I watched the Irish women's World Cup qualifying play-off win over Scotland last night, and I was delighted with their success. I was saddened to hear that a pro-IRA song was sung by a group of the players in the dressing room after the match. Some of them may not even appreciate the significance of the song, 'Ooh ah, up the "RA"', but that does not excuse their participation in it. When Limerick won the All-Ireland hurling title in 2018, players and supporters sang the IRA-associated song 'Sean South of Garryowen' in the Croke Park dressing room and elsewhere. The book *Lost Lives* by David McKittrick et al., lists and tells a brief story of 3,600 of those who were killed in the most recent campaign of violence in Northern Ireland. We owe a debt of thanks to Republic of Ireland manager Vera Pauw not only for the success of the Irish women's team but also for her very detailed apology for this unacceptable insult to the victims of violence. In August 2022, Sinn Féin vice president Michelle O'Neill responded to a question about IRA violence by saying: 'I think at the time there was no alternative …'. In human interactions, there are always peaceful alternatives to political violence. There has never been a proper and genuine apology by the present Sinn Féin nor by its predecessors who went on to become Fine Gael and Fianna Fáil for the unjustified violence that was perpetrated in the name of the Irish people. If all the peoples of Ireland are to be genuinely and peacefully united, our Irish leaders need not only to apologise for past unjustified killings but also to renounce such violence in the future.

No. 259.
The Irish News 25 November, 2022
Irish Neutrality Suffering Death by a Thousand Cuts

In recent times, our Irish Government is doing all it can to end Irish neutrality against the wishes of the Irish people. The Fine Gael ard fheis passed a motion to effectively scrap the triple lock on sending Irish soldiers on overseas missions by eliminating the need for a UN mandate. Our Defence Forces have become so run down due to lack of government support that it seems like our government wants to decommission our Defence Forces and invite NATO or a European Union defence alliance to defend our country, thereby ending the sovereignty of the Irish people and the Irish State.

Our government's unconstitutional agreement allowing the British Royal Air Force to engage in military operations within Irish sovereign airspace was just another step towards fully abandoning Irish sovereignty. The most serious ongoing breach of Irish neutrality has been our government's decision in 2001 to turn Shannon Airport into a US-forward air base to wage illegal wars in the Middle East.

A further retrograde step is due to happen this weekend.

Today four NATO warships of the Royal Netherlands Navy have been permitted to visit Cork harbour. HNLMS *Karel Doorman* (A833) will be docking at the Cobh Cruise Terminal. HNLMS *Zeven Provincien* (F802) is due to dock at Marino Point. HNLMS *Groningen* (P843) is due to dock at North Custom House Quay. HNLMS *Van Amstel* (F831) is due to dock at JJ Horgan's Wharf. The democratic republic, that was hard fought for a century ago, was meant to achieve government of the people, by the people, for the people. That vision seems to be rapidly disappearing in Ireland, Europe, and in the wider world as the abuses of military power are replacing the rule of law and basic morality. Irish neutrality is suffering death by a thousand cuts.

No. 260.
Irish Daily **Mail 28 November 2022**
NATO and EU Military Alliances Compromise Neutrality

It's not so long ago since some soldiers of a NATO army were killing innocent civilians in Northern Ireland, as demonstrated by the conviction on 25 November of former British soldier David Holden of the manslaughter of Aidan McAnespie in 1988. On the same day, four NATO naval vessels were visiting Cork, and NATO soldiers at Kilworth in Co Cork were participating in exercises to assess the basic capabilities of Irish soldiers and their use of artillery fire support in complex missions with foreign forces. Such aggressive training by NATO forces has contributed to the killing of innocent civilians in the Middle East and elsewhere. The training and military experiences of Irish soldiers have been largely focused on genuine peacekeeping and this is far more appropriate for the soldiers of a genuine neutral state. The only complex missions that Irish soldiers should be undertaking with foreign forces should be United Nations peacekeeping missions. Irish Defence Forces are increasingly entangled with NATO and EU military forces. We now have a new name for the developing EU army or 'battlegroups'. It will henceforth be called The EU Rapid Deployment Capacity (RDC) and our government has committed up to 120 Irish soldiers to this foreign military alliance. Our government falsely claims that all this is not in breach of 'military' neutrality. All of the above are in clear breach of any concept of genuine neutrality as defined by international law. May Aidan McAnespie, and all those innocent people killed by all aggressive military forces, rest in peace.

No. 261.
Irish Examiner, **10 December 2022**
Justice Comes, Albeit 53 Years Too Late for Dónal de Róiste

In these present times of wars and widespread injustice, it is good to see some flickers of candlelight as some justice is achieved. The government's apology to Dónal de Róiste and his family is to be welcomed even if it comes fifty-three years late. Minister for Defence Simon Coveney's statement said: 'Clearly, the security situation in Ireland in 1969 was far different than what it is today. However, while a decision to retire Mr de Róiste from the Defence Forces in these circumstances, and on the basis of the documentation considered at the time, was found by the reviewer to be reasonable, the review has determined that no national security concerns should have prevented Mr de Róiste from being afforded the most basic procedures of natural justice and the right to defend himself and his good name.' The suggestion that the 'documentation considered at the time, was found by the reviewer to be reasonable' seems to excuse those military officers who perpetrated this injustice of their responsibilities to conduct such an important legal process justly and fairly and in accordance with military law and the constitution. These responsibilities applied just as much fifty-three years ago as they do today.

No. 262.
Irish Daily Mail 16 December 2022, *Irish Independent* 31 December 2022
Death of an Irish Peacekeeper

It is with deep sadness that we heard the news that an Irish peacekeeping soldier in Lebanon, Private Seán Rooney, was killed and three others injured, including Trooper Shane Kearney, who is in a serious condition. This emphasises the real risks that Irish and other peacekeeping soldiers and civilians take on a daily basis. Peacekeeping duties are of vital importance for humanity, and far too few resources are given to making peace compared to making wars. The loss of a soldier on peacekeeping duties is tragic but justified. The losses of millions of soldiers, and far more civilians, in countless unjustified wars are totally unjustified. All wars in this age of weapons of mass destruction, that include automatic rifles as well as nuclear weapons, are unjustified. There are always better peaceful ways of avoiding, preventing, and ending wars. The present war in Ukraine is no more justified than the dreadful wars that destroyed Afghanistan and Iraq and so many of their people.

This brings to eighty-nine the number of Irish soldiers who have died on overseas duties. This is a very high casualty rate for a very small army. However, it emphasises the importance of Irish neutrality. If the Irish Government abandons Irish neutrality and joins NATO or a European Union defence alliance, Irish soldiers will end up dying in unjustified wars, and worse still, Irish soldiers will be involved in the killing of innocent people in unjustified wars. Our thoughts and condolences are with the families of these brave soldiers.

May Private Seán Rooney, who gave his life for peace, now rest in peace, and may his sacrifice not be in vain. May Trooper Shane Kearney make a full recovery.

No. 263.

Sunday Independent **1 January 2023 (un-edited version)**

In 2023, Ireland Must Do What Is Right for Humanity

The year 2022 has been a relatively good year for most Irish people (except our most vulnerable children and homeless). The government has used the bonanza of corporation tax, not to fund the health services or the housing crisis, but mainly to benefit those already well off. Ireland has been very much an outlier compared with most of humanity, many of whom have experienced war, starvation, human rights abuse, dire poverty, and the destruction of their living environment. Due to its privileged position on the UN Security Council, the Irish Government was in a unique position throughout 2022 to use our traditional altruistic foreign policy, the foundation of which has been our policy and practice of active neutrality, towards promoting international peace and justice. Shamefully, it failed to do so, and instead joined the militaristic coalition of the West against the Rest. Apart from fulfilling our humanitarian duties to give shelter to Ukrainian refugees, which we generously did, Ireland had nothing of value to give towards the defence of Ukraine, except our now abandoned ability to promote peace. Irish and European Union treatment of other refugees and asylum seekers from the most impoverished and conflict-torn regions of the Middle East and Africa has been in marked contrast with our genuine humanitarian response to Ukrainian refugees. Sally Hayden's book, *My Fourth Time, We Drowned* documents the shocking reality that our European Union has abandoned its duties to rescue the drowning and provide asylum for refugees of all ethnic backgrounds. The undeclared famine in the Horn of Africa and Yemen is a crime against humanity given that there is no overall shortage of food throughout the world. Ireland must stop standing idly by and do what is right because it is right.

No. 264.
Irish Independent 9 February 2023
Rescue Response in Syria Will Be Lesser Due to World Politics

The multiple tragedies that are increasing by the hour due to the earthquakes in Turkey and Syria require a well-coordinated rescue and humanitarian response from the international community. Ideally, there should be no differentiation in the responses to this huge emergency regardless of whether the victims are in Turkey, or in Turkish- or US-occupied northern Syria, or in Idlib province, which is controlled by Syrian rebels, or in the large areas of Syria controlled by the Syrian Government, that were devastated by the earthquakes. The reality is that due to national and international factors, the Syrian victims of these earthquakes are likely to receive far less assistance than those in Turkey. The conflict in Syria since 2011 has already caused huge suffering and deaths as well as destruction to buildings and infrastructure. In addition, sanctions imposed by the US, the EU (including Ireland), and many other countries have also caused multiple deaths. These sanctions are now contributing to the death toll and suffering of all sections of the Syrian people. These unjustified sanctions that impact mostly on the most vulnerable, especially children and the elderly, should be ended immediately. It is the duty of the international community and of all members of the United Nations to respond to such emergencies in an equitable and caring manner. Countries like Ireland should focus their responses on those most in need. All human lives are equally important.

No. 265.
Irish Daily Mail 30 January 2023, *The Irish News* 2 February 2023.
We Should Learn from the Swiss on Neutrality

This week, the President of Switzerland Alain Berset ruled out any involvement in sending weapons to Ukraine. He said that Switzerland had a unique quality of neutrality, and that Switzerland's role, as reflected in the Geneva Conventions, is so much more important than joining a parade of weapon providers. 'Today, it is not time to change the rules against exporting weapons. Neither is it time to change the rules of neutrality. On the contrary, it is time to recall our basic principles, to stay committed to them and find a right path for the country in this situation.' Switzerland, he said, has 'a different role from other states'. Ireland should also have a different role from other states. In this most dangerous time for humanity, the Irish people and our Irish Government should consider these words very carefully and follow the example of Switzerland. Those who denigrate Swiss and Irish neutrality ignore the benefits of positive neutrality for the citizens of these two countries and for humanity as a whole. There is no perfect version of neutrality, but war in this 21st century is madness. The Swiss and Irish governments should be actively promoting peace in Ukraine and elsewhere. The alternative may well be that we are moving closer to World War III and the likely use of nuclear weapons.

No. 266.
Irish News 13 February 2023, also in *Irish Daily Mail* and *Irish Examiner*.
All Human Lives Are Equally Important.

The multiple tragedies that are increasing by the hour due to the earthquakes in Turkey and Syria require a well-coordinated rescue and humanitarian response from the international community. Ideally, there should be no differentiation in the responses to this huge emergency regardless of whether the victims are in Turkey, or in Turkish- or US-occupied northern Syria, or in Idlib province which is controlled by Syrian rebels, or in the large areas of Syria controlled by the Syrian Government, that were devastated by the earthquakes. The reality is that due to national and international factors, the Syrian victims of these earthquakes are likely to receive far less assistance than those in Turkey. The conflict in Syria since 2011 has already caused huge suffering and deaths. In addition, sanctions imposed by the US, the EU (including Ireland) and many other countries have also caused multiple deaths. These sanctions are now contributing to the death toll and suffering of all sections of the Syrian people. These unjustified sanctions should be ended immediately. It is the duty of the international community and of all members of the UN to respond to such emergencies in an equitable and caring manner. All human lives are equally important.

No. 267.

Irish Independent 20 February 2023

Too Many Women Are Being Forced Out of Irish Politics.

I listened to the interview with Fianna Fáil TD Anne Rabbitte on RTÉ news on 19 February 2023 concerning the incident on the 4th of January last, when a bag of excrement was thrown at her during a public meeting in Gort, Co. Galway. Apart from serious legal aspects, this was a cowardly, ignorant, and unacceptable act against one of our Irish citizens who also happens to be an elected legislator and a Minister of State. I was saddened but not surprised to hear Anne Rabbitte say that she does not intend to contest the next election. Women of her calibre are needed in Dáil Éireann. Throughout the history of this State, far too many women have been excluded not only from politics but also from religion dominated by the Catholic Church, and from many other aspects of Irish society, including employment opportunities. While some progress has been made in recent times, the proportion of women in Irish politics is still far too small. Throughout the history of the State so far, less than 10 per cent of those elected to Dáil Éireann have been women, in spite of them representing more than 50 per cent of the population. The present Dáil still has only 22.5 per cent women. Such imbalance in any society is counterproductive and dangerous. Women are also far more likely to be subjected to violent sexual assaults than men, and the recent increase in the number of women being murdered in Ireland is also of serious concern. The Irish State is still failing to treat all its citizens equally and justly.

No. 268.
Irish Examiner 4 March 2023
Irish Government Active in Supporting War

When asked on RTÉ Radio on Sunday, February 26, if the Irish Government's decision to send Irish Defence Forces personnel to train Ukrainian soldiers was a breach of Irish neutrality, An Táiniste Micheál Martin TD denied this was the case and stated: 'We are all anti-war.'

Mr Martin was a senior minister in successive governments that allowed the US military to use Shannon Airport and Irish airspace during the US/NATO wars against Serbia, Afghanistan, and Iraq. All of these wars were in breach of the UN Charter and in breach of Irish neutrality.

Ireland was elected to the UN Security Council for a two-year period in 2021 based substantially on its record as a neutral state actively promoting international peace and justice yet failed shamefully to live up to its important responsibilities to promote peace in the conflict between Ukraine and Russia. Ireland has no credible capacity to promote and support wars, yet has had a proud tradition of promoting peace and justice internationally. Now our government is actively supporting wars and reducing our traditional commitment to genuine UN peacekeeping.

The Irish people have strongly supported the peace process within Ireland and our government should likewise be supporting international peace.

No. 269.
The Irish Times **17 March 2023**
The International Criminal Court

The Minister for Foreign Affairs, Micheál Martin TD, stated in a CNN interview on 14 March that: 'Ireland has been supporting the International Criminal Court (ICC) as it prepares to open a case against Russians involved in the war in Ukraine.' Of course, Ireland should be supporting the ICC and the rule of international laws in all cases. There is evidence that war crimes have been committed by Russia and by Ukraine. Virtually all modern wars involve war crimes due to the indiscriminate use of powerful weapons. The Ukraine War brings the added risks of nuclear war and catastrophic damage to nuclear power stations. Successive Irish Governments remained silent when the US and its NATO allies invaded and overthrew the Afghan and Iraqi Governments and committed serious war crimes. A genuinely neutral Ireland should condemn all those who commit war crimes and should make every effort to promote peace in all violent conflicts. Mr Martin was quoted as saying: 'China should use its influence to get Russia to stop this war', and 'I'd be careful of language around mediation at this stage.' Being 'careful of language around mediation' combined with sending Irish soldiers to train Ukrainian soldiers is likely to perpetuate this war until either Ukraine, supported by NATO, defeats Russia or Ukraine is defeated and destroyed by Russia. Yes, China should use its influence to get Russia to stop this war, but Ireland should also get all sides in this war to stop this war.

Ireland's proud history of promoting international peace and justice has now been abandoned. The fatalities in the Ukraine conflict have likely exceeded 200,000 so far. How many more must die in Ukraine before the Irish Government, and others including the UN, will do their humanitarian duty to promote peace?

No. 270.
Irish Examiner **20 March 2023**
Remaining Neutral in All Aspects of War

Minister Eamon Ryan, while in Hong Kong, quoted Daniel O'Connell as justification for Ireland's support for Ukraine in its war against Russia. Ryan stated that: 'There was a famous Irish patriot, Daniel O'Connell – The Liberator – and he said one line and I think it's appropriate here: Nothing that's morally wrong can be politically correct.' Daniel O'Connell was a dedicated pacifist who would have been appalled at the carnage in Ukraine. He was dedicated to peaceful, non-violent means throughout his public life. 'Not for all the universe contains would I, in the struggle for what I conceive my country's cause, consent to the effusion of a single drop of blood, except my own.'

In typical Irish Government doublespeak, Eamon Ryan said: 'While Ireland remained a militarily neutral country, it was not neutral on the war itself' (CNBC Asia, March 15). A genuinely neutral country should remain neutral in all wars. The overwhelming majority of Irish people want the Irish Government to pursue a policy of active positive neutrality promoting international peace and justice. In this 21st century, the proliferation of weapons of mass destruction and the reality that wars create mass destruction of our global environment means that all wars are morally wrong.

The Irish Government and the Green Party in particular should be promoting peace by peaceful means only. St Patrick would be equally appalled at his festival being used to promote the continuation of wars in Ukraine and elsewhere.

No. 271.
Article in Irish Foreign Affairs magazine, March 2023
Ireland, Neutral, Non-Aligned, or NATO Belligerent?

The system of international relations and rule of international law since the end of the Cold War has become very complex and very dangerous. We need to understand the complexities and real dangers and the existential crises that face humanity right now and into the future. We are already in a multipolar global system as the US, with less than 5 per cent of the world's population, attempts to impose by military means the stranglehold that it has enjoyed over the global economic system including its access to an undue share of the worlds depleted resources. The US defeat in Vietnam demonstrated the limitations of US power. The possession and threatened use of nuclear weapons and Mutually Assured Destruction, gave the US and Soviet Union relative power throughout the rest of the Cold War. With the end of the Cold War, the US sought to restore or create its own unipolar hegemonic control and seemed to be succeeding for a while until it went on to repeat many of its Vietnam mistakes in Iraq and Afghanistan.

To survive as an imperial power, the US needs the resources that Russia has, but it needs NATO and other allies as its enforcers in what has become the equivalent of a global criminal protection racket. First, the rule of international law, of which the UN Charter is the foundation, needed to be overcome and pushed to one side. The power of veto by the five permanent members of the UN Security Council (the P5) was the mechanism used to achieve this, with the support of US P5 allies, Britain and France. The first step in this process was the US and NATO war against Serbia in 1999, in clear breach of the UN Charter. This was followed by the war against Afghanistan in 2001 and Iraq in 2003 and the overthrow of their governments without the required approval of the UN Security Council. The US and NATO had now successfully hijacked the proper role of the UN and placed themselves beyond the rule of international laws. NATO expansion up to the borders of Russia now posed an existential threat to Russia, to which Russia felt obliged to respond. Russia responded carelessly and recklessly, and arguably walked into a US/NATO-laid trap. In the meantime, the European Union has been virtually absorbed into NATO, with Sweden and Finland abandoning their neutrality and about to join NATO. This means that of the twenty-seven EU member states, twenty-three will be full members of NATO. Austria, Ireland, Malta, and Cyprus are not full members of NATO but Austria, Ireland, and Malta are members of NATO's Partnership for Peace (PfP), and the neutrality of Cyprus is questionable given that more than half of Cyprus is occupied or controlled by NATO members Britain and Turkey. What this may well mean for Ireland is that the Irish Government may opt not to fully join NATO, and therefore still claim that we are militarily neutral, or non-aligned or whatever, but will sign up for an EU defence alliance and thereby enter NATO by the back door. Ireland's membership of PESCO is a step in that direction, just like our membership of PfP.

Ireland was prevented from joining the United Nations for ten years by disputes between the two superpowers and possibly because of our wisdom in staying out of World War II. When we did join in 1955, we upgraded our negative WWII neutrality to positive active neutrality, promoting international peace and justice and encouraging the decolonisation process. Because of our huge diaspora and kinship ties with the US, we have remained closely, and arguably too closely, associated with US economic and geopolitical interests.

The Non-Aligned Movement

Throughout the Cold War, attempts were made to establish a third force in international relations that became known as the Non-Aligned Movement.

The Non-Aligned Movement (NAM), describes itself as an international organisation dedicated to representing the interests and aspirations of developing countries and has up to 120 member states, so it is a very loose grouping of states. The idea first came to prominence at the 1955 Bandung conference in Indonesia in 1955 and was officially founded in Belgrade in 1961 under the leadership of Josip Tito of Yugoslavia, Gamal Abdel Nasser of Egypt, Jawaharlal Nehru of India, Kwame Nkrumah of Ghana, and Sukarno of Indonesia. Neutrality was never one of the objectives of the NAM, and they encouraged national self-determination against all forms of colonialism and imperialism and abstaining from allying with either of the two superpowers (the United States and the USSR). If Ireland were to join the NAM, we would find ourselves with some strange bedfellows, including North Korea, Saudi Arabia, Pakistan, and India (both states with nuclear weapons), Afghanistan, Belarus, Eritrea, Ethiopia, Libya, Myanmar, Somalia, and Syria. Neutrality is not high on the agenda of any of these countries, so by joining the NAM, Ireland would be abandoning its traditional neutrality. The effectiveness of the NAM is also problematic. Just as neutral states are being encouraged or threatened towards abandoning their neutral status in recent times, with Sweden and Finland having done so in 2022, many members of the NAM have likewise been targeted by belligerent powers. In 1965, President Sukarno of Indonesia was overthrown in a military coup led by Army Colonel Suharto but actively supported by the US CIA, in which up to one million Indonesian communists and those suspected of being left-wing were murdered. Suharto remained in power in Indonesia with active US support for thirty-two years until he was forced to resign in 1998. Coincidentally, former US President Barack Obama lived as a child in Indonesia from 1967 to 1971. His mother, who had married an Indonesian, worked with USAID during this period, and USAID was closely associated with the CIA in Indonesia during these times.

Dr Pat Walsh asks: 'If Ireland is non-aligned then why is it not a member of the Non-Aligned Movement?' He also writes that: 'The Non-aligned Movement represents what independent Ireland historically stood for – anti-colonialism, independence, and neutrality.' In this he is only partly correct. Independent Ireland historically did stand for anti-colonialism and independence, and neutrality, but neutrality has not been and is not a feature of the NAM. Many of the NAM members also do not comply with the requirement of 'the absence of bilateral military agreements or foreign military bases'. Dr Walsh also argues that membership of the NAM would: 'give Irish neutrality the substance it lacks, which it has not really had since World War II'. I disagree with this. During World War II Irish neutrality, while fully justified, was a negative self-interested type of neutrality, while our neutrality after we joined the UN in 1955 became a much more active positive neutrality promoting international peace and justice and supporting the decolonisation process.

The Irish people, or the people who have lived on the island of Ireland, have a long history of belligerence, and a shorter history of peace and neutrality. We should begin by undertaking the difficult task of trying to define who or what the term 'the Irish people' means. As far as we know, Ireland has only experienced human occupation within the past 10,000 years or so. I worked in the Afar region of Ethiopia in 2010 and visited the site where the remains of a lady known as Lucy were discovered. She and her people lived in this East African Rift Valley area over three million years ago, so our human history in Ireland has been of relatively short duration by comparison. We are all blow-ins here in Ireland, and very many Irish have also blown-out in the meantime into almost all the countries of the world. We were colonised in Ireland but became colonisers not only as part of the British Empire but also participated in the colonisation of the America's north and south, and many other areas, and as colonisers we were not always the most humane. We were fighters in every clime, in every cause but our own, especially after the flight of the Wild Geese. As I write these words, plans are afoot to return the remains of Patrick Sarsfield to Ireland. He was fatally wounded at the Battle of Landen in Belgium in 1693. Perhaps his remains could be returned to Limerick, the city of the broken treaty stone?

In my view, it is the Irish people, including our Irish diaspora, whose interests we should protect and defend rather than the proverbial Four Green Fields or the territory of Ireland. In the context of modern warfare, the territory of Ireland is incapable of being defended against a major or even a mid-level modern power, and it would be suicidal economically and in reality to attempt to do so. The only wise defence policy for Ireland is to maintain a small well-trained defence force that would be equipped and trained to engage in guerrilla warfare in the event of a hostile invasion, as a deterrent to any such invasion. This has never been the defence policy of successive Irish governments, even during World War II, when defence policy was based on very lightly armed brigade and division-level formations. We built fake armoured cars to fool the invaders, then seemed to forget they were fake armoured cars, and sent them with Irish peacekeepers to Congo, where their limitations were tragically exposed.

Including the Irish Diaspora is important in my view as many of them were involuntary emigrants due to persecution in Ireland prior to independence and due to involuntary emigration since independence caused by dreadful government economic policies and corruption.

The best interests of all Irish people can only be achieved by the pursuit of international peace and justice. While the economic policies of Éamon de Valera were disastrous, especially his economic war with Britain, his support for the League of Nations and later for the United Nations and his pursuit of Irish neutrality especially during World War II were fully justified and established a legacy that subsequent generations of Irish people have identified with and supported.

Since the foundation of the Irish State in 1922, we have experienced several bouts of civil conflicts, all connected with the failure to achieve independence for all of Ireland. However, the Irish State had not participated in foreign wars as a state, until our successive governments began abandoning our neutrality after the end of the Cold War by supporting US wars of aggression. I grew up near Ballyseedy in Co Kerry where one of the worst war crimes was committed by the Irish Free State forces a century ago on 7 March 1923, and as a teenager, I attended the unveiling of the memorial in 1959 at Ballyseedy. Four years later, I joined the Irish Defence Forces, which was still being labelled as the Free State Army by republicans.

Definition of neutrality: It is essential to clarify what the term neutrality means from an international law perspective as well as from an Irish perspective. The Hague Convention V on Neutrality 1907 defines the rights and duties of neutral powers, Article 2 states that: 'Belligerents are forbidden to move troops or convoys of either munitions of war or supplies across the territory of a neutral Power' and Article 11 states that 'A neutral Power which receives on its territory troops belonging to the belligerent armies shall intern them, as far as possible, at a distance from the theatre of war.'

In March 2003 I took a High Court constitutional case against the Irish Government on the issue that allowing the US military to use Shannon Airport to wage wars in the Middle East was in breach of Articles 28 and 29 of Bunreacht na hÉireann and in breach of international laws on neutrality. During this case, international law expert Professor Ian Scobbie defined international law on neutrality in an affidavit as follows:

Oppenheim-Lauterpacht contains a useful definition of neutrality. It states:

Neutrality may be defined as the attitude of impartiality adopted by third States towards belligerents and recognised by belligerents, such attitude creating rights and duties between the impartial States and the belligerents. Whether or not a third State will adopt an attitude of impartiality at the outbreak of a war is not a matter for International Law but for international politics…[A]ll States which do not expressly declare the contrary by word or action are supposed to be neutral, and the rights and duties arising from neutrality come into existence, and remain in existence, through the mere fact of a State taking up an attitude of impartiality, and not being drawn in to the war by the belligerents. (Oppenheim-Lauterpacht 1952 653-654).'

Professor Scobbie went on to say that: 'the core concept of the customary institution of neutrality is the neutral's attitude of impartiality which excludes such assistance and succour to one of the belligerents as is detrimental to the other, and, further, such injuries to the one as benefit the other. But it requires, on the other hand, active measures from neutral States' (Oppenheim-Lauterpacht 1952 654). In traditional doctrine, neutral States must prevent belligerents from using their territory and resources for hostile purposes during war. This extends beyond the conduct of hostilities on neutral territory to prohibit, for instance, the transport of troops and war materiel over neutral land territory. This was expressly prohibited by 1907 Hague Convention V, Article 2.

Judge Kearns ruled against me and in favour of the Irish Government on the constitutional issues of Articles 28 and 29, on the questionable basis that Article 29, subsections 1, 2, and 3 were only advisory and 'that these provisions are entirely addressed to other nations and not to individuals ... They are ... more akin to the kind of assertion one might find in the preamble to a convention, or a treaty agreed between sovereign States'.

The 'individuals' involved are the people of Ireland who voted by referendum on 1 July 1937 to establish Bunreacht na hÉireann as the foundation of democracy in Ireland and this constitution was directed primarily and applicable to the Irish people and to the Irish Government and not to foreign states as suggested by Judge Kearns.

On Article 28, Judge Kearns argued that the issue of separation of powers between the Government, the legislature, and the judiciary made it inappropriate for the court to intervene in such government decisions. The phrase used by Judge Kearns 'without proof of quite exceptional circumstances' ignores the reality that extraordinary circumstances were occurring in Iraq involving the unlawful killing of tens of thousands of people, and that US military use of Shannon Airport was facilitating these crimes. The issue of separation of powers also implies that the judiciary does have such powers and responsibilities under the constitution, but in this case, the High Court failed to use or apply such powers and responsibilities.

The High Court did, however, rule in my favour on the issue of whether the Irish Government was in breach of international laws on neutrality by allowing the US military to use Shannon Airport.

'The court is prepared to hold therefore that there is an identifiable rule of customary law in relation to the status of neutrality whereunder a neutral state may not permit the movement of large numbers of troops or munitions of one belligerent State through its territory en route to a theatre of war with another.' However, the court failed to follow up on this ruling by imposing any form of sanction or criticism on the Irish Government for its breaches of international laws. In the intervening period between 2003 and the present time, the Irish Government has continued to be in breach of international laws on neutrality and in breach of a High Court ruling by allowing US troops to transit through Shannon Airport.

Given the likelihood that Ireland north and south will become a united state in the foreseeable future, it remains to be seen whether this united Ireland will be a neutral state or will choose to join NATO as a compromise towards the Unionist minority who may insist on remaining part of the NATO alliance. A united Ireland as a member of NATO would have no credible claim to be a sovereign independent state. However, the issue of the sovereignty of states is a questionable and contested one. Germany discovered recently that its sovereignty was not all it might be, when on the 26th of September 2022 the Nord Stream gas pipelines were blown up, most likely by the US, in an act of economic war against Germany and Russia.

Since the end of the Cold War, successive Irish governments have been eroding and degrading Irish neutrality to such an extent that Ireland is no longer a neutral state.

This began when successive Irish governments allowed the US military to transit through Shannon Airport during the first Gulf War in 1991, continued with the NATO war against Serbia in 1999, and followed on with the wars of aggression and overthrow of the governments of Afghanistan in 2001, Iraq in 2003, and Libya in 2001, and the attempted overthrow of the government of Syria.

When asked on RTÉ Radio on Sunday the 26th of February if the Irish Government's decision to send Irish Defence Forces personnel to train Ukrainian soldiers was a breach of Irish neutrality, An Táiniste Micheál Martin TD denied that this was the case and stated that: 'We are all anti-war.' Mr Martin was a senior minister in successive Irish governments, including in 1999, 2001, and 2003, when the Irish Government allowed the US military to use Shannon Airport and Irish airspace during the US/NATO wars against Serbia, Afghanistan, and Iraq. All of these wars were in breach of the UN Charter and in breach of Irish neutrality.

Ireland was elected to the UN Security Council for a two-year period in 2021 based substantially on its record as a neutral state actively promoting international peace and justice yet failed shamefully to live up to its important responsibilities to promote peace in the conflict between Ukraine and Russia. Ireland has no credible capacity to promote and support wars, yet has had a proud tradition of promoting peace and justice internationally. Not only are our government actively supporting wars, and reducing our traditional commitment to genuine UN peacekeeping, but it has also allowed the strength of the Irish Defence Forces to fall below 8,000 personnel and denied them the necessary resources to provide adequate working conditions and essential equipment.

The Irish people have strongly supported the peace process within Ireland and our government should likewise be supporting international peace.

The following are ten reasons why Ireland must not join NATO or any defence alliance or the Non-Aligned Movement, and must restore its positive neutrality.

Reason 1: The first and most important reason for Irish neutrality is for the well-being and physical safety of humanity, including the Irish people. Since the first Gulf War in 1991, up to five million people have died across the wider Middle East for war-related reasons, including one million children. All these wars were unjustified and illegal and now the death toll is being added to by the horrific war in Ukraine. Ireland has facilitated these wars and is still doing so by allowing millions of US soldiers and weapons to use Shannon Airport as a refuelling air base, in breach of international laws on neutrality and making Ireland actively complicit in these millions of war deaths.

Reason 2: The primary duty of all Irish governments is to defend the lives and interests of Irish people. The Irish people include all those living in Ireland and our diaspora scattered around the world. Promoting international peace and justice must therefore be the top priority of the Irish Government and this can only be achieved by peaceful means. One of the youngest victims of the 9/11 terrorist attacks on the United States was an Irish girl, four-year-old Juliana Clifford McCourt.

Reason 3: Irish independence and sovereignty was achieved at great cost during a time when up to 50,000 Irish soldiers were being slaughtered fighting for the British Empire. Our freedom, sovereignty and neutrality are inseparably linked – if we lose one, we lose all three. The Third World War may already be in its early stages. Joining military alliances now could cost the Irish people far more than 50,000 lives in unjustified future wars. NATO has become a global protection racket acting in gross breach of the UN Charter and the rule of international laws. Russia is now doing likewise in Ukraine.

Reason 4: The imperial wars of the past are now replaced by resource wars by the most powerful states to perpetrate the theft of scarce vital resources from the least powerful states. The rule of international law is vital for small countries like Ireland and for those countries and peoples impoverished by exploitation by powerful countries, including the US and Russia, and the European Union. Ireland must take the side of the most vulnerable peoples of the world and must not join those who are perpetrating war crimes. In this 21st century, all wars are war crimes.

Reason 5: Ireland has neither the resources nor the constitutional mandate from the people to get involved in unjustified wars. All wars in this 21st century have been and are unjustified due to the exceptional dangers of catastrophic consequences. There are always peaceful alternatives to wars and violence and Article 29 of the Irish Constitution obliges Ireland to pursue the path of peace and avoid involvement in wars.

Reason 6: Ireland was elected to the UN Security Council for a two-year period beginning in January 2021. This was the fourth time that we, as a small country, achieved such an important international position, and our positive neutrality was a significant factor in achieving this. Unfortunately, our Irish Government has failed to use this vital opportunity to help to promote peace in various conflicts. Our government has supported US-led aggression in the Middle East and is supporting the US/NATO alliance which is using the tragic Ukrainian conflicts as a proxy war with Russia. It was Ireland's duty as a member of the UN Security Council to make every possible diplomatic effort to promote peace between Russia and Ukraine and we have failed to do so.

Reason 7: The success of the Irish economy in recent decades has been substantially helped by the high priority given by successive Irish governments to the education of our children. This has been possible partly because we have not been spending (or wasting) lots of money on armaments and defence spending. Foolish recent proposals by Ireland to purchase a squadron of fighter jets and other military equipment including a multi-role large naval vessel will result in less financial resources being available for vital services such as education, health, and social services for our most vulnerable citizens.

Reason 8: Geographical location has been a vital factor in enabling Ireland as an island on the western periphery of Europe to maintain its neutrality, especially throughout World War II. While being a peripheral island has many economic disadvantages, we must cherish the security advantages it affords us.

Reason 9: While the risk of a nuclear war is a possible threat, the existential damage to our living environment is no longer just a threat, it is a reality that is happening and intensifying daily. The militarisation of Europe and the wider world is a major contributor to this environmental damage, and this is exacerbated by the environmental destruction and pollution caused by wars. The US, NATO, and other powerful countries are implementing and actively planning for the use of outer space and undersea spaces towards achieving full spectrum military dominance. Artificial intelligence, replacing soldiers with robots, and the increasing use of unmanned military vehicles, aircraft drones, and undersea drones, are becoming a reality.

Reason 10: Ireland is sometimes spuriously accused of benefiting from NATO's so-called security umbrella. Throughout the Cold War, NATO and the USSR terrorised the world with the threat of a nuclear Holocaust. This nuclear terrorist threat is now more immediate and more serious. NATO's security umbrella could become the reality of horrific mushroom clouds leading to the extinction not only of humanity but all living things on Planet Earth. If Ireland joins NATO or an EU military alliance and continues to facilitate US military use of Shannon Airport, this could make Ireland a 'legitimate military target' by countries attacked by the US and NATO.

Conclusion: Ireland must do what is right in the long-term interests of humanity and the Irish people and must avoid what is cynically expedient in the short term. Positive neutrality means working ceaselessly to promote international peace with justice. Peace without justice is just a temporary ceasefire.

'They're lying to us. We know they're lying to us. They know we know they're lying to us. And yet, they continue to lie.' - Alexander Solzhenitsyn

No. 272.
The Irish News 30 March 2023
EU Bombs for Peace

At a meeting in Brussels on March 20, attended by Peter Burke TD, Minister of State for European Affairs and Defence, the EU decided to use the European Peace Facility to spend €2 billion to supply Ukraine with 155mm artillery shells which will be used to kill thousands of Russians and Ukrainians in eastern Ukraine. This is the sort of international immorality George Orwell tried to expose. Our Irish Government is also contributing €3m towards the International Criminal Court war crimes investigations in Ukraine but for three decades ignored the war crimes committed by the US and its NATO and other allies in Iraq and Afghanistan. All war crimes must be investigated, and the perpetrators brought to justice. The best way to prevent war crimes is to prevent wars by promoting peace by peaceful means. Since Sweden and Finland abandoned their neutrality, Ireland,

Austria, Cyprus, and Malta are the only EU states not full members of NATO. NATO has effectively taken over the EU. The US has been using NATO as its enforcer to maintain its stranglehold over the global financial system and access to an undue share of the world's limited resources. How many more innocent Ukrainians must die?

No. 273.

Irish Independent 11 April 2023

We Must Advocate for Peace Worldwide, Not Just at Home

The visit to Ireland by US President Joe Biden to celebrate the 25th anniversary of the Good Friday Agreement (GFA) should be used to strengthen the peace process in Ireland and to promote international peace, rather than just be used for US presidential electioneering purposes.

Successive Irish governments have been justifiably portraying the peace process in Northern Ireland as a positive example of how other conflicts internationally could be resolved. The GFA includes the following in its Declaration of Support: 'We reaffirm our total and absolute commitment to exclusively democratic and peaceful means of resolving differences on political issues, and our opposition to any use or threat of force by others for any political purpose, whether in regard to this agreement or otherwise.'

The word 'otherwise' in this statement indicates that these principles should also be applied to other conflicts at international level in keeping with the Irish Constitution.

Consecutive Irish governments have reneged on their constitutional, humanitarian, and international law responsibilities by actively supporting US-led wars in the Middle East by allowing the US military to transit through Shannon Airport.

While the Irish Government has justifiably criticised the Russian invasion of Ukraine, it has wrongfully failed to criticise the US and its NATO allies' invasions and wars of aggression in Serbia, Afghanistan, Iraq, Libya, and elsewhere.

No. 274.
The Irish News 4 May 2023, *Irish Examiner* 6 May 2023
Are Mistakes of Rwanda Being Repeated in Sudan?

The present conflict in Sudan once again demonstrates the abject failure of the UN and the international community to prevent or stop conflicts in Africa that have amounted to genocide and widespread human rights abuses. In 1994, the international community stood idly by as up to a quarter of a million Rwandan people were brutally slaughtered. This conflict then spilled over into the Democratic Republic of Congo, igniting a conflict that is still ongoing causing several more million deaths. European and Western lives are given priority over the lives of the rest of humanity. The US and NATO intervened eventually to stop the conflict in Bosnia in 1995, although their attempts to impose democracy there have arguably failed.

Little has been learned from the twenty-year US-led unjustified war of vengeance waged against the Afghan people. In the resulting 2021 evacuation chaos, military dogs were given priority over Afghans who worked with Western forces and whose lives were in danger. No accountability has been achieved for the ongoing trauma that the Afghan people are still going through. While most Western citizens have been successfully evacuated from Sudan, far too little consideration is being given to the trauma being suffered by the citizens of Sudan. How many Sudanese refugees will be allowed into Fortress Europe? Many of these conflicts in Africa and the Middle East have roots in European colonial abuses.

There is now a serious risk of the present Sudan conflict deteriorating into crimes against humanity. When a popular uprising overthrew the autocratic government of Omar al-Bashir, their efforts to establish democracy were thwarted by the two main perpetrators of this present conflict, General al-Burhan and RST leader General Dagalo / Hemedti both of whose forces were implicated in the Darfur genocide.

The United Nations is once again being prevented from doing its primary task of maintaining international peace by several of its most powerful states who are pursuing their national interests at the expense of the most vulnerable members of humanity.

No. 275.

Irish Independent 17 May 2023

Where is 'Register of Damage' For Victims of US Conflicts?

Taoiseach Leo Varadkar is attending a Council of Europe summit meeting in Iceland on 16 May for the purpose of creating a 'register of damages' for those who have suffered from the ongoing war in Ukraine. This is an 'ah but what about letter'. Of course, a 'damage register' should be established for all conflicts and those responsible for such damage and related war crimes should be fully held to account. It begs the question, why have there been no similar meetings to establish a 'damage register' for the wars of aggression waged by the US and its NATO and other allies in Serbia, Iraq, Afghanistan, Libya, Syria, Yemen and elsewhere? And why has there been no accountability for the very serious war crimes and crimes against humanity committed against the peoples of these non-European countries? Up to five million people have died due to war-related reasons in these conflicts and untold infrastructural and environmental problems have been caused by these unjustifiable wars. The Council of Europe may well argue that its focus is primarily on Europe, but surely the United Nations and other international bodies such as the International Criminal Court should have initiated and carried out such a damage register and taken steps to hold all those responsible for such crimes accountable.

No. 276.
Irish Examiner **26 May 2023.**
Second-Hand Ships Not Up to the Task for Naval Service
Recently, the naval service took possession of two ships to work on day-long surveillance patrols in the Irish Sea and off the southeast coast. The naval service does need suitable new ships to undertake its important duties, but these were not 'new ships'. They were second-hand ships originally built for the New Zealand Navy. However, they were found to be unsuitable for use on the high seas or rough sea conditions, and were confined to inshore duties only. If these ships were a mistake for the New Zealand Navy, then their purchase was arguably a mistake by the Irish Government. Commodore Michael Malone seemed to acknowledge the limitations of these ships when he said they will 'enhance the patrol profile of the Naval Service on the East and Southeast Coast'. The most important duties and operations of the Irish Naval Service are off the northwest, west, and southwest coasts. It is not just a matter of the Naval Service returning to 'its mandated number of hulls'. These ships are not 'a step forward in capability' but more likely a step backwards. The report said these ships 'will also be available for maritime rescue operations' yet, such operations most often occur in difficult weather and sea conditions. Lieutenant General Seán Clancy, when the ships were ceremonially handed over to Ireland in March, said these ships will allow the naval service to 'tackle the dynamic and ever-changing maritime environment that we operate in 365 days a year'. This is a questionable statement.

No. 277.
Irish Daily Mail, **30 May 2023.**
Environmental Crisis Needs to Be Tackled Not Neglected
Dublin Airport has a car parking crisis. It had 28 million passengers in 2022 and is seeking planning for up to 40m passengers. Ryanair orders 300 Boeing 737-max-10 aircraft. The vast bulk of these flights and aircraft are used for avoidable tourism and are causing serious damage to the environment. Farmers are critical of plans to rewet state-owned bogland in

case it might cause rewetting on their own neighbouring bogland, which should never have been drained in the first place. Huge costs are being incurred to try to prevent coastal flooding of properties that should never have been built too close to the coast, or in floodplains. Our government politicians are arguing over how much to spend on buying voters for the next election while failing to deal with the housing crisis and the more serious environmental crisis. Wars and the militarisation of Europe and the wider world are huge contributors to the environmental crisis. Council of Europe leaders justifiably seek to hold Russia to account for its war against Ukraine, yet they and Ireland remained silent when NATO and EU states bombed Yugoslavia in 1999, and waged wars of aggression in Iraq, Afghanistan, and elsewhere in contravention of international laws. Positive active neutrality and peace in Ukraine are supported by the majority of Irish people, yet the Irish Government is holding an arguably undemocratic forum, the object of which is likely to be the abandonment of Irish neutrality. The war in Ukraine poses a huge risk of nuclear disaster. Environmental destruction exacerbated by wars is causing a global refugee crisis, famine, and human rights abuses, yet Ireland and the European Union are failing to live up to their and our humanitarian responsibilities. Too many governments, and too many Irish and global citizens, are behaving selfishly and failing to address the environmental crisis that threatens the existence of all future generations.

No. 278.
Irish Examiner 15 June 2023
At a Crossroads on a United Ireland

After a century of independence, the Republic of Ireland has reached a crossroads on our journey to take our place among the nations of the world. If we continue down the road of genuine peace and reconciliation on the Island of Ireland, a united Ireland is on the horizon, but this must be the unity of the people of Ireland rather than of the four green fields. For such a small country with limited resources, Ireland has played an important altruistic role in promoting global peace and justice. This is now under threat by the determination of successive governments to abandon a policy of active neutrality, that is supported by most Irish people, and become entangled with EU and NATO Western military alliances that are promoting global domination and exploitation at the expense of the majority of humanity. The top-down consultative forum organised by the Department of Foreign Affairs is intended to take us down the road of militarism and exploitation by Fortress Europe or US-led NATO full spectrum dominance. The war in Ukraine is doing colossal damage to the people of Ukraine and Russia. The Irish Government was in a unique position as a member of the UN Security Council throughout 2022 to help promote peace between Ukraine and Russia but chose instead to support those who were determined to use the conflict in Ukraine as a proxy war against Russia. Historically, the people of Russia and Ukraine have suffered hugely from wars and human rights abuses. Now, this conflict has the potential to have catastrophic consequences for all of humanity. It is vital that the people of Ireland engage with these forum sessions in Cork, Galway, and Dublin, to persuade the Irish Government to respect the democratic wishes of the Irish people to promote global peace and justice instead of wars and military domination that are destroying the global environment.

No. 279.

Irish Examiner 17 June 2023
Med Mission Leaves Gap Off Our Coasts

The LÉ *William Butler Yeats* has departed for its six-week Mediterranean Operation Irini mission to enforce a UN embargo on arms shipments into Libya. This is a pointless mission since Libya has been awash with arms since NATO helped overthrow its government in 2011. This mission should not have been authorised when most of the other Naval Service ships are tied up due to lack of crew members. It leaves an unacceptable gap in its duties to provide emergency marine duties off our Irish coasts.

This coincides with news of the dreadful tragedy that hundreds of migrants are likely to have drowned when a migrant ship from Libya sank near the coast of Greece. It's been reported that about 100 children were packed into the hold of the ship. Most of them are believed to have drowned. The European Union Frontex agency, and the Greek Coast Guard, had been monitoring this ship for up to twelve hours prior to the disaster, and failed to offer any practical assistance until it was too late, thereby failing in their international laws of the sea duties. The presence of an Irish Naval Service ship off the coast of Libya imposes duties on the crew of that ship to provide emergency rescue services for migrants fleeing from Libya. This may be in conflict with its Operation Irini mission. The Irish Government should now either change the mission of the LÉ *William Butler Yates* from enforcing the arms embargo to rescuing migrants in danger of drowning or order the return of this ship to its duties off the Irish coast.

No. 280.
The Irish Times 7 July 2023
Ireland and Its Neutrality

Sir, In the recent consultative forum on International Security Policy there was a lot of discussion from government-appointed panel members on the removal of the triple lock so as to allow Irish Defence Forces personnel to serve on overseas missions that do not have a mandate from the United Nations. This would include NATO and European Union missions. The US/NATO-led occupation of Afghanistan ended in chaos in August 2021, with up to a quarter of a million people killed. Two hundred twenty-six Irish soldiers served with these NATO missions over a fifteen-year period. In Conor Gallagher's book *Is Ireland Neutral*, Gallagher records details of an interview with retired Lieutenant Colonel Ray Lane (page 135), who served as a bomb disposal expert with NATO in Afghanistan, in which he says that Lt Col Ray Lane: 'was also involved in the more aggressive side of the response; helping to track down and kill Taliban bombers. This included assisting US forces in directing airstrikes against targets responsible for IED attacks'. This suggests that a senior Irish officer from a neutral country was involved in the killing of Afghan soldiers who were fighting to free their country from foreign occupation. Britain's Prince Harry is reported to have written in his autobiography that he had killed twenty-five Taliban soldiers. The Irish Defence Forces, Óglaigh na hÉireann, owes its origins to the freedom fighters who fought to free Ireland from foreign occupation. Yes, the triple lock should be amended, to ensure that Dáil Éireann and UN approval is needed for any number of Irish soldiers to be sent on foreign missions.

Yours etc, Edward Horgan (Commandant retired)

No. 281.
Irish Examiner **12 July 2023**, *The Irish News* **13 July 2023**
The New RTÉ Will Have to Be Independent

The problems that have been exposed in the management of RTÉ are getting the attention they deserve. Misuse of publicly funded broadcasting can have important implications for matters of democracy and justice in Ireland and globally. Privately owned and commercial media sources are also subject to similar abuses and may be far less amenable to the sort of accountability we are now seeing at RTÉ. Mainstream media globally, including Irish media, are heavily influenced by US and Western commercial media. RTÉ does some good investigative reporting on some national and international issues but has been falling short in several important areas. Examples include its recent reporting on Israeli aggression in which RTÉ gave airtime to Israeli Prime Minister Netanyahu seeking to justify the military attack on Jenin refugee camp. On July 10, Oliver Callan, standing in for Ryan Tubridy, gave an extended uncritical interview with Evan Thomas promoting his book *Road to Surrender* justifying the atomic bombing of Hiroshima and Nagasaki. RTÉ news reporting on the European Union, NATO and the war in Ukraine has arguably been unduly uncritical. Public broadcasting should not become a government broadcasting service. The reorganised RTÉ must promote a more independent form of investigative journalism prioritising the most important national and international issues, as befits its role as part of the fourth estate.

Edward Horgan, Castletroy, Limerick.

No. 282.
Irish Examiner 1 August 2023
Never Too Late to Do What Is Right

Paul Hosford highlighted the issue of the US military use of Shannon Airport in his article 'US plane that carried weapons through Shannon was not checked for cluster bombs' (July 27). In spite of continuously stating that Ireland is a neutral country and using this to help gain membership of the UN Security Council for 2021 and 2022, successive Irish governments have allowed aircraft associated with the US military and the CIA to refuel at Shannon Airport over the past three decades. The US and its NATO and other allies were waging wars that included the overthrow of the governments of Afghanistan and Iraq, and carrying out unjustified military aggression against Serbia, Libya, Syria, and elsewhere. US military use of Shannon Airport made the Irish Government, and by default the Irish people, complicit in the deaths due to war-related reasons of millions of people, including an estimated one million children. Thirty-nine years ago, a courageous group of Dunnes Stores workers went on strike to protest against apartheid human rights abuses in South Africa. Their names were Mary Manning, Karen Gearon, Liz Deasy, Michelle Gavin, Sandra Griffin, Theresa Mooney, Vonnie Munroe, Cathryn O'Reilly, Alma Russel, and Tommy Davis. It is now time for equally courageous workers at Shannon Airport to refuse to refuel and service aircraft associated with the US military. It is never too late to do what is right. It will not bring back those who have already died, but will help to prevent more unjustified deaths in the future, just as the actions of the Dunnes Stores workers helped to end apartheid in South Africa.

No. 283.
Irish Independent 1 August, 2023. Also published in the *Irish Examiner*
Sinéad Was a Woman of Peace, So Warplane Tribute Was Deeply Inappropriate

Sinéad O'Connor, in addition to being a beautiful singer, was also a committed activist for human rights. She would be appalled at the headline and photograph in the *Sunday Times* on July 30.

It read 'Highest tribute to incomparable singer', with a photo of a World War II Lancaster Bomber and three Irish Air Corps aircraft at the Bray Air Show.

The caption explained that a Lancaster bomber from the Battle of Britain had been flown in a tribute to Sinéad O'Connor.

On the night of February 13 into February 14, 1945, 254 Lancaster Bomber aircraft dropped 500 tons of high explosives and 375 tons of incendiaries (firebombs) on the city of Dresden, Germany, killing about 25,000 people. Most of those killed were civilians.

No. 284.
Irish Examiner 14 August 2023
Two Wrongs Do Not Make a Right

Cliff O'Hanlon (Dresden was not the only target, letters August 7) takes me to task for my letter criticising the Lancaster Bombers being used to commemorate the death of Sinéad O'Connor. I sympathise with Cliff O'Hanlon and with all those who have lost friends and relatives in wars. Those of us who served in the Irish Defence Forces knew many of those who lost their lives on UN peacekeeping duties.

He seeks to justify the firebombing of Dresden on the basis that it was requested by the Russians because Germany had a radio station in Dresden that was monitoring the Russian advance. The firebombing of Dresden cost the lives of about 25,000 people, mainly civilians. Two wrongs never make a right. O'Hanlon lists some of the British cities bombed by Germany 'where the innocent suffered in the insanity of war'. I agree fully with his characterisation of war as insanity and with his concerns for the innocents who suffer in wars. Modern 21st-century wars are so horrific that only peaceful means must be used to resolve conflicts.

No. 285.
The Phoenix 23 March 2023
Affairs of the Nation, Pillars of Society, Edward Horgan

DUBLIN (March 10, 2023) – Recently acquitted of criminal damage to a US Navy warplane in Shannon Airport six years ago, the seventy-seven-year-old ex-military officer, commandant Edward Horgan, must be one of the most resilient (and formidable) anti-establishment campaigners Ireland has seen for many years. He has been in and out of Irish courts and Garda holding cells down the years in his campaigns for peace and he has returned his military and UN decorations and his presidential commissioning certificate in protest at the government's participation in the Iraq War (given the US military's transit to the Middle East via Shannon).

He is a founding member of the Shannon Peace Camp and a leading member of the Peace and Neutrality Alliance. And in his writings and ideas – as enunciated to peace activists and defenders of Irish neutrality – Horgan has become the most effective human face of the peace movement in Ireland over several decades.

Horgan could have become a senior member of the officer class, had he played the game with the top brass and relevant ministers. He describes the highlight of his military career as his appointment in 1983 as officer commanding the 1st tank squadron.

In 1985, Horgan became senior instructor in armoured warfare at the Command and Staff School, where he says he had to teach future senior commanders of the armed forces military strategy based on manuals from the British and US armed forces, which 'I knew were almost totally inappropriate towards defending the territory and people of the Irish Republic.'

As Horgan puts it: 'I had concluded that Ireland did not have the resources to defend its territory by conventional military means and that it could only be defended, as our independence had been achieved, by guerrilla warfare.

'The counterargument was that if we had a squadron of fighter aircraft and a brigade of tanks and other associated military equipment, we could defend Ireland against any likely aggressor. Saddam Hussein and Muammar Gaddafi were to discover to their cost that hundreds or even thousands of slightly out-of-date tanks and aircraft were useless against the conventional weapons of NATO. Their armies were obliterated in the first days of US/ NATO-led attacks on their countries and their unfortunate conscript soldiers were slaughtered in their thousands.

'Algeria and Vietnam had demonstrated the success of the guerrilla warfare alternative,' he said.

'Our Military College experts got around this conundrum by the clever trick of designing all military exercises as if the invading forces always had just a little less military power at their disposal than we had. No sensible military power would invade a country like Ireland without employing an attacking force about three times the strength of our defending forces. However, since we had a force of less than 10,000 soldiers and given that we had no combat aircraft or modern battle tanks, we tailored our imaginary enemies accordingly.

'When I suggested at exercises debriefs that guerrilla warfare was the only sane option, but that this needed to be planned carefully well in advance, I was told that this was neither army nor government policy, and was told to teach the officially approved doctrines.

'After six months in this appointment, I decided I had had enough of military life, so I opted for early retirement. I had enjoyed most of my twenty-two years' military service and did not want to spend a further twenty years cynically teaching or applying military training that I knew was fundamentally wrong.'

International Experience

There is something fundamental about this disagreement with the military and political establishment as Horgan stuck to the ideas and principles of the Irish anti-colonial experience against the new, 'modern' officers and politicians anxious to be in step with their transatlantic superiors.

For the next decade or so, Horgan worked in senior security and safety employment in places such as Aughinish Alumina in west Limerick and Trinity College Dublin, before spending several years working on democratisation and election supervision in over twenty countries.

He also spent several years boning up on international politics and peace analysis, securing more than one postgrad degree on such topics to accompany his international experience, which by now had transformed him into a deeply committed peace campaigner.

Many such activists pinpoint various EU treaties between the mid-1980s and late noughties [the decade from 2000 to 2009] as the process whereby Irish ministers turned against the honourable policy of non-alignment and neutrality that had formerly distinguished Irish foreign policy. These treaties began with the 1987 Single European Act and were followed by the 1992 Maastricht Treaty, the 1998 Amsterdam Treaty, the 2002 Nice Treaty, and the 2008 Lisbon Treaty. The latter two were initially rejected by Irish voters who subsequently endorsed them following reassurances from the EU that Irish neutrality would not be compromised by the treaties.

In an *Irish Times* (IT) article just after the Lisbon Treaty was endorsed in a second vote in 2008, Horgan demolished the superior D4 view of neutrality as espoused by IT Peter Murtagh days earlier, who dismissed 'insular… neuralgic and myopic arguments over neutrality'.

In his simple but authentic and most persuasive style, Horgan wrote: 'On March 20th, 2003, the government invoked the status of neutrality by declaring Ireland a neutral state, but contravened the Hague Convention by allowing US troops to use Shannon Airport for its war on Iraq. An implied condition of neutrality is that states do not enter into military alliances, such as NATO, or an EU army if such develops.'

He also wrote: 'Peace must be created by peaceful means, not warfare. In exceptional circumstances peace must be enforced by legitimate UN authority, not by self-appointed vigilantes such as the US, the UK, or the North Atlantic Treaty Organisation [NATO]'.

Horgan claimed that he and his allies support an active, positive neutrality that reflects the past policies of Éamon de Valera and Frank Aiken, 'active supporters of the League of Nations and the UN'.

Here again, Horgan reflects the divide between the values of anti-colonialism that were reflected in Fianna Fáil governments and some other parties in the first fifty years of the state and the new establishment that thinks it is somehow internationalist to be part of the Western war machine.

A most interesting if non-intellectual argument that determined just which ideas about neutrality would – or would not – become available to readers of the liberal *Irish Times* came quickly. Horgan found that, since that article fifteen years ago (August 2008), the paper of reference has not published any further articles presented to it by the peace campaigner. Like others – northern republicans and Eurosceptics in particular – such censored individuals eventually give up composing and submitting articles that jar with the Tara Street line.

The year before this exchange, Horgan had taken the government to the High Court, claiming that the government's facilitation of armed US troops' journey to Iraq, via its stop-off at Shannon, was unconstitutional on two grounds and was also 'a breach by the state, as a neutral state, of the customary rules of international law and is thereby unconstitutional' (under Irish law).

BUSH VISIT

Judge Nicky Kearns dismissed all three grounds of Horgan's case but, on the issue of neutrality and international law, he conceded that 'the court is prepared to hold therefore that there is an identifiable rule of customary law in relation to the status of neutrality, whereunder a neutral state may not permit the movement of large numbers of troops or munitions of one belligerent state through its territory en route to a theatre of war with another'.

However, Kearns concluded: 'Where a conflict arises, the rule of international law must in every case yield to domestic law.'

Horgan's next incursion was rather more dramatic and he, along with two other anti-war activists, caused a commotion when they entered an 'exclusion zone' in the Shannon Estuary in June 2004, when then-US President George W. Bush was visiting Ireland. Two boats were launched from the LÉ *Aoife* while a helicopter circled overhead as the three cockleshell heroes were pursued and confronted by the forces of the state that night.

At Ennis District Court, Judge Joseph Mangan dismissed charges against the three of refusing to obey an order to leave the exclusion zone. The judge also dismissed the charge of entering the exclusion zone without permission after he rejected the state's application to amend the charges against the three.

In recent years, Horgan's main political and peace activity is that of letter writer to newspapers and contributor to others in tracts that both intellectually arm his supporters and persuade others to adopt the cause. His writings on Palestine, Yemen, Syria, and the other larger theatres of war and carnage such as Ukraine are textbook examples of lucid, knowledgeable, and persuasive political polemics. As his day job, he also manages the Centre for Care of Survivors of Torture in Dublin.

Naming the Children

However, Horgan's main project these days is the Naming the Children campaign, an effort to name as many children as possible in the first Gulf War in 1991 to the present day.

Horgan writes: 'When we include the dreadful statistic that up to half a million Iraqi children died as a result of US-driven UN sanctions on Iraq in the 1990s, one begins to realise that the total number of children who have died as a result of these wars may be as many as one million.' (The Iraq figure is a United Nations statistic).

Horgan made much of this campaign when arraigned before the Dublin Circuit Criminal Court in January, along with Dan Dowling, on charges of trespass at Shannon Airport and causing criminal damage to a US Navy aircraft (writing 'Danger, danger, don't fly' on the plane). Horgan presented a folder to the arresting Garda with the names of up to 1,000 children who had died in the Middle East.

He spent much time explaining to the jury and a most attentive judge Martina Baxter that his only intent was to 'try and minimise the number of people who are being killed in the Middle East, especially children. So that's why and I believe that I did have lawful excuse.'

Horgan added that his 'subsidiary' reason for going into the airport was to highlight the wrongdoing of the government at Shannon and 'the failure of the Gardaí, under instructions from the government, I'm presuming, to search the planes'.

The efforts that the state prosecutor, barrister Jane McCudden, made to paint Horgan as some extreme political agitator may not have been the best tactic, as he batted aside such accusations with ease.

The jury did not take long to acquit the two of criminal damage but presumably felt compelled to convict on the trespass charge, whereupon Judge Baxter ordered that they each pay €5,000 to a women's refuge in Clare. Passing sentence, she also described both men as displaying 'upstanding character, composure and dignity' at all stages during the trial. 'You are upstanding people; you have behaved with courtesy and dignity throughout,' Judge Baxter said.

Horgan's old-world charm and civility, as recognised by the judge and others, are merely part of his armoury, which at bottom is a clear, well-read analysis of global politics and militarism and an ability to express it succinctly in an Irish context.

EU-NATO COOPERATION

Never was such analysis so needed as our 'statesmen' – Micheál Martin, Leo Varadkar, and even Green Party leader Eamon Ryan – begin to behave like European leaders in the run-up to the Great War in 1914, a mad rush that even drew in what are now called the parties and leaders of European social democracy; all except Ireland's James Connolly.

A specific development this year – that was either unnoticed or deliberately downplayed by the mainstream media and body politic – was the joint declaration on EU-NATO cooperation, delivered in mid-January. It spoke of EU/NATO 'shared values' and the grave threat to Euro-Atlantic security posed by Russia's aggression in Ukraine, before warning of the 'growing strategic competition' posed by 'China's growing assertiveness'.

It also emphasised repeatedly the need for EU-NATO unity. But the real message in the fourteen-point statement came in number eight, which said: 'NATO remains the foundation of collective defence for its allies and essential for Euro-Atlantic security. We recognise the value of a stronger and more capable European Defence that contributes positively to global and transatlantic security and is complementary to and interoperable with NATO'.

This is a clear statement by the EU that, while its plans for militarisation of the union are still on train, it is NATO that calls the shots in the Western alliance from now on and plans for an EU army that would be independent of and even a rival to NATO have now been recognised as pipe dreams.

Horgan is well aware of such developments – caused by the Russian invasion of Ukraine and NATO's meddling in the first place. One expects to hear from Horgan on this issue in due course. In the meantime, the pacifist warrior was at it again this weekend with a letter to the *Sunday Independent*. In it, he attacked Micheál Martin for breaching Irish neutrality as a minister in past governments and in the current Cabinet that has agreed to send Defence Forces personnel to train Ukrainian soldiers.

Comment: I decided to include some of the conclusions from my PhD Thesis as the final item in this book, as it sums up much of my thinking on matters of peace, justice, and fairness.

No. 286.
Thesis Edward J. Horgan, University of Limerick, 2008
The United Nations – Beyond Reform? The Collective Insecurity of the International System and the Prospects for Sustainable Global Peace and Justice

Summary of Thesis Conclusions:

This thesis finds that the system of international relations, including the United Nations that has been in existence since 1945, but which is based on the older Westphalia system, is no longer adequate to ensure a satisfactory system of international peace and security, or to ensure the very survival of humanity. Thomas Turner states that even though the international system is undergoing another transformation stage in the post-Cold War era: "(u)nlike the other transition points 1815, 1918 and 1945 – the end of the Cold War has yet to yield new institution to replace those born after the Second World War.".[1] This research recommends that humanity should look to a more dynamic functionalist approach towards the attainment of a comprehensive working peace and common human security system for all humanity's individuals, based on functional multi-level cosmopolitan governance underpinned and regulated by a constantly evolving, or dynamic, system of global jurisprudence. The Westphalia system and its subsequent developments through the Concert of Vienna, League of Nations and on to the United Nations all developed as a result of catastrophic wars. Following the introduction of weapons of mass destruction in 1945, ostensibly to defend humanity from harm, humanity can no longer afford to wait for violent conflicts to be the catalysts for change. Peace and security gradually developed by peaceful and creative means, rather than the contradiction of attempting to impose peace and

---

[1] Thomas Turner, *The Congo Wars: Conflict, Myth & Reality* (New York: Zed Books, 2007), p. 149.

security quickly by violent and destructive means, is the only safe way forward for humanity.

The United Nations organisation has been attempting to achieve international peace and security for over sixty years. It has failed to do so and has failed catastrophically in conflicts in Asia, the Middle East and Africa. The UN could continue to perform many useful purposes, including providing a forum for member states, and providing an international set of structures in what should be seen a graduated matrix of human societal regulatory structures from the individual and the local to the global. In this age of increasing globalisation, an internationally based United Nations does not provide the necessary levels of authority, independence, neutrality, or structural foundation to achieve peace and security for humanity. A more effective system of dynamic global governance and jurisprudence is needed that will have the capacity and resources to provide comprehensive human security for the vast majority of humanity. This global governance system could oversee an expanded role for the UN in policing conflicts throughout the world. The UN and humanity do not need four or five self-appointed policemen who are curtailing the UN from achieving international peace and security. These 'policemen' need to be policed. The veto-wielding P-5 states have prevented the UN from evolving to meet the security needs of humanity. Humanity needs the UN to be the world's policing peace force, but not a collective security armed force. A superior regulatory governance system is needed to oversee the UN and other international systems.

The question posed in the title of this research project – The United Nations – Beyond Reform? – is intended to be both pessimistic and forward looking. The pessimistic conclusion of the thesis is that the UN is indeed beyond or incapable of being reformed in the timescale needed to ensure a satisfactory level of peace and security for humanity, given the urgent threats facing humanity in the twenty-first century. However, this research project looks beyond the existing limitations of the UN and speculates on what ought to be the system of human security at global level, and how this might be achieved. The concepts of 'collective security' and the 'international system' implied in the second part of the title – The Collective Insecurity of the International System and the Prospects for Sustainable Global Peace and Justice – have been analysed leading to the conclusion that both collective security and peacekeeping are flawed concepts for the maintenance of peace and security for humanity, and that the international system, such as it is, is already dangerously outdated. The prospects for sustainable global peace and justice are poor in the short term, but are achievable in the long term provided that the UN and the present international system are both transformed and superseded by more appropriate systems of global governance and global jurisprudence.

Did this thesis in general and this chapter in particular answer the research questions posed in Chapter 1?

There are no simple answers to the problems of peace, security and survivability facing humanity at the beginning of the twenty-first century, just as there have been no simple answers to such questions throughout human history. However, the following answers have been established by this research:

1. Is the key objective of the UN, the maintenance of international peace and security, still a valid and a necessary objective for humanity? The conclusion is that the maintenance of international peace and security is a more important objective for humanity now than at any time since the foundation of the UN. However, creating peace is a vital prerequisite towards maintaining peace.
2. Has the UN achieved this key objective in each of the case study regions examined, and in a wider international context? This research project concludes that the UN has not achieved this objective in any of the case study areas nor in the wider global context.
3. If the UN has failed to achieve its key objectives, why has it failed? The UN has failed to achieve this objective for a wide variety of reasons, including, a flawed Charter, inadequate authority, support and resources, inadequate leadership within the UN and within the international community and abuse of power by the UN's P-5 group of states.
4. If the UN has failed on the broader front to achieve its objectives, can it reform or be reformed to achieve these key objectives? The reluctant answer to this question is that the UN does not have the capacity or the will to either reform or be reformed due to the inherent blocking mechanism in its charter, particularly the power of veto invested in the P-5 group of states, and due to its limited status as an international organisation of states rather than as a supranational or global regulatory organisation.

5. If such reform is not possible, or so difficult as to be unlikely, in what alternative ways can the key objectives of the UN be achieved? A dynamic functionalist approach should be used to supersede the UN with more appropriate systems of global governance and global jurisprudence.
6. Should the UN be either transformed to enable it to achieve these objectives, or be replaced by a new organisation or organisations that will be capable of achieving these objectives? The answer to this question is that the transformation or replacement of the UN should not be pre-programmed in advance but should occur in a gradual but dynamic way in response to the changing human security needs of humanity.
7. How can, or how might, such transformation of the international system be achieved? A dynamic functionalist approach should be used to achieve change where change is possible, and to bypass and explore alternative solutions to the UN and the existing international system. Of critical importance will be the gradual evolution of the existing system of international law into a more comprehensive system of global jurisprudence combined with the evolution of the existing international security system into a dynamically developing system of global governance.

David Mitrany wrote that: "Promissory Covenants and Charters may remain a headstone to unfulfilled good intentions". He went on to add: "… but the functional way is action itself, and therefore an inescapable test of where we stand and how far we are willing to go in building up a new international society."[2] Emperor Haile Selassie comments on the League of Nations apply equally to the need for UN reform over seventy years later. "Is it the Covenant that needs reform? What undertakings can have any value if the will to keep them is lacking? It is the international morality which is at stake, not the articles of the Covenant."[3]

International morality has progressed too little since 1936. Kenneth Waltz outlines the realist perspective. "Force is a means of achieving

---

[2] David Mitrany, *A Working Peace System: an argument for the functional development of international organization* (London: Chatham House, 1943), p. 55.
[3] Adam Lebor, *Complicity with Evil: the United Nations in the Age of Modern Genocide* (New Haven: Yale University Press, 2006), p. 20.

the external ends of states because there exists no consistent, reliable process of reconciling the conflicts of interest that inevitably arise among similar units in a condition of anarchy."[4]

The solution to the problems posed by both Haile Selassie and Waltz is to introduce morality and governance into the anarchic international system, and put in place a reliable process of reconciling the conflicts of interest between states. Dag Hammarskjöld's quote from Markings may still be relevant.

The international status quo post bellum (1945–2008) is a form of madness in the global marketplace, or survival-space. The UN is a critical part of this international madness. So far too few have stopped to seriously question whether the very existence of the UN in its immutable form, is a form of madness. The alternatives to a very flawed UN have not been adequately explored.

This thesis begins the process of identifying the critical limitations of the UN and the need for alternatives to the UN, but much more needs to be done as suggested in the recommendations made above. This thesis rejects or challenges, the status quo, including the United Nations, towards the maintenance of international peace and security. It moves things forward first by amassing evidence of the UN's failures and of its lack of capacity to reform to address these failures. It then questions key concepts of international relations, particularly the concepts of collective security, peacekeeping and multilateralism. It proposes the rehabilitation of Mitrany's functionalism in a more dynamic format towards overcoming the obstacles that are preventing the achievement of international peace and security.

David Mitrany summed up the functionality aspects of his theory in his 1944 pamphlet, The Road to Security, which was a critique of the draft UN Charter.

> The turning point in international security will come not through constitutional texts, but by working out of new economic relationships; it will come when the Economic and Social Council

---

[4] Kenneth N. Waltz, *Man the State and War* (New York: Columbia University Press, 1959), p. 238.

will have acquired greater meaning and influence than the Security Council.[5]

Comprehensive human security is needed as urgently now as it was in 1944. The international system, including the United Nations, needs to be transformed into a dynamic system of functioning global governance in which global jurisprudence and the rule of law, exercises effective restraints over the rule and abuses of power.

Warfare raging out of control added to other stresses – overpopulation, environmental damage, drought, and extravagance – that pushed the Classic Maya civilization into decline and collapse.[6]

Déjà vu, again, on a global scale?

I will end with a few final words. Words have enabled human communication and have led to amazing scientific and technological developments over past millennia. But words used injudiciously can cause grief, just as not all scientific and technological developments have been beneficial for humanity. Words once spoken cannot be unspoken, just as an exploded so-called smart bomb or nuclear bomb cannot be unexploded. Yet remaining silent when our words should shout out may be a life sentence or death sentence for many innocents. We must not allow fear of being wrong or being criticised to silence us. These three words – LETTERS WORDS SENTENCES can be understood in different ways. It is my hope that the letters, words and sentences I have used in this book and have had published previously may in some small way help to commute or prevent some of the death sentences that are so recklessly imposed on so many innocent people, most especially innocent children, by unjustified wars of aggression.

Shakespeare had Hamlet saying that he read 'words, words, words' and George Bernard Shaw penned the words 'I'm so sick of words' for Eliza Doolittle. These letters, words, sentences of mine are far more prosaic than those of these two great writers, but they do represent my views and experiences as I trudged along the byways.

---

[5] David Mitrany, *The Road to Security* (London, National Peace Council, 1944), p.20.
[6] Guy Gugliotta, "The Maya: Glory and Ruin", *National Geographic*, August 2007, p. 97.

I will finish by repeating this quotation from Dag Hammarskjöld, who was by far the best UN Secretary General, taken from a little book called Markings, published after his death and his probable assassination in 1961. He tried to make peace in the Congo and paid for his efforts with his life. Six decades later the Congo is still in chaos. One of the richest countries in the world with poorest and most exploited people.

'The madman shouted in the marketplace. No one stopped to answer him. Thus, it was confirmed that his thesis was incontrovertible'.

Some madmen now seem to have gained control of our global asylum.

Printed in France by Amazon
Brétigny-sur-Orge, FR

15836464R00201